The Gardens
of
Gertrude Jekyll

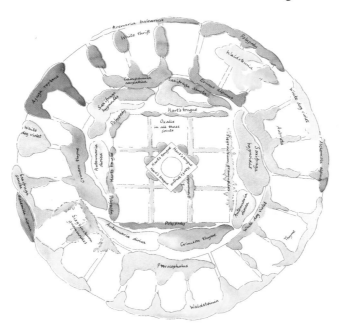

The Gardens of Gertrude Jekyll

RICHARD BISGROVE

Special photography by Andrew Lawson

LITTLE, BROWN AND COMPANY
BOSTON · TORONTO · LONDON

First American Edition

ISBN 0-316-09657-1

Library of Congress Catalog Card Number 92-53850

Library of Congress Cataloging-in-Publication information is available.

10 9 8 7 6 5 4 3 2 1

Published simultaneously in Canada by Little, Brown & Company
(Canada) Limited

Printed in Italy

Half-title page
The sundial planting at Pednor
House, Buckinghamshire.

Frontispiece
Carpets of stachys and pillars
of rosy-mauve sweet peas
harmonize with the grey of the
castle walls in Miss Jekyll's
planting at Lindisfarne,
Northumberland. The warmer
colours of heleniums and orange
poppies provide contrast.

Contents page
The Great Plat at Hestercombe,
Somerset. Miss Jekyll's
favourite bergenias edge each
bed of Lutyens's parterre,
emphasizing the pattern, while
delphiniums contribute the
necessary height. Roses
insinuate themselves among the
bolder plants, flowering
throughout the summer, and
small groups of white lilies add
sparkle to the scheme.

CONTENTS

INTRODUCTION

Gertrude Jekyll has long been renowned for the wonderful gardens she designed between the closing years of the nineteenth century and her death in 1932. Now, more than a hundred years since she began her work, she is recognized as the most significant influence in the design of today's gardens.

There remains, though, a widespread misunderstanding about the nature of Miss Jekyll's contribution to garden design, resulting in a stereotyped view of her as the 'inventor' of the herbaceous border or as the obliging producer of colour borders by the yard to fill in blank shapes left by architects in their clever garden plans. This misunderstanding threatens to conceal from gardeners much of the wealth of experience which she accumulated in her long and industrious life.

Fortunately, new editions of all Gertrude Jekyll's books have become readily available, so it is now much easier to study her ideas at first hand than it was even ten years ago. However, in addition to her output as a writer – thirteen books and over a thousand published articles – Miss Jekyll also left over two thousand plans for some 250 gardens. These working copies of her design schemes, accumulated over the years in the workshop of her home at Munstead Wood, were acquired by the American landscape architect Beatrix Farrand, and, on her death in 1959, were bequeathed to the School of Environmental Design at the University of California, Berkeley. There they form the Reef Point Collection, named after Beatrix Farrand's summer home in Maine. The Reef Point Collection constitutes an astonishing record of Miss Jekyll's versatility as a garden designer and shows clearly that painstaking attention to detail that she applied to all her many interests.

The Gardens of Gertrude Jekyll brings together a representative sample of her plans and for the first time makes them accessible to everyone interested in gardening. Miss Jekyll worked hard to achieve the apparently effortless abundance which characterizes her gardens and it has not been easy to summarize these efforts. Every one of her two thousand

drawings was examined in the preparation of this book, and the forty-seven plans finally included were chosen after the painful elimination of over 150 outstanding examples of her work. The final selection, though, does represent the widest possible range of situations, scale and character.

As Miss Jekyll's working copies, the plans were not intended to be read by anyone else. The combination of her quick, decisive handwriting, her last-minute alterations as the plan was refined, and the smudging which has occurred with age, means that it takes a practised eye to decipher the plans, a sound knowledge of botanical history to translate plant names into their currently accepted equivalents, and experience in design and planting to understand the significance of her choice and arrangement of plants.

For *The Gardens of Gertrude Jekyll*, each plan has been carefully redrawn and relabelled (in a hand more legible than Miss Jekyll's own!). Her mix of common and botanical names has been kept, retaining the character of the original, but botanical names have been brought up to date. The plans have also been coloured, making it easy to see at a glance the general effect intended in each scheme. The text analyses each plan, bringing out often subtle details of form, foliage and seasonal change, and these details are related to Gertrude Jekyll's general principles of garden design. Specially commissioned photographs of Jekyll gardens and of modern plantings in the Jekyll tradition bring to life plants and plant associations throughout the book.

My main objective in writing *The Gardens of Gertrude Jekyll* has been to foster a wider understanding of the basic principles underlying Miss Jekyll's garden plans. The sifting and selection, redrawing, colouring and analysis of her plans have all been directed to this end. No attempt has been made to modify the plans to adapt them to some stereotyped notion of 'modern circumstances'. Each Jekyll plan was designed for a particular situation and I have no wish to promulgate the idea that the substitution of a few undemanding potentillas or ground-covering golden conifers for dahlias, antirrhinums or clematis-wreathed delphiniums will result in an all-purpose, all-year-round and trouble-free Jekyll garden. This would not only be a delusion: it would miss the whole point of Miss Jekyll's approach to gardening and to life – her knowledge that it is the purposeful striving towards perfection, and not its attainment, which is important to a full and satisfying life.

Of course it is possible, with care, to adapt and select from Jekyll plans and to translate them to the context of a small, labour-saving garden. Equally, the owners of large and perhaps overgrown gardens can find inspiration by studying the way that Miss Jekyll was able to create a garden out of a wilderness with a minimum of well-directed effort. But first it is necessary to grasp the principles behind the plans.

One excellent way to achieve this understanding is to copy the plans. Miss Jekyll herself spent many days during her student years in London making copies of Turner's paintings in the National Gallery, in order better to understand his marvellous use of colour. By tracing over her plans in *The Gardens of Gertrude Jekyll*, while following the accompanying text, it is possible to see very clearly how plant groups are built up and plant associations developed. By using information in the text to study different aspects of each scheme – seasonal changes in flowering, variations in foliage colour and texture, or distribution of evergreens perhaps – the full impact of her designs gradually emerges.

Increasing experience and discrimination are the fruits of this effort. It becomes possible to absorb the principles rather than to mimic details, and to reap the satisfaction of original composition, a satisfaction thought by Miss Jekyll to be 'the nearest thing we can know to the mighty forces of creation'.

Miss Jekyll's delight in using a few good plants at a time is evident in this sunny corner at Hestercombe. Grey-leaved giant thistles and rounded hummocks of santolina establish the character of the scheme, harmonizing in colour and sculptured quality with Lutyens's handsome stonework. Garlands of fragrant roses are balanced by slender Madonna lilies on the opposite side of the grass panel. Rosemary, which supports the lilies both physically and visually with its own vertical growth, is repeated on the upper level, pushing through the balustrade to soften the architecture and unify the whole garden.

GARDEN MAKING

A painterly vision for today's gardeners

Munstead Wood, Surrey

The Deanery, Berkshire

In order to understand why Miss Jekyll holds such an important place in the making of today's gardens, it is necessary to consider briefly the background to her gardening activities.

Born in London in 1843, Gertrude Jekyll lived through the peak of Britain's industrial and imperial expansion. She was five when her family moved to Bramley in Surrey. When, at the age of thirty-five, she went back to Surrey after living for nearly ten years in Berkshire, she described her return as a coming home from exile. In her new home at Munstead, near Godalming, she became part, but a conscious part, of a traditional way of life, in a quiet backwater of Surrey heathland between the increasingly bustling main roads and commuter railways to London.

In 1861, while still living at Bramley, she enrolled at the South Kensington School of Art to study painting. This was the year in which William Morris founded Morris, Marshall, Faulkner and Co. in Red Lion Square, Bloomsbury, only a stone's throw from the British Museum. Morris exerted a profound influence on Miss Jekyll's ideas. He had a catholic interest in painting and weaving, dyeing and printing, engraving and poetry. Through his new company he promoted the production of stained glass, handmade furniture and the materials of interior design in general. He studied and translated Icelandic sagas and drew sharp contrasts between the noble age of medieval craft guilds and his own modern era of industrialized mass production of crude, shoddy goods in inhuman factory conditions. All this and more was distilled in a philosophy that expounded the importance of art to life itself, the unity of the aesthetic arts, and the necessity of combining heart, hand and eye in the creative process – the underlying principles in what came to be known as the Arts and Crafts Movement.

All this struck a responsive chord in Gertrude Jekyll: the ideas advocated by the Arts and Crafts Movement were already encapsulated in her way of life, frugal but richly creative. As a student, she met Morris. She also attended lectures by his guiding light, John Ruskin, the leading publicist of the Pre-Raphaelite Brotherhood and of the Arts and Crafts Movement. At Kensington Miss Jekyll studied colour theory. She spent many hours in the National Gallery studying Turner's paintings and was inspired by the glowing harmonies and impressionist use of colour in what Ruskin described in his

lectures as 'Turner picturesque'.

Her studies in London and travels abroad, to Greece and Italy, North Africa and Switzerland, in the company of a close circle of intellectually gifted friends, heightened her awareness of the traditional values and traditional techniques around her and strengthened her determination to retain these traditions in her own life, in her writing and in her designs. Miss Jekyll herself practised many crafts: tapestry and embroidery, metal-work, woodwork, painting and, later, the new technique of photography. For her own house, Munstead Wood, she carved a wine-cellar door with graceful festoons of grapes and grape leaves and her many books were illustrated in large part by her own carefully chosen photographs.

The concept of the unity of the arts, as preached by Morris, is very apparent in all Miss Jekyll's work. The tendrils of her wooden vines bear witness to close observation of the living plant, perhaps the claret vine (*Vitis vinifera* 'Purpurea') which grew on the wall behind the flower border at Munstead Wood. Her embroidery pattern for the Guild of Needlework shows both the abundance and the discipline characteristic of her gardens, while the elegant sweep of the tulip stems or lily petals in the embroidery can be seen time and time again in the delineation of garden paths in her many plans for wild gardens.

It was gardening, though, which came to be the constant activity around which her daily life was increasingly orga-nized. When she moved back to Surrey with her mother, she developed the garden of the family home, Munstead House, moving fruit trees from their former home at Wargrave in Berkshire and creating a pergola, wild garden and long flower border. By 1880 the garden was sufficiently notable to merit visits from Dean Hole (the first President of the National Rose Society) and from William Robinson, editor of *The Garden*. In 1883 Miss Jekyll acquired her own plot of land, Munstead Wood, on the other side of the lane from Munstead House. There she shaped what quickly became a garden of legendary beauty admired by artists and gardeners alike.

Miss Jekyll first met William Robinson in 1875 at the offices of *The Garden*. Robinson had already made his mark as an acerbic critic and prophet of gardening styles. He was passion-ately enthusiastic about gardening as an activity and waxed eloquent on the sophisticated pruning techniques, intensive

pages 8–9 The early summer borders in the kitchen garden at Munstead Wood, shown here in an autochrome made in Miss Jekyll's time. Pale blue, yellow and white iris and lupins against a dark yew hedge capture the freshness of the season, while occasional deeper tones in the falls of the iris add a note of warmth.

Opposite In Miss Jekyll's embroidery pattern, a profusion of flowers, subtly contained within a square, is drawn with lines that are simultaneously natural and controlled. There are clear parallels with her garden plans.

Above A woodland walk at Munstead Wood, in the early years of this century. Slender birch (carefully thinned for picturesque effect), a fern springing casually from a stone, a loose group of dark-leaved rhododendrons – painstaking effort has created an effect of inevitability.

vegetable cultivation methods and mushroom production he had seen in France, but his enthusiasm stopped short of greenhouse exotics and their use in garish and grandiose bedding displays. In their stead he praised the wild garden and the hardy flower garden, places in which the true beauty and natural grace of individual plants could be displayed and appreciated.

Gertrude Jekyll shared Robinson's enthusiasms. She became a regular contributor to *The Garden*, and wrote a chapter on 'Colour in the Flower Garden' for his most important work, *The English Flower Garden*, first published in 1883. However, her taste in plants was more catholic: she argued energetically in defence of colourful bedding plants, pointing out that it was not the plants' fault that they were used in ignorant and foolish ways. In her later years Miss Jekyll published a book on *Annuals and Biennials*, dwelling at length on the value of their long-lasting bright colour in the garden, whereas Robinson, when he somewhat reluctantly included a chapter on 'Summer Bedding' in later editions of *The English Flower Garden*, added a footnote to remind his readers that it was there only for the sake of completeness and that he had not written it himself.

Robinson's distaste for bedding became an obsession, and in successive editions of *The English Flower Garden* he launched a verbal tirade against architects for meddling in gardens when, in his opinion, they were rarely capable, even, of designing decent buildings. In 1892 Reginald Blomfield attempted to put Robinson firmly in his place, publishing *The Formal Garden in England*, and thus bringing to the surface the deep divisions which had always underlain extreme opinions in garden making.

Blomfield saw 'landscape gardening' as a mere copying of nature, with the copy produced inevitably being inferior to the original; it represented an abdication of the designer's responsibility to his art. For Blomfield design was an intellectual abstraction relating to mass, void and proportion and involving the studied interplay of geometrical forms, while gardening was simply a necessary evil. The job of the gardener, as servant of the architect, was to prevent wayward plants from obscuring the plan so carefully worked out on the drawing board. For Robinson, on the other hand, 'Nature' represented that perfection of harmonious beauty to which

the humble gardener should ceaselessly aspire. Plants were the raw material and the *raison d'être* of gardens, while terraces, walls, steps and other architectural impedimenta were to be kept to the absolute minimum necessary to support a house on a sloping site. Fountains, statues and all other artifice (including especially the artifice of massing exotic plants raised in artificial greenhouse climates) were to be avoided at all costs.

Battle lines were drawn. Six months after the publication of *The Formal Garden*, Robinson published *Garden Design and Architects' Gardens*, an apoplectic response to Blomfield's gibes. In October of the same year, only three months later, Blomfield published a second edition of *The Formal Garden* with a lengthy preface refuting Robinson's words and pouring scorn on his ideas. The main effect of this flurry of verbal abuse was to implant in the minds of a generation of the gardening public the notion that a garden could *either* be designed *or* be interesting.

The greatest single contribution of Gertrude Jekyll to garden making must be in demonstrating beyond any doubt that this dichotomy of design and plantsmanship was foolish nonsense. Garden design was not the seeking after a theoretical style divorced from the sordid practicalities of

Left An early autochrome shows clary (*Salvia sclarea*), sweet scabious and tall pink hollyhocks – all traditional cottage garden flowers – their colours blending in a gentle harmony. Variegated apple mint in the foreground and the bold spikes of white antirrhinums insert a clearer, brighter note.

Right The spring garden at Munstead Wood, in Miss Jekyll's time. The spring garden was tucked into a triangle of ground between the main flower border and the kitchen garden with its twin borders for early summer and autumn. While the main colour was provided by thin streams of tulips, irregular patches of aubrieta and arabis, and drifts of wallflowers in carefully chosen hues, the foliage of epimediums and peonies adorned the garden long after the main flowering season had passed.

double-digging, staking and deadheading, but the seeking after beauty and harmony with all the strength and patience and skill at one's disposal. In a period of semantic warfare, she was bilingual, speaking both art and horticulture.

This role as peacemaker was made much more significant by her meeting, in 1889, the young architect Edwin Lutyens. Although painfully shy, Lutyens had a quick wit and a fierce dedication to his chosen profession of architecture. He shared with Miss Jekyll a deep admiration for traditional craftsmanship and, like her, combined enormous breadth of vision with painstaking attention to detail. Perhaps one of the most delightful examples of this was his design for the nursery clock in the Imperial Palace at New Delhi. While wrestling with the complexities of literally miles of avenues and acres of elaborately carved stonework for the palace, he designed a clock for the children's nursery in the form of a starchily uniformed manservant, with one eye to receive the clock key, the other for the chimes and an inane grin containing the arc of the slow/fast adjustment.

Despite, or perhaps because of, the great differences in their dispositions, Gertrude Jekyll and Edwin Lutyens formed a close friendship, travelling the Surrey lanes in her dog-cart to study traditional building techniques and offering each other mutual advice and support. The picturesque effects of innumerable vernacular buildings and the simple gardening ways of the cottagers were thus absorbed into a complex and malleable ideal, from which emerged hundreds of quietly restrained country houses set in abundant cottage gardens.

One of the first fruits of their collaboration was Miss Jekyll's own house, Munstead Wood, which Lutyens skilfully dovetailed into her already notable and rapidly maturing garden. Such was the sympathy between architect and gardener that the union of house and garden was immediate and complete.

The house, with its deep roofs, tall chimneys and massive walls of local stone, is approached discreetly by a quiet path from the lane. Behind the house a shaded north court with its overhanging gallery is embroidered with *Clematis montana* drooping into the pale green and white of *Viburnum opulus*. Lilies, hostas, ferns and tall campanulas in pots repeat the refreshing coolness of colouring at ground level. From this cool retreat low steps flanked by pots of geraniums and

maiden's wreath (*Francoa ramosa*) lead along paths lined with aromatic sweetbriar roses to the pergola, thence to the main flower border, and finally to the quieter charms of the grey garden and the spring garden of bulbs and hardy ferns. The larger part of the garden is organized into grassy rides leading into what had been the scrubby regrowth of woodland felled fifteen years earlier, now transformed by skilful felling and grouping of trees into a series of delicate woodland pictures.

At Munstead Wood the range of expression possible in gardening is already apparent, from the leafy shade of the

Left A nut walk underplanted with spring bulbs and other early flowers provides a delightful link between different areas of the garden. At Munstead Wood the nut walk led from the north court of the house to the pergola at one end of the main flower border. The nut walk shown here is in a private garden at Tonbridge, Kent. Charming and full of incident at the beginning of the year, when herbaceous borders, rose gardens and similar features have barely started into growth, the tapestry of spring flowers beneath the nut trees gradually gives way to greenery as the leaves expand, creating a cool green tunnel as a foil to bright summer flowers elsewhere.

Right Munstead Wood, Surrey

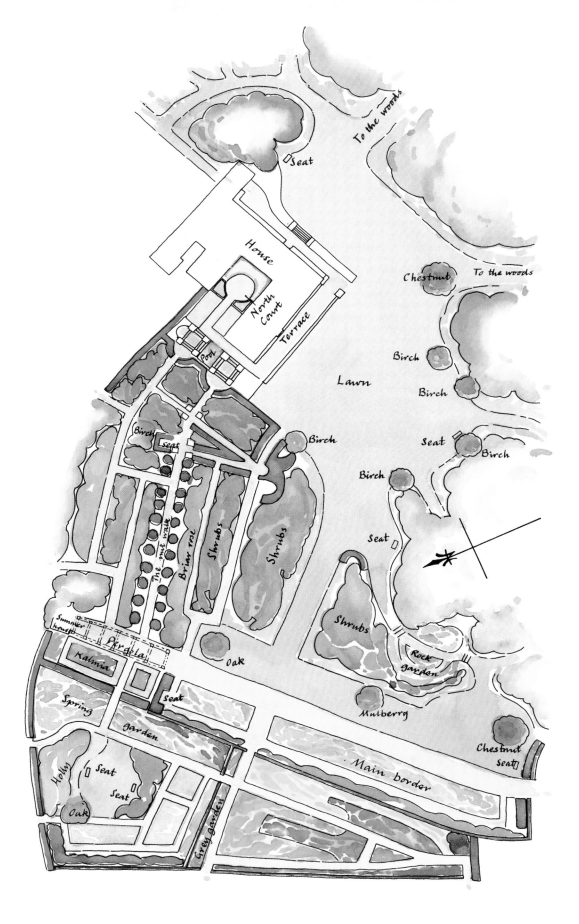

north court to the bright reds of geraniums in terracotta pots by the steps; from the tranquil woodland rides to the delicate brilliance of blue scillas and muscari, white hyacinths and yellow narcissi among young leafage of ferns in the spring garden; and in the splendour of the main border, where soft greys and blues at either end built to a colourful climax of gorgeous reds and oranges in the centre. Everywhere is a balance of generosity and modest restraint.

In 1901 came Lutyens's single most significant commission, The Deanery at Sonning in Berkshire. Within ancient walls encompassing a mere 0.8 hectares/2 acres of land, Lutyens planned a house for Edward Hudson, a friend and near neighbour of Miss Jekyll. The Deanery was especially important for Lutyens in that he found in Hudson a kindred spirit who, as proprietor of *Country Life*, published enthusiastic descriptions of Lutyens's work to a wide and discriminating audience of potential clients. It was of still greater importance to the world at large in demonstrating the possibilities for complete interpenetration of house and garden.

The massive oak door of The Deanery opens from the busy village street into a covered passage alongside an open court with a small central pool. The transition from public thoroughfare to quiet oasis is complete and instantaneous: the tinkling rill, meandering through a carved stone channel from a lead tank into the pool, creates echoes of a Moorish paradise. Straight ahead of the outer door lies the front door proper to the house, opening on to a passage leading through the house and out on to the main upper terrace. To the left of the front door a vaulted arch of brick and chalk connects the little entrance court to the main garden, opening first on to the herb garden and a transverse view of the pergola. Beneath the pergola, a path leads forward, past the little rose garden, past the spring garden of magnolias against the old wall on the left, to emerge between broad pillars of yew on the upper terrace. From here the main path leads out, via circular steps, to the orchard thickly planted with bulbs; or one might take instead the lateral flight of steps wrapping around the terrace wall, and descend to the lower terrace with its long central rill, to

Left While we cannot copy nature, we can learn from it 'that quality which, in painting, is known as "breadth".' Broad swathes of narcissi, planted beneath trees at Dyers Hill House in Charlbury, Oxfordshire, create a wonderful freedom of effect. In the orchard at The Deanery late-flowering narcissi provided the culmination to a succession of bulbs that flowered for nearly eight months of the year.

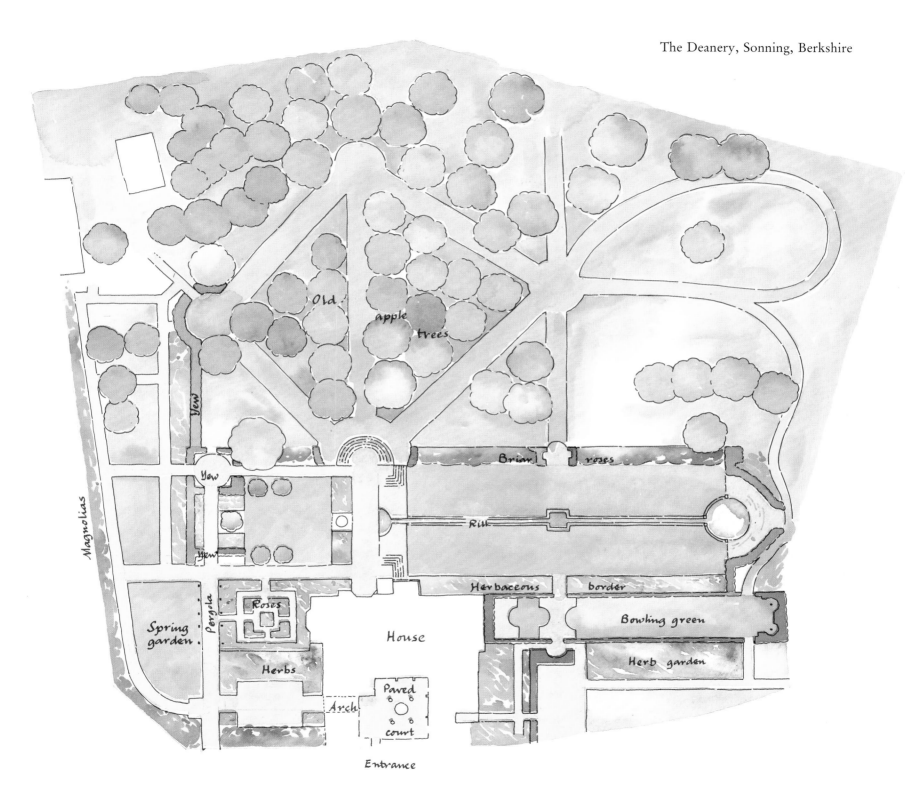

The Deanery, Sonning, Berkshire

reach the orchard and lower lawn by a different route.

The Deanery garden is a masterpiece of understatement. Gentle changes of level define the spaces. Separation of one space from another is achieved by compact blocks of yew, by pergola pillars and by openwork walls of half-round tiles. The stonework is exquisitely detailed but always softened by Gertrude Jekyll's sympathetic planting; the plants are there to support the garden but never overpower it by their presence. Christopher Hussey, Lutyens's biographer, said of The Deanery that it 'virtually settled that controversy, of which Sir Reginald Blomfield and William Robinson were for long the protagonists, between formal and naturalistic garden design.

Miss Jekyll's naturalistic planting wedded Lutyens's geometry in a balanced union of both principles.'

Lutyens went on to discover the exhilaration of classical architecture and the challenge of its disciplined proportions, producing at Folly Farm, Gledstone, Hestercombe, and ultimately New Delhi, examples of what he humorously dubbed 'High Wrennaissance', in deference to Christopher Wren. But he continued to produce surprises, not least in the picturesque magnificence of Castle Drogo, a granite castle built between 1910 and 1930 on the edge of Dartmoor for Julius Drewe, and his remodelling of Lindisfarne Castle on Holy Island, where he worked again for Edward Hudson.

However, circumstances were changing rapidly as the new century advanced. The decline of private wealth, the austere simplicity of the Modern Movement in architecture, and most of all the increasing separation of architectural design and traditional building skills from mechanized construction using mass-produced components, led to Lutyens's increasing isolation from the mainstream of his profession. He was dismissed by younger architects of the new school, although a close look at such buildings as his extension to Folly Farm would have shown surprising similarities with the massive simplicity of Frank Lloyd Wright's houses in America, for example, or Peter Behrens's and Walter Gropius's monumental brick buildings in Europe.

Miss Jekyll never lost favour in this way, in spite of new housing estates, new small gardens and a labour saving mentality. Her books continued to be in demand from public libraries and her ideas lived on in the work of such gardeners as Lawrence Johnston at Hidcote Manor, Vita Sackville-West at Sissinghurst Castle, Constance Spry (who was influenced by Miss Jekyll's thoughts on flower arranging), and Graham Stuart Thomas, a director of Sunningdale Nurseries and adviser on gardens to the National Trust.

In the post-war years of burgeoning car ownership and increasing leisure, the gardens created and conserved by such people were visited by growing numbers of increasingly discerning enthusiasts. Even as Miss Jekyll's books were finally disappearing from library shelves, the ideas they contained were being rediscovered by a public raised on a diet of new colour magazines and garden visiting, and thirsty for inspiration to guide their own attempts at garden making.

This rediscovery coincided with an era of environmentalism, anti-modernism, a cry for humanity and spirituality in daily life as a release from our materialistic age – circumstances reminiscent of those that led to the founding of the Arts and Crafts Movement, of which Miss Jekyll was an integral part.

By 1982, fifty years after her death, Miss Jekyll had become a national heroine. Ten years on, we have arrived at a situation in which even garden centres display their plants in colour-coordinated groups.

Why has Miss Jekyll's influence been so pervasive? The main reason must lie in the simultaneous depth and breadth of her approach to gardens and gardening. She saw garden making as a fine art, ranking, as it had done in the eighteenth century, with painting, poetry, music and sculpture. However, she also recognized that the translation of an artistic conception of a garden into reality required a wide range of practical horticultural skills. She studied with extraordinary diligence the materials of her art.

Significantly, Miss Jekyll never spoke of herself as a garden designer and rarely used the phrase 'garden design'. For her, *gardening* summed up the activities which resulted in satisfying and beautiful gardens, just as *painting* created works of art on canvas. Garden planning, plant knowledge and plant cultivation were as interdependent in the making of gardens as were picture composition, familiarity with pigments and canvas, and skill in applying paint to canvas in the production of a major painting. It is possible to draw many analogies between Miss Jekyll's garden making and practices in other arts and crafts. Indeed it is difficult not to: her many books are full of comparisons between plant textures and fabrics and between the painter's and the gardener's use of colour; her writing in those books verges on the poetic and her numerous garden plans are charming drawings in their own right.

A second reason for her significance as a garden maker is the universal application of her ideas. She did not set out to create or promote a particular style of garden, but to work steadfastly and patiently towards perfection in the garden, while understanding that perfection could never be achieved. Although she worked in the main on what we would now consider very large gardens, she never confused quantity with quality, arguing that 'The size of a garden has very little to do with its merit. It is the size of the owner's heart and brain and goodwill that will make his garden either delightful or dull.' Her influence was much more profound and her designs were

At Greywalls, Gullane, in East Lothian, the sophisticated curves and counter-curves of Lutyens's stonework merge effortlessly into the simpler geometrical patterns of cross paths. Small groves of trees create a rapid change of atmosphere, from sun to dappled shade. Here, any semantic distinctions between formal and naturalistic garden design are blurred.

'Rhododendrons where the copse and garden meet.' Miss Jekyll's photograph shows a natural stand of birch, carefully thinned, and a cultivated group of rhododendrons, carefully planted, in a quieter part of the garden at Munstead Wood. It was garden scenes such as this, exploiting and enriching the genius of the place, which led Lutyens to describe Miss Jekyll as 'an Artist, old and experienced in the way of plants'.

infinitely more varied than the caricature of colour-border manufacturer admits. Among the drawings in the Reef Point Collection there are schemes for stunning displays of bedding plants and cool woodland walks, for rose gardens and rock gardens, soft grey borders and bold plantings of rich dark green, plans for whole gardens and charming details. Many of her plans were commissioned by architects, but as many more were for garden owners themselves.

Correspondence from her clients shows a deep respect, often verging on awe, for her abilities, and she repaid this trust by careful and sympathetic attention to their wishes. At Dungarth, near Huddersfield, she began by suggesting minor alterations to the house in order to forge an easier link between house and garden, an idea which her client, Mrs Sykes, received with enthusiasm. In replying to Miss Jekyll's questions about the site, Mrs Sykes explained that some planting in the garden had already been done by local nurserymen working to her 'amateurish instructions. ... When it was begun I had no idea that it was possible to appeal to you.'

Often Miss Jekyll would take an amorphous, fragmented and uninspiring plot and, by carving rides and walks through established woodland or by distributing trees and shrubs about an open paddock, she was able to create a garden rich in harmony and variety. In her first American commission, for Mr and Mrs Glendinning B. Groesbeck in 1914, she began by positioning the new house on its virgin site. Grace Groesbeck wrote that 'Mr Groesbeck and I have come to the conclusion that your idea of the position for the house is best ... we had thought of putting [the other buildings] at the foot of the hill ... but I want you to understand that we do not wish to thrust our ideas upon you ... as of course your ideas are infinitely better and we have perfect confidence in whatever you decide is best.' And this despite the fact that Miss Jekyll was never able to visit the rolling site in Ohio.

Much of the correspondence remaining with her plans testifies to the care and personal attention which the proud owners felt Miss Jekyll had devoted to their particular garden and their particular needs and to their trust in her judgment. Other letters also refer in glowing terms to Miss Jekyll's generous hospitality and to the delights of tea at Munstead Wood.

Gertrude Jekyll had a great respect for the architectural profession and, because she was able to understand what they were striving for in their designs, she was able to work with rather than for them. With Edwin Lutyens in particular, the garden schemes for which she planned the planting evolved after much consultation on the aims, the general strategy and the possibilities of the site. Together they worked on schemes ranging from the relatively modest cottage gardens of Millmead and Crooksbury to the remarkable settings and gardens for Lindisfarne Castle and Castle Drogo. In arguing for a fence rather than a ha-ha at Castle Drogo, Lutyens wrote to his client, Julius Drewe, suggesting that 'Mr Veitch and Myers should lay their scheme before Miss Jekyll, who is a great designer, an Artist, old and experienced in the way of plants and a lover of the Wilderness & moorland.' He urged Drewe to visit Miss Jekyll at Munstead to obtain her opinions at first hand. Three days later he wrote to Miss Jekyll explaining that 'the fence can tic tac about to suit planting and its needs, horticultural and pictorial', confiding to her that 'Veitch is to do the work and their sketches chill my liver.'

A third reason for Miss Jekyll's importance, and a vital one in understanding her particular relevance to modern garden design, lies in her painstaking attention to detail. Even in the largest of her gardens there were small fragments, odd and awkward corners directly comparable in scale with the small gardens of a modern housing estate. Because these fragments received as much careful thought as the more conspicuous elements of the design, her plans for them now offer many ideas for the owner of the small modern garden. Similarly, in the longest border, the plant associations were planned to the last lily, so it is possible to take a small part of a Jekyll plan, a combination perhaps of three or four good plants, and to use it as the basis for a tiny bed or border. This is not, of course, to imply that any Jekyll border might be cut into 3m/10ft sections and pasted about willy-nilly; there is a fundamental difference between cutting a painting into small squares and

The elderly Gertrude Jekyll, photographed by Mr Cowley, editor of *Gardens Illustrated*, in the spring garden at Munstead Wood. Her vision was poor and her health failing, but still no detail escaped Miss Jekyll's searching eye.

extracting from it a delightful and self-sufficient vignette.

For Gertrude Jekyll gardening was never a matter of style or fashion. The garden was not an end result but a process, a process inevitably involving the making of mistakes but offering in return that serene satisfaction which comes from tireless dedication to a job well done. It is that quality which ensures for her a lasting place in an increasingly makeshift world.

GARDEN CHARACTER

It was an unwritten rule of Miss Jekyll's planning that every garden should have a character, a personality, or as Lutyens said in a debate on garden design at the Architectural Association in 1908 (having spent the previous weekend at Munstead Wood to rehearse Miss Jekyll's words) 'a backbone – a central idea beautifully phrased'. The garden was not merely a collection of plants but a work of art arising first as an idea in the mind of an artistic creator.

Garden design, then, is an art. Any artistic creation demands the ability to keep in mind the whole idea while working on its constituent parts, to consider simultaneously the materials and the concept. Just as a sculptor 'releases' the finished form from an apparently shapeless rock, or a painter gives substance to an idea by building up successive brushstrokes on a canvas, so the designer of a garden creates a unified scheme from many disparate elements of site and planting. The 'applied' artist (if it is possible to make such a distinction) must have in mind, too, the needs of a client. This unity and simultaneity of vision is evident in the work of both Gertrude Jekyll and Edwin Lutyens.

Above *Rosa virginiana*

Pages 22–3 Simple formality softened by a profusion of well-chosen plants was characteristic of Miss Jekyll's flower gardens. The tradition is continued in these borders at the House of Pitmuies, in Scotland.

The thumbnail sketches with which Lutyens explained and illustrated his thoughts in so many letters to Miss Jekyll were not whimsy – picturesque building shells into which the requisite accommodation would somehow be shoehorned at a later date. They were polished solutions to the social, structural and aesthetic requirements of a particular commission, designed simultaneously from the inside and the exterior. In the same way, Miss Jekyll's gardens were not mere assemblages of details, or pattern book templates into which she could paste a suitable number of herbaceous borders. Each garden scheme represented a totality, within which the study of the whole site and its potential suggested subordinate parts of varied character, while the parts united to form a balanced composition both harmonious and varied.

The range of Miss Jekyll's schemes was extraordinary, but it can be illustrated quite neatly by comparing the three American gardens which she designed: the Groesbeck garden in Ohio (1914), the garden designed for Mr and Mrs Stanley Resor in Greenwich, Connecticut (1925) and the Old Glebe House garden in Woodbury, Connecticut, commissioned by Annie Burr Jennings in 1926.

In her plan for the new property of Mr and Mrs Glendinning B. Groesbeck in Perintown, Cincinnati (referred to in the Jekyll archives as 'Elmhurst' because Grace Groesbeck wrote to Miss Jekyll about the project from the family home of that name), Miss Jekyll suggests the new house be sited at the head of a valley running through the property. She then marshals the steep slopes below into a complex cascade of steps, clearly Italian in inspiration. Each flight of steps descends to meet a terrace walk across the slope – walks that are straight to begin with, then curve around the hillsides, connecting eventually with long informal flights of steps to other levels. One walk terminates in a circular rose garden with twenty-five granite pillars swagged in climbing roses.

The rough grassy slopes between the levels are punctuated with casually distributed 'groups of *Rosa lucida* [now *R. virginiana*] and other native roses with low native bushes – *Rubus nutkanus* [now *R. parviflorus*] etc. in rough grass', plants so often used by Miss Jekyll in her English wild gardens but here literally at home. Below the steps a wide vista of rough grass sweeps down to the river, while on either side the planting merges into 'bushes and trees of wild character', framing the

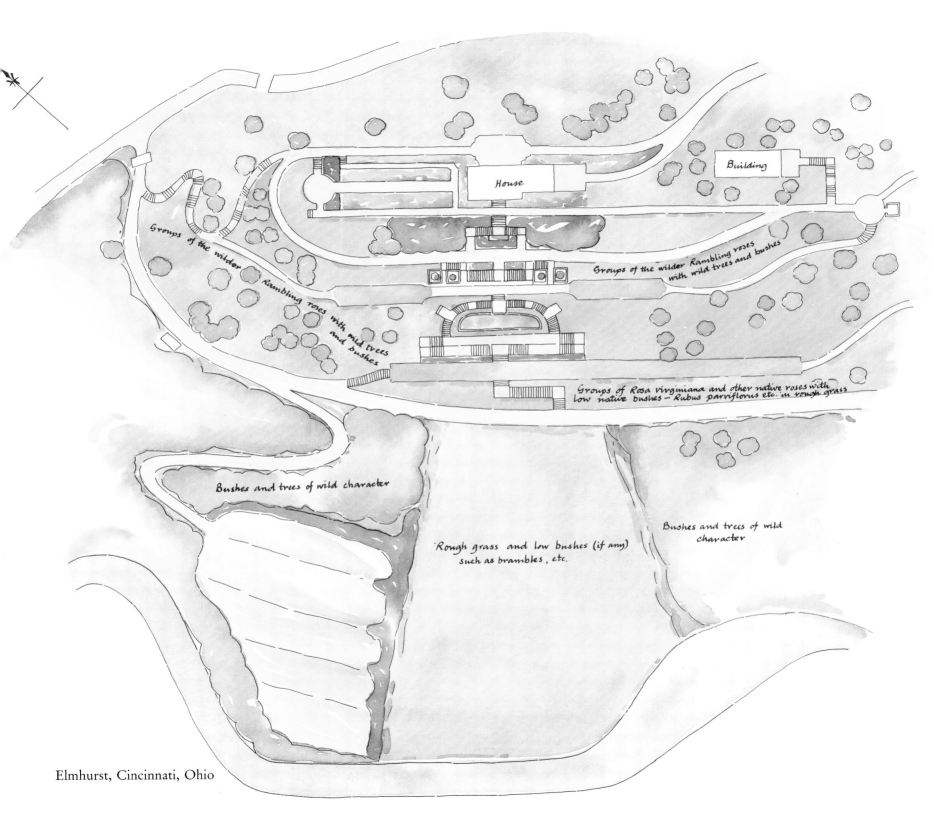

Building

House

Groups of the wilder Rambling roses with wild trees and bushes

Groups of the wilder Rambling roses with wild trees and bushes

Groups of Rosa virginiana and other native roses with low native bushes — Rubus parviflorus etc. in rough grass

Bushes and trees of wild character

Rough grass and low bushes (if any) such as brambles, etc.

Bushes and trees of wild character

Elmhurst, Cincinnati, Ohio

Azaleas, rhododendrons and young spring foliage in a woodland setting at Ramster, in Surrey. Concentrating flowering plants into long irregular drifts interleaved with ferns and other foliage creates a sense of depth. In summer the pale green leaves of azaleas merge with expanding fern fronds within the heavier framework of evergreen rhododendrons, while autumn brings warm tones of yellow, red and rusty brown.

view, and, on the north-west flank, concealing a large, terraced kitchen garden.

The owners of the second American garden, Helen and Stanley Resor, were introduced to Miss Jekyll by Edward Hudson. They visited Munstead Wood in 1924 and their new house, 'Cotswold Cottage', in Greenwich, Connecticut, shows a close affinity with the steep roofs and massive stone chimneys at Munstead. Miss Jekyll's plans for the Resor garden, in sharp contrast to those she did for the Groesbecks, contain hardly a single straight line. The drive snakes boldly around the grassy hillside, dividing around a circular mound of savin (*Juniperus sabina*) to arrive at a simple circular forecourt. This leads by short paths to the merest suggestion of formal gardening within the thick hedges immediately around the house.

Mr and Mrs Resor travelled every summer, rendering any elaborate flourishes of summer gardening at home redundant. Instead Miss Jekyll designed for them a delightful scheme of gently meandering paths, merging on the steeper slopes into easy flights of steps and weaving through a tapestry of naturalistic, often native, planting. The European savin (a favourite of Miss Jekyll's), hardy hybrid rhododendrons and spreading yews merge with North American junipers, spruces and *Mahonia aquifolium* against a backdrop of hemlock and Douglas fir for winter greenery. Within this firm framework of varied greens there are groups of azaleas, spindle (*Euonymus europaeus*), *Berberis thunbergii*, *Cotinus coggygria*, amelanchier, rubus, crab apples and *Cornus florida*, the American flowering dogwood. Together, these shrubs and small trees provide a wealth of spring blossom and autumn foliage.

The hard angle of the hedge below the south corner of the house is broken by a group of another American native used freely in Britain by Miss Jekyll, *Aesculus parviflora*. Flowering in late summer, this might have welcomed the Resors home on an occasional early return and would, like the summer-flowering *Rosa wichuraiana* planted liberally about the hillside for its glossy greenery and freedom of growth, ensure that the garden was never without interest.

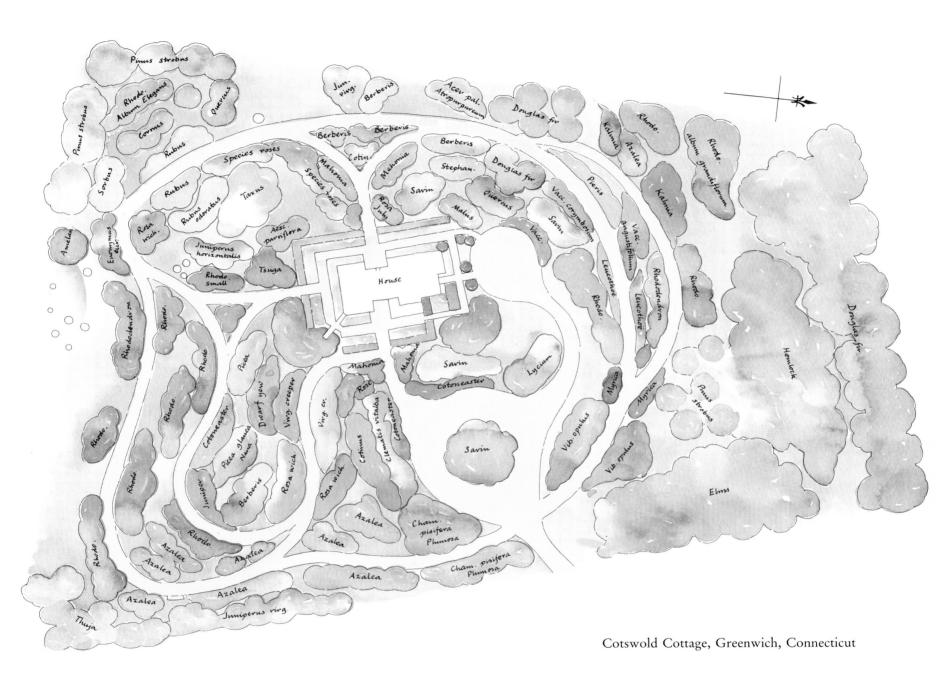

Cotswold Cottage, Greenwich, Connecticut

The Old Glebe House in Woodbury dated back to 1695. After a thirty-year-long threat of demolition, it had been saved and restored in 1925. In 1926 Miss Jennings, a founder member of the Seabury Society for the Preservation of Glebe House, visited Miss Jekyll at Munstead and asked her to provide plans for an old-fashioned garden around the house. The resulting scheme is straightforward but far from dull. It would have delighted William Morris.

Within a surrounding fence (of materials appropriate to local traditions), a good hedge provides both durable enclosure and a backdrop for the flower border. The new path leads directly to the front door, shaded by a large plane tree, then branches to right and left, to contain narrow borders against the house. A small formal garden at the back of the house (an earlier attempt at historical gardening) is replanted with roses, while the remainder of the rear garden, screened behind a hawthorn hedge, is divided by straight service paths into six plots for vegetables. In terms of its plan the Old Glebe House garden is simple in the extreme, but its planting is rich and varied.

The narrow, shady borders flanking the front door are simply and symmetrically planted: lilacs by the door, mahonia beneath the windows and dark mounds of *Viburnum tinus* to anchor the corners of the house. On the two sunniest sides of the house the planting is of China roses and rosemary, linking with the quartered rose garden at the back of the house. From this small garden-within-a-garden, the path continues between borders of iris (for early summer) and more roses, this time edged with pinks and punctuated by the vertical stems of sweetly fragrant Madonna lilies, to emerge finally through an arch of climbing roses on to the main lawn.

Against the remaining wall, the scheme is one of apparently sharp contrasts: lavender and China roses in the more open part of the border, Lent hellebores and (beyond the rose arch) lily of the valley where the shade is more prolonged. However, both *Viburnum tinus* and *Helleborus orientalis* (the Lent hellebore) have foliage of so dark and distinguished a green that they associate well both with yellow-greens, including the pale yellow-green of grass, and with grey foliage. They draw the roses, with their correspondingly dark, glossy foliage, the

Left A straight border edging a rectangular lawn, at Tintinhull House in Somerset. As at the Old Glebe House, a simple plan is enriched by skilfully planned planting. Drifts of salvia, *Echinacea purpurea*, phlox, galega and eupatorium in front of the buddleja produce a quiet harmony. Lighter thistle heads of *Eryngium giganteum*, white roses and arching sprays of tall grasses introduce points of variety to prevent the harmony becoming monotonous.

Right The Old Glebe House, Woodbury, Connecticut

pale lavender and grass into a picture of subtle unity.

Views from the house, across a lawn punctuated by fortuitously positioned trees, are contained on three sides by a flower border. This starts by the willow tree, with a sparkling colour scheme: dark *Hebe brachysiphon*, paler laurel and golden holly, with dark *Iberis sempervirens* (perennial candytuft) and variegated *Euonymus fortunei radicans* edging the border. The white flowers of the candytuft and hebe, with the graceful white wreaths of *Spiraea × vanhouttei*, *Leucanthemum maximum* (Shasta daisies) and dahlias, extend the flowering season from spring to the first frosts.

Among this array of green and white, pale lavender erigerons and pink anemones introduce a second idea, small strands of warmer colouring which gradually intensifies towards the sunniest corner of the garden, with dark red hollyhocks and antirrhinums, strong yellow heleniums, oenotheras and rudbeckias and scarlet monarda. Around the corner, this rich colouring mellows: fuchsias and centranthus, the dusky red-brown spikes of *Polygonum affine*, peonies and other pink flowers and finally white flowers and grey foliage again: Shasta daisies, Madonna lilies, lavender and stachys.

Half-way across the garden the border is interrupted by the gate. At this point the main colour scheme is varied by a symmetrical grouping of tree ivy and bergenia, stachys and lavender, dark green and silver foliage echoing the scheme at the corner of the house – a sharp contrast of foliage, but one which succeeds because of the way in which the plants are skilfully woven together. Beyond the gate, the colour scheme flows on as before: clear blue anchusas and, later in the year, delphiniums among predominantly white flowers; then, carefully separated from the clear blues by a good group of *Rosa virginiana* and Lawson cypress, the softer greys and lavender-blues of echinops, *Salvia virgata* and *Iris pallida*, edged with long drifts of nepeta, *Hosta sieboldiana* and, around a seat, aromatic bushes of rosemary. Finally the planting returns to white and pale greens, with an edging of variegated euonymus and neat green *Hebe buxifolia* against a backdrop of dark green holly.

White flowers among green create a sparkling, refreshing effect in Miss Jekyll's plan for the borders at the Old Glebe House. In this planting at Hadspen House in Somerset the theme is developed through white Shasta daisies above dark bergenia leaves, bold curving stems of white centranthus, airy sprays of *Crambe cordifolia*, and trails of white verbena. Pale roses introduce the first warmer tones.

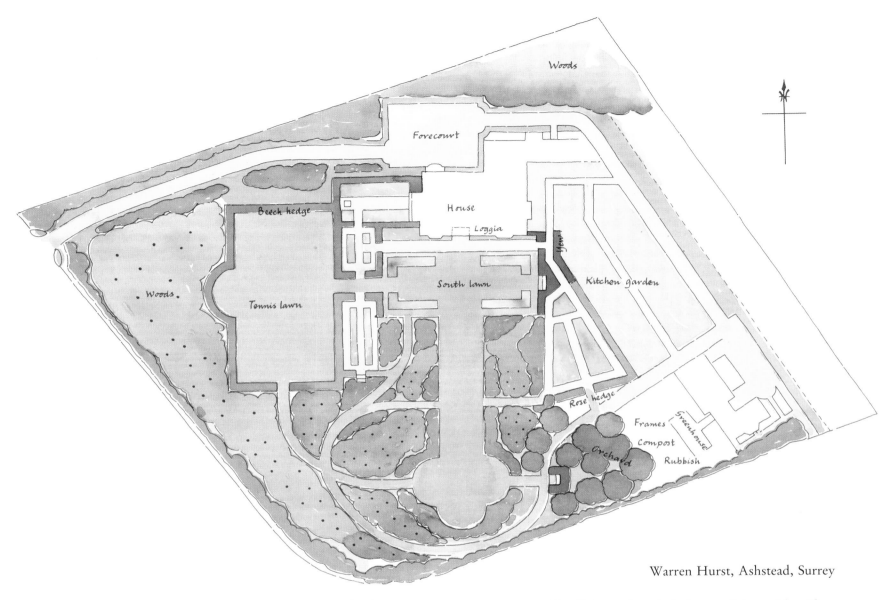

Warren Hurst, Ashstead, Surrey

Many characteristics of Miss Jekyll's use of plants are apparent in the Old Glebe House borders: the repeated use of hollyhocks, antirrhinums and dahlias, irises and peonies, each in a range of colours to emphasize a changing colour scheme, while the planting is unified by the repetition of their distinctive forms; the use of bergenias and other emphatic plants at key points, and so on. The Old Glebe House shows vividly the variety of mood which Miss Jekyll could create within an apparently quite simple garden scheme.

These three American gardens clearly illustrate the variety of Miss Jekyll's garden plans. Among the diversity of her far more numerous English gardens it is impossible to identify a 'typical' garden, but Warren Hurst at Ashtead, in Surrey, perhaps encapsulates the components of a Jekyll garden most succinctly. The drive enters discreetly at one corner of an irregular plot, closely bordered by banks of evergreens save for a brief glimpse of the woodland garden at the entrance. Two subtle changes in alignment separate the middle section of the drive from both the entrance gateway and the forecourt, creating a psychological 'air-lock' between the garden and the outside world. Beyond the second bend the vista along the drive terminates in the forecourt, but the drive itself continues

31

to the service quarters, the kitchen garden and orchard, the gardener's cottage and stables.

On the south side of the house a deep loggia connects house and garden with a wide grass vista extending to a boldly sculpted enclosure of three semicircular alcoves surrounded by greenery. Immediately below the house this main vista meets a broad cross axis: a formal lawn that stretches between enclosing hedges of beech, before expanding to form the largest garden compartment, the tennis lawn. These two main axes, penetrating both the depth and the breadth of the garden, are then connected by curving walks through woodland, developing a completely different sense of freedom of line and planting, while the smaller spaces around the house and between the major formal lawns are filled with a secondary necklace of small enclosed flower gardens.

The result is a garden of great complexity, with a maze of small paths opening on to and from the main vistas, and of wide variety, from the severely geometric to informal woodland. By virtue of the interplay and transition between formal and informal, though, it retains an overriding sense of unity.

A similar degree of diversity on a distinctly smaller scale can be seen in the plan for the White House at Wrotham in Kent. Here the starting point was a very bland garden with a grass tennis court terraced into the slope (the hatchings indicating the banks can be discerned on Miss Jekyll's plan), dominating the house and slightly skew to it. Rows of fruit trees backed the court, only thinly disguising the boundary of the garden and in no way reducing its angularity.

Miss Jekyll's solution was to reduce the scale of the garden by creating a lawn of sculptured outline, now parallel and perpendicular to the house, within the former tennis court, and to conceal the harsh lines of the embankments beneath dense shrub planting. These shrub masses are permeated by winding paths and bordered on their inner and outer edges by more purely decorative planting carefully chosen to provide a distinct edge to the path.

On the cool, east-facing side of the garden, the shrubs are mainly of dark and glossy greens: bay and phillyrea, laurustinus, cotoneaster and Miss Jekyll's much-loved *Daphne pontica*, with holm oak and the deciduous but dark and glossy

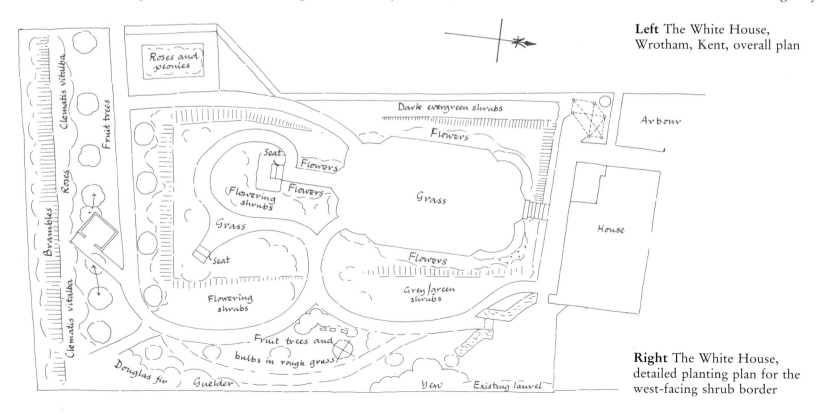

Left The White House, Wrotham, Kent, overall plan

Right The White House, detailed planting plan for the west-facing shrub border

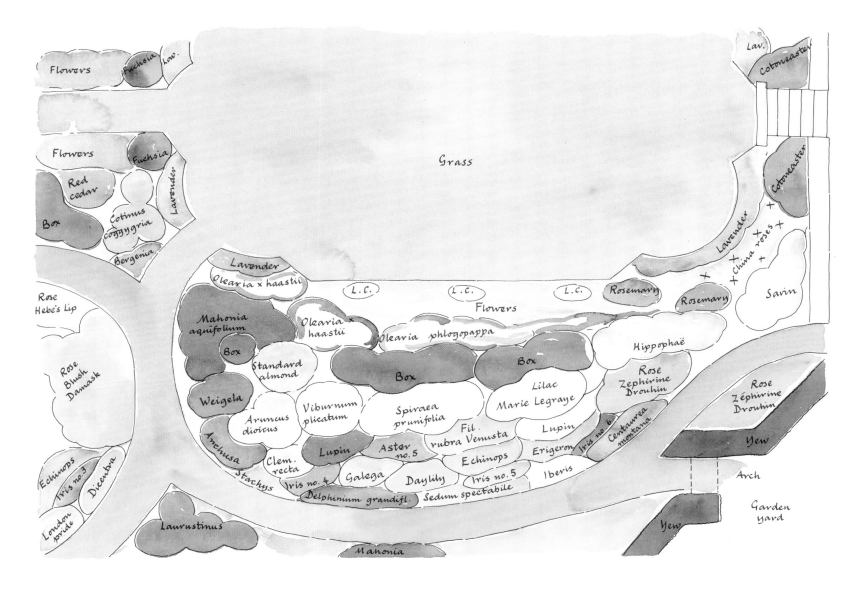

Labels on plan: Flowers · Fuchsia · Low. · Lav. · Cotoneaster · Flowers · Fuchsia · Lavender · Red cedar · Grass · Box · Cotinus coggygria · Bergenia · Cotoneaster · Lavender · Rose Hebe's Lip · Lavender · Olearia x haastii · L.C. · L.C. · L.C. · Rosemary · China roses · Savin · Flowers · Rosemary · Mahonia aquifolium · Olearia x haastii · Olearia phlogopappa · Hippophaë · Box · Rose Blush Damask · Box · Standard almond · Box · Lilac Marie Legraye · Rose Zéphirine Drouhin · Rose Zéphirine Drouhin · Weigela · Aruncus dioicus · Viburnum plicatum · Spiraea prunifolia · Fil. rubra Venusta · Lupin · Iris no. 6 · Centaurea montana · Yew · Anchusa · Lupin · Aster no. 5 · Erigeron · Echinops · Iris no. 3 · Dicentra · Stachys · Clem. recta · Iris no. 4 · Galega · Daylily · Echinops · Iris no. 5 · Iberis · Arch · London pride · Delphinium grandifl. · Sedum spectabile · Garden yard · Laurustinus · Mahonia · Yew

Rosa virginiana. In the south-facing alcove near the house these dark but often muted greens merge into China roses with a contrasting edging of pale, grey-leaved lavender. Lavender and roses also fill the alcove on the opposite side of the steps down from the house, but on this sunnier side of the garden (shown on the detailed plan), the grey theme established by the lavender is continued with savin (*Juniperus sabina*) and hippophaë, olearias, grey-green lilacs and *Spiraea prunifolia*. The spine of fine-textured box, with dark-shadowed but light-surfaced leaves, is ideally suited to its key role of continuing but containing the generally soft colouring.

At the farther end of the lawn, in the area beyond the limits of the detailed plan, dark and light plantings meet in the mid-green foliage of common flowering shrubs – forsythia and weigela, berberis and rubus, ribes and spiraeas. Important places are reserved, though, for *Cotinus coggygria*, one of the best shrubs for harmonizing with both grey-green and yellow-green foliage, and for the twin red cedars (*Thuja plicata*) that provide an emphatic evergreen backdrop to the fiery autumn colours of the cotinus.

Beyond this main garden the thin margin of fruit trees is gently diversified: one tree has been eliminated and two have been moved (to make room for a small pavilion), thus breaking the regimented rhythm of the trees. The grass, planted with bulbs, has a curving path mown through it to complement the curves of the permanent paths in the new plan, and the rigid boundary of the garden has been disguised with irregular groups of yew, hawthorn and guelder rose. Near the corner of the garden, Douglas firs shelter and half-conceal a garden seat.

Along the southern edge of the garden the naturalistic quality of the planting continues, but the narrow glade between boundary and shrub bank is opened out as the path rounds the corner beyond the firs: arching mounds of wild clematis, rambling roses and brambles tumble down the steep bank at the end of the garden, defining its boundary without obstructing the view. This lower walk, straight and quietly formal within its now irregular avenue of fruit trees, reveals a small rectangular garden of roses and peonies (a favourite combination of Miss Jekyll's). A gently curving path slopes up through dark green shrubbery, returning finally to the main lawn.

In many instances, certainly in the case of her American gardens and even in Kent or Berkshire, Miss Jekyll never saw the gardens she so carefully planned, being increasingly unable or unwilling to travel any distance as she grew older. In this she seems to have broken the golden rule to 'consult the genius of the place in all' and is therefore looked upon askance by many twentieth-century landscape architects. However, she was well aware of the difficulties presented by not knowing a site at first hand. Unable to consult the *genius loci* in person, she asked for, and received, careful surveys, often annotated by her client to show tree spread, views, shade, and so forth, and she asked questions constantly, receiving long and detailed letters in reply. Even so, there had to be a degree of trial and error in her commissions – and not always because *she* did not know the site!

For Borlases in Berkshire, designed for Nathaniel Davidson in 1918, the first plan sent to Miss Jekyll by Captain Davidson (from his military base in Derby) showed a square field which he hoped to add to an existing garden. She sent in return a few suggestions for improving the existing garden and a plan for the proposed extension, a straightforward and more or less self-contained shrub garden, with paths radiating from an octagonal yew-hedged enclosure against the wall. After a long delay occasioned by 'medical boards and other business of war', Davidson wrote gratefully – and with abject apologies – to say that the plan would not quite work because the boundaries of the field, which he had guessed to be at right angles, were in fact far from square. A correct plan, obviously the work of a skilled surveyor, was proffered.

The result was a second plan from Miss Jekyll, showing an altogether bolder scheme with the octagon moved towards the centre of the garden, wide cross paths radiating from four of its sides and narrower paths winding in gentle counterpoint to the formal scheme connecting the new garden to an existing informal pond. All the compartments between the paths are filled with evergreen and white-flowered shrubs intermingled with ferns, bamboos, white willowherb and other plants of similarly refreshing grace.

Miss Jekyll's ability to design from a distance was, of course, greatly facilitated by the patient interest of her clients, by the efforts of their knowledgeable gardeners and the availability of experienced nurserymen to implement her plans. Furthermore, in an era when intensive horticultural activity was taken for granted, thorough cultivation guaranteed the results of her planting schemes regardless of native soil types. One plan of Gledstone, for example, is annotated by the gardener to warn Miss Jekyll that, although most of the borders had been dug and enriched to a depth of 1.2m/4ft, one had been cultivated only to 45cm/18in, because of a last-minute change in the layout of the garden!

Opposite *Cotinus coggygria*, one of the most versatile garden shrubs, was much used by Miss Jekyll. The pale green foliage of the species is an ideal intermediary between yellow-green and grey-green foliage, while the purple form seen here introduces a velvety richness. Both forms colour brilliantly in the autumn, often providing as a bonus the feathery panicles of flowers which earn the plant its common name of smoke bush.

Above While Edwin Lutyens learned much from Miss Jekyll about the making of a home and garden, she benefited from his architectural skill. Her bold geometrical treatment of the shrub garden at Borlases is reminiscent of Lutyens's Great Plat at Hestercombe, shown here. Four panels of grass radiate from the centre of the Plat to form diagonal vistas through Miss Jekyll's luxuriant planting.

The extent to which Miss Jekyll succeeded in creating a detailed scheme from a distance is well illustrated by her plans for Durmast in the New Forest. A survey of the existing garden presents a typically depressing starting point: a scattering of quite interesting trees in rough grass or heath around an amorphous lawn with a small rock garden on one side and a meanly proportioned rose garden – some distance from the house and at an odd angle to it – on the other.

The solution is ingenious. Capitalizing on the awkward but unalterable orientation of the wall behind the rose garden, Miss Jekyll extends a new axis perpendicularly from the house into the garden and repeats the odd angle of the wall on the other side of this new axis. The result is a much larger, kite-shaped rose garden enclosed within the existing wall on one long side and a new shrub border embracing the summerhouse on the other. Between the rose garden and the house the ground is shaped into new paths and borders parallel to the house and extending the pattern of the rose garden. While combining to form a unified scheme, the new borders are carefully positioned and proportioned to incorporate or avoid mature trees, and one path takes on a gently curved alignment to connect the rose garden with the less formal outer parts of the garden. The drive, meandering inconsequentially through the trees in the initial plan, is reinforced by evergreen shrub planting at strategic points to create an elegant but informal forecourt and to separate the drive from the garden proper. Finally, a marginal note on the plan advises, 'keep hedge low if good views to forest'.

Clearly the owner did not consider the views to be of great merit: in a revised plan, the open boundary has been replaced by a raised bank and wall, planted with a mixture of native and garden plants. The quartered plan of the sunk garden at the south-west end of the house has also been modified by combining two of the four beds into a larger border.

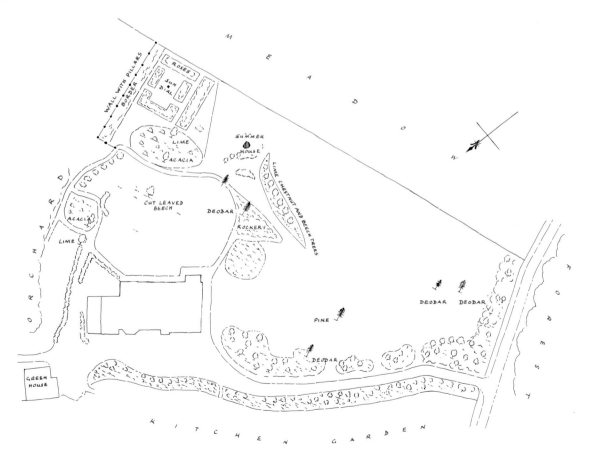

Plan of the original garden at Durmast, Burley, Hampshire

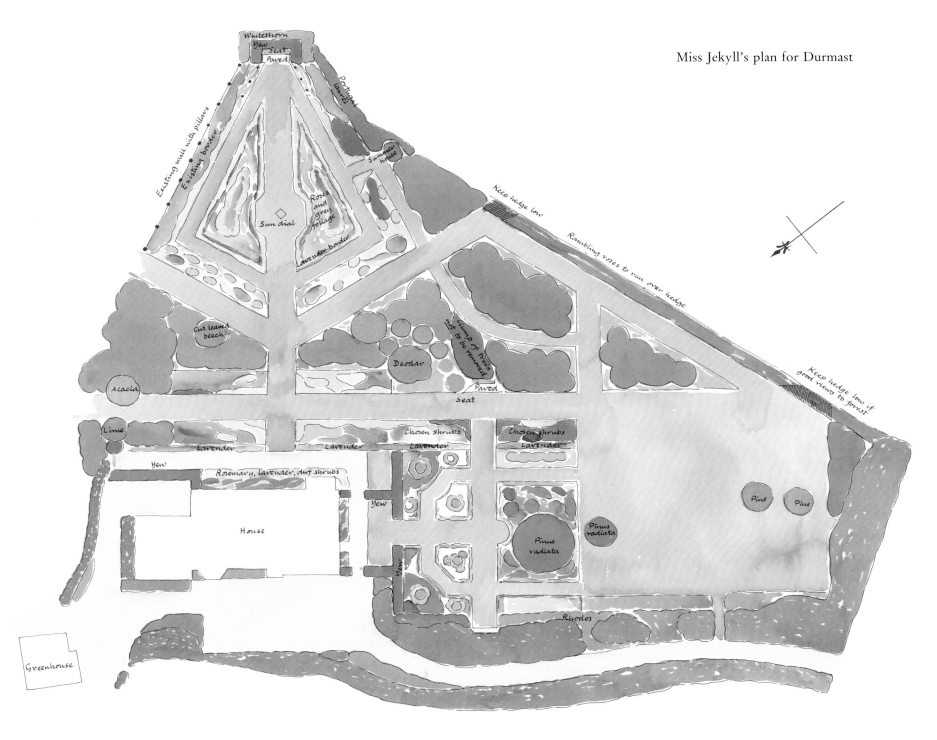

Miss Jekyll's plan for Durmast

Whitethorn
Yew
Seat
Paved

Portugal laurel

Existing wall with pillars

Existing border

Summer house

Roses and grey foliage

Sun dial

Lavender border

Keep hedge low

Rambling roses to run over hedge

Cut leaved beech

Clump of trees not to be removed

Deodar

Acacia

Paved
Seat

Keep hedge low if good views to forest

Lime

Chosen shrubs
Lavender

Chosen shrubs
Lavender

Lavender

Lavender

Yew

Rosemary, lavender, dwf shrubs

Yew

Pinus radiata

Pine

Pine

Yew

Pinus radiata

House

Rhodos

Greenhouse

A plan for the planting around
the sundial at Pednor House,
Buckinghamshire

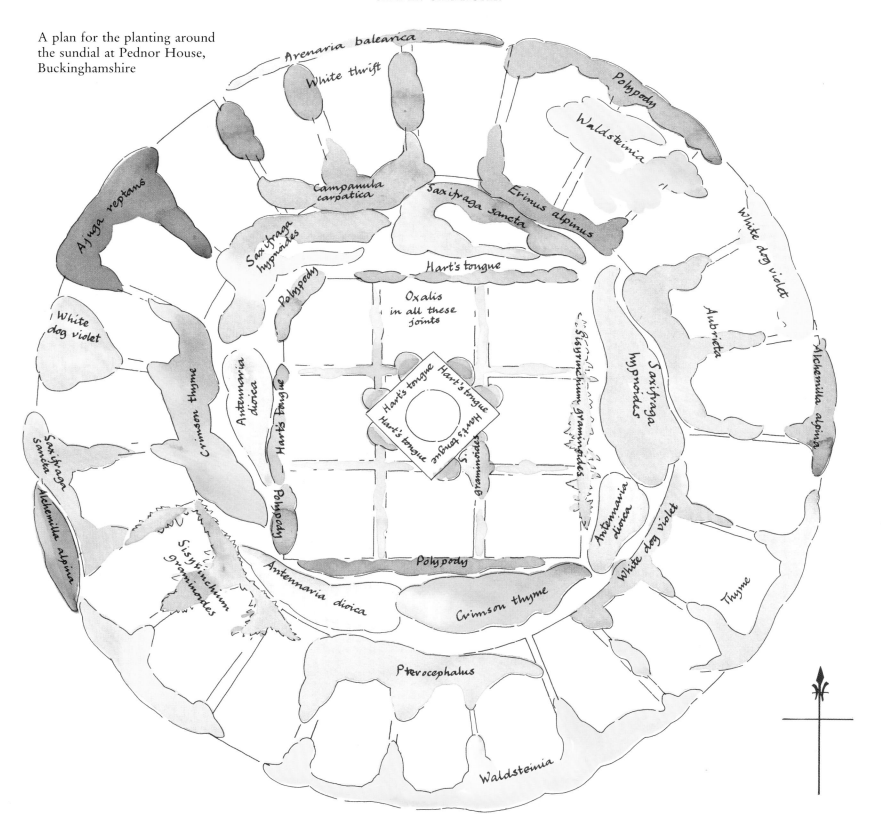

Right A plan for the roof of garden sheds at Highmount, Guildford, Surrey

Below A sketch of a topiary hedge for the Old Parsonage, Gresford, Clwyd, North Wales

The final result is a garden plan original in concept, varied in its parts but unified and utilizing the site to the full. There are no left-over parts. This does not imply, though, that the garden has been rigidly constrained by an arbitrary pattern. It is simply that by careful attention to detail, weaving existing plants into the new design and ensuring that each small piece plays its full part in the overall scheme, a garden has been created without waste, yet without proclaiming to the world at large 'I am designed'.

Jekyll plans range from whole gardens, such as at Durmast, to the most delightful details. At Pednor House in Buckinghamshire, for instance, a request from the distinguished architectural practice of Forbes and Tate for a planting plan around a sundial brought in response a finely detailed scheme with tufts of hart's tongue fern and creeping colonies of polypody springing from the base of the sundial and its plinth, the joints of which are etched in frail oxalis. Surrounding this central plinth are clumps, drifts and spreading patches of mat-like thymes and antennaria, hummocks of saxifrage, thrift and dog violets, spiky sisyrinchium, wide-spreading waldsteinia and ajuga all carefully disposed in repeated and irregular groups to provide a low mosaic of flowers and foliage throughout the year.

At Highmount, a suburban garden in Guildford for which nearly thirty plans were supplied, one plan was for the roof of garden sheds. In *Colour Schemes*, Miss Jekyll avowed 'I hold that nothing unsightly should be seen in the garden.' When a shed for stakes and other sticks had to be constructed at Munstead Wood, with a roof of galvanized iron because of the low pitch, she covered the iron sheets with 10cm/4in of peaty soil and planted it with sedums and other plants which flourish in hot, dry places. The plan for Highmount, clearly inspired by the success of her experiment at Munstead, shows elegant drifts of *Sedum spurium* in crimson and pink, with white *Sedum oppositifolium*, all interspersed among rounded hummocks of the taller *S. telephium* for its later flat heads of dusky pink. An edging of the trailing, bright yellow *S. reflexum* on one corner and patches of the softer pale violet *S. ewersii* at a safe distance on either side complete the scheme.

Both the sundial surround and this tiny roof plan show what might be achieved today, with a little thought and care, even in the most inhospitable back yard of cracking concrete and unsightly roofs.

Finally, the little sketch of a hedge for the Old Parsonage at Gresford, Clwyd, North Wales, seems to capture the essential character of Miss Jekyll's designs in a way that no larger scheme could do. Carefully controlled lines in elegant sweeps result, quite surprisingly, in homespun cottage garden topiary of a charming and wrily humorous domestic quality – a far cry from the terraced *tour de force* of the Groesbeck garden!

PLANT
ASSOCIATIONS

Combining colours, forms, textures

Pollards Park, Buckinghamshire

Grayswood Hill, Surrey

Newchapel House, Surrey

Field House, Clwyd

The Manor House, Upton Grey, Hampshire

Gertrude Jekyll was an accomplished garden designer: the examples in the previous chapter show her ability to create garden plans which were straightforward but often surprisingly inventive. However, it was her planting design which made her gardens exceptional. While Lutyens and other architects frequently resorted to elaborately detailed masonry and a certain amount of geometrical bravura to impress their clients and to satisfy their own creative appetites, Miss Jekyll produced plans which were distinctly simpler. Her steps and walls, summerhouses, pools and other architectural features are well proportioned and eminently practical, but she preferred to leave architectural elaboration to the architects and to rely on plants to give expression to her ideas. Where her sparkling plant associations were combined with Lutyens's architectural fireworks, the results were awe-inspiring.

For Miss Jekyll the choosing of plants, and especially the weaving together of plant groups, had a special fascination. 'Slowly', she said in her first book, *Wood and Garden*, 'comes the power of intelligent combination, the nearest thing we can know to the mighty force of creation.' Anyone who has appreciated two instruments playing in harmony, or the beauty of two plants carefully juxtaposed, will know that profound sense of gain: one plus one equals far more than two.

Examples of Jekyll combinations are to be seen in profusion in every one of her plans, but it is important to make a few general observations before launching into individual examples to show the range of plant associations.

Oriental philosophers have recognized for more than two thousand years the wholeness which comes from the meeting of two extremes: day and night, water and rock, male and female. The unity is expressed in the symbol of yin and yang, dark and light shapes opposing each other in their colour and their swirling motion, yet combining to form a complete circle. Two such pairs of extremes characterize the gardens and planting schemes of Gertrude Jekyll: discipline and generosity, harmony and contrast.

A combination of discipline and generosity is not so paradoxical a concept as it might seem. If one considers Miss Jekyll's own personality, there is ample evidence of her abundant kindness and hospitality, her easy tolerance of ignorance in beginners to gardening and her empathy with children. Equally, though, it is not difficult to sense beneath that ample

Pages 40–41 In the garden at Hadspen House, in Somerset, grey thistles and spiky globe artichoke combine with clear blue delphiniums, paler blue symphytum and soft salvia, in a haze of misty colouring. *Crambe cordifolia* enlivens the planting with its crumpled dark green foliage and clouds of honey-scented white flowers.

Above Within this simple planting at Hadspen, each small flower contributes to the overall effect. Here the emerging buds of *Anthemis tinctoria* underpin fragrant yellow roses and slender spikes of creamy lupins. Lilies and greenish yellow alchemilla introduce a sharper note in the foreground, with blue geraniums to provide contrast.

generosity a formidable strength of character, an intolerance of fools, and an inviolable sense of right and wrong. As Lutyens confided in a letter to his wife, 'Bumps rampant is an awful sight!' Her generosity was not hypocritical; nor did it reflect casual sloppiness, a temporary casting off or relaxation of an iron discipline. Rather, it represented the genuine overflowing spirit of a generous person confident of right and wrong and thankful of her place in a world marvellously wrought by a generous Creator.

In exactly the same way, her planting schemes were not excesses of shapeless plants imposed on an architectural framework to disguise its harsh angularity. Plants were there to fill out the basic idea, the backbone, and to create a series of enchanting garden pictures furnishing the central spine and reliant on it for support and unity.

Harmony and contrast, too, resolve from apparent extremes to inseparable partners, for without an underlying harmony there can be no meaningful contrast; without contrast there is no frame of reference for appreciating harmony.

Planting in drifts, as suggested by Gertrude Jekyll, allows the plants in flower at any one time to build up into colourful compositions, while earlier- and later-flowering plants fade into the background. Here, at Powis Castle in Wales, the drifts create a strong sense of rhythm and harmony.

Harmonious colour planning, in effect a horticultural 'theory of relativity', is perhaps Miss Jekyll's greatest technical contribution to garden design. It was a direct result of her training at the Kensington School of Art. Here she was taught that human colour perception was greatly influenced by the need of the brain to 'see', through the eyes, a 'normal' world, a world in which a completely reflective surface would appear white. If, for example, one were shut in a room painted in a uniform bright orange, the brain would gradually adjust the messages received from the eyes and suppress orange until it convinced itself that the world was normal – that is, white. The truth would only be revealed when one left the room to discover a world painted white minus orange – that is, bright blue!

In her books, Miss Jekyll recounted many examples of colour deception, of looking through a hole torn in a burdock leaf to appreciate the blue colouring in a distant landscape which the brain 'knew' ought to be green; or of staring hard at an orange French marigold and then, after a minute or so, gazing at its leaves to see them as bright blue. Her most amusing example was of awakening from half-sleep in her painting shed to see a blue horse with a bright orange spot on its flank. This strange apparition was caused by afternoon sunlight pouring through a knot hole in the wall on to a white horse she had been using as a model for her painting. The warm sunshine threw a spotlight on to the horse's coat, which was otherwise illuminated by the cold bluish light from a large north window. The saturation of the eye with one colour so that its complementary colour would then be seen in enhanced brilliance was the basis of Miss Jekyll's management of contrast.

Colour was not all, of course. Miss Jekyll ended *Colour Schemes* on an apologetic note: 'If in the foregoing chapters I have dwelt rather insistently on matters of colour, it is not that I under-rate the equal importance of form and proportion, but that I think that the question of colour, as regards its more careful use, is either more commonly neglected or has fewer exponents.' In practice her use of form and texture was at least as important as her colour planning in achieving the balance she sought between harmony and contrast.

In modern gardening the need for contrast is emphasized to excess. Small gardens erupt in blue-grey conifers sprouting from golden heathers, while larger gardens mix purple cotinus and berberis with yellow robinia, golden elder and *Lonicera* 'Baggesen's Gold', *ad nauseam*. Miss Jekyll understood the need for a prevailing sense of harmony within which carefully planned contrasts of form, texture and colour could excite rather than jar the senses.

To some extent, of course, this balance of harmony and contrast was made easier by the scale of her gardens. With acres at her disposal there was space for separate compartments, time to saturate the eye with glowing orange before moving into the next garden with greys and lavenders rendered luminously brilliant by contrast; there was space to move from misty schemes of grey and pink through masses of handsome dark green, and into brightly colourful flower gardens. But there are innumerable examples among her plans of the management of contrast on a smaller scale: bright borders with a dark background, grey gardens surrounded by borders of rich orange, or subdued associations of dark green on one side of a terrace answering soft plantings of grey, pink and lavender on the other – ideas directly applicable to the small garden.

What is more important, even her largest schemes are characterized by minute attention to detail. In addition to the major contrasts between one garden compartment and another, there are invariably lesser contrasts within each part: spikes of gladiolus emphasizing the cloudy softness of gypsophila; lilies of crystalline whiteness dropped into the border to ensure that dark reds appear rich rather than sombre; bold groups of bergenia underpinning the frothier components of a border to prevent the airiness degenerating into an insipid blur. Each large plan contains within it dozens of potential smaller schemes to inspire the owner of even the smallest garden.

One significant unifying element in Miss Jekyll's plant associations is her use of plants in long, thin, flowing groups – 'drifts' was the word she adopted to describe them. These Jekyll drifts are very apparent in her flower borders, but they can also be seen in the interweaving groups of holly, oak, thorn and other natives in her woodland plantings, and in the interplay of plant groups and open space in her wild gardens. In her borders, the drifts have a practical purpose in that while a considerable quantity of each plant is revealed when in flower, its thin trail disappears as it ceases to flower and other plants come into prominence. There is, though, a secondary effect in that the planting is unified by the repetitive flow, just as a picture is given character by the brush-strokes of the artist.

Drifts are not inevitable, however. Among the drifts there are sharper points of emphasis – *Lilium candidum* perhaps, or white broom in shrub borders. On occasions her groundwork of flowing drifts gives way dramatically to short stabs of planting, never more so than in the long flower border at Brackenbrough, in Cumbria, where the drifts of soft-coloured and rounded perennials at either end of the border appear, on plan, to collide in the sharp dabs of yuccas, cannas, dahlias and tall hollyhocks, like waves crashing on to a half-submerged rock (see pages 70–71). Often, too, flowing drifts lap around the static, solid forms of yuccas, euphorbias or other statuesque plants, as in the designs for the main border at Munstead Wood, and for the lovely grey garden at Chinthurst, Surrey.

The balance of discipline and generosity, harmony and contrast, which characterizes Miss Jekyll's planting schemes is beautifully illustrated in a plan of Pollards Park, Buckinghamshire, a quiet, contemplative planting in soft colours.

Discipline is apparent in the geometry of the garden, a circular compartment some 25m/80ft across, enclosed within twin borders each 30m/100ft along the front edge. A feeling of abundant generosity results from the repeated drifts of stachys, *Senecio bicolor* ssp. *cineraria* and santolina edging the borders in nearly symmetrical masses, flowing forward over the path; and from the rounded forms of phlomis, gypsophila and lavender backed by trailing *Clematis* × *jackmanii* and everlasting pea in pink and white.

In an unusually pervasive expression of harmony, the borders are devoted completely to flowers and foliage of the softest colours – pink, white, lavender, purple and grey. Instructions on the plan direct the gardener to remove the yellow flowers from the santolina and senecio. There are to be no sharp contrasts here. However, the vertical accents of

In a planting at Mottisfont Abbey, in Hampshire, statuesque spires of Madonna lily (*Lilium candidum*) are inserted with studied irregularity between long drifts of pale pink *Linaria* 'Canon Went', deeper perennial wallflowers and roses. While the lilies repeat the vertical lines of the wallflowers and the slender linaria, their bold stems and glistening white flowers stand out emphatically.

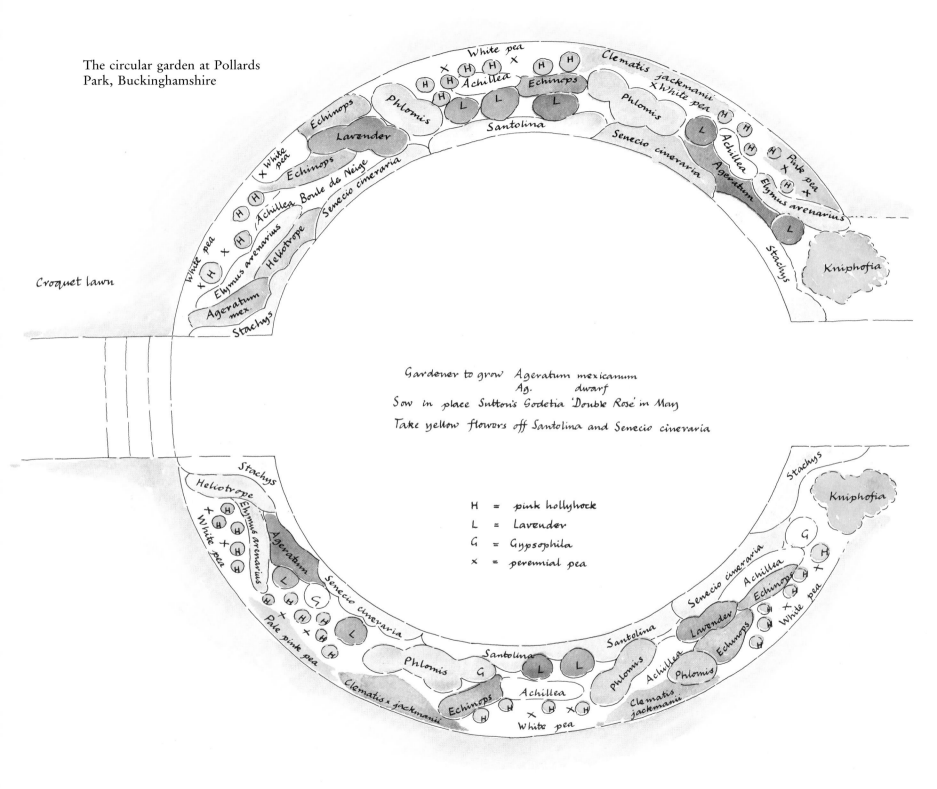

The circular garden at Pollards Park, Buckinghamshire

White pea

Achillea

Echinops

Clematis jackmanii

Phlomis

Phlomis

Echinops

Santolina

Lavender

White pea

Senecio cineraria

White pea

Achillea Boule de Neige

Echinops

Senecio cineraria

Pink pea

Achillea

Ageratum

Elymus arenarius

Heliotrope

Elymus arenarius

White pea

Croquet lawn

Ageratum mex.

Stachys

Stachys

Kniphofia

Gardener to grow   Ageratum mexicanum
                   Ag.   dwarf
Sow in place Sutton's Godetia 'Double Rosé' in May
Take yellow flowers off Santolina and Senecio cineraria

Stachys

Heliotrope

Elymus arenarius

White pea

Ageratum

Senecio cineraria

Stachys

Kniphofia

Senecio cineraria

Achillea

Echinops

Pale pink pea

Lavender

White pea

Phlomis

Santolina

Phlomis

Clematis x jackmanii

Santolina

Phlomis

Echinops

Achillea

Achillea

Echinops

Clematis jackmanii

White pea

H = pink hollyhock

L = Lavender

G = Gypsophila

x = perennial pea

hollyhocks and of silver-leaved elymus enliven the border, and the placing of the circular grey garden at the end of the double borders of glowing orange allows the strategic positioning of two large clumps of orange kniphofia where the two compartments meet.

The elymus, so important for the insistent vertical note of its foliage, carries the grey colouring back into the borders on three of four corners (a subtle break with symmetry), with rounded mounds of lavender filling out the central sections. Phlomis (with its gentler yellow flowers and larger leaves) and misty gypsophila add variations on this subtle theme of rounded softness.

Within this framework of pale grey are set the flowers: purple spikes of lavender, of course, and the quiet buff-yellow of phlomis, but also the more positive flowers of pink holly-hocks encircling the garden, the blue globes of echinops above its dark green and grey foliage, and dense white heads of *Achillea* 'Boule de Neige' on spreading masses of fine dark foliage. The achillea is usually placed beside or in front of the echinops so that the darkness of leaf is absorbed, by virtue of the white undersides of echinops foliage, into the general scheme. Behind and among the hollyhocks are everlasting peas, white in the main but with two pairs of pale pink to introduce a minor variation, followed by rich purple *Clematis × jackmanii* (the original, rather thin-petalled form, as Miss Jekyll thought the colour of 'Superba' too red). Long drifts of greyish purple ageratum, as soft in texture as in colour, and richly scented heliotrope complete the scheme on plan, but the gardener is also directed to sow godetia (Sutton's 'Double Rose') in late spring through any of the thinner patches of the border, binding the whole scheme into a continuous picture of marvellously soft colouring. At the entrance to the garden those two important clumps of dark-leaved and fiery orange kniphofias in the main border intrude just sufficiently to serve as a constant frame of reference to eyes attempting to adjust themselves to seeing the softness of colouring as the normal state of the world. (The cost of Miss Jekyll's plants for the grey garden amounted to £6 11s!)

The tranquillity of this open, circular garden, lined with misty colours, must have been quite enchanting – a calm oasis of grey and pink after a rigorous afternoon of croquet on the adjacent lawn.

Grey is also the predominant impression created by the lower garden at Grayswood Hill in Surrey, but the character of Grayswood Hill is totally different from the ethereal calm of Pollards Park.

In *Colour Schemes* and elsewhere Miss Jekyll expressed her regret that her own 6 hectare/15 acre garden was too small to accommodate all the ideas she would like to try. 'One of my desires that cannot be fulfilled is to have a rocky hill side in full sun, so steep as to be almost precipitous … I would have great groups of Yucca standing up against the sky and others in the rock face, and some bushes of this great *Euphorbia* [*E. characias* ssp. *wulfenii*] and only a few other plants, all of rather large grey effect.' At Grayswood Hill she found at least partial fulfilment of her desire.

Rosemary, phlomis and santolina in free-flowing masses are interwoven with yuccas (*Yucca gloriosa*, *Y. recurvifolia* and the smaller *Y. filamentosa*), with *Euphorbia characias* ssp. *wulfenii* and the stiff swords of *Phormium tenax*, all plants of bold form yet muted grey colouring, with the sharp yellow flowers of the euphorbia repeating the colouring of the phlomis nearby. While these bolder plants are arranged in deep groups of three or five plants, standing out in silhouette from the slope, the smaller plants at their feet are arranged in long drifts, parallel to the path, underscoring the scheme. Pale helianthemums, grey othonna, fine-textured buglossoides and woolly white santolina flow around and beneath the bolder plants, merging gradually into taller rosemary on one side and *Brachyglottis* (*Senecio*) 'Sunshine' on the other, and thence into the background of taller shrubs and trees.

These taller plants include *Cistus laurifolius* and the darker *C. × cyprius* (aromatic Mediterranean associates of the phlomis, rosemary and santolina). There is the smooth-leaved form of laurustinus, *Viburnum tinus* 'Lucidum', matching the cistus in its glossy leafage, and *Rosa virginiana*, richly glossy too, but deciduous and colouring brilliantly before leaf fall. Among these rounded forms a thin trickle of cypress adds the staccato rhythm of repeated verticals, with the equally dark but bold, jagged and glossy foliage of acanthus reinforcing the Mediterranean allusion.

Thus, on the main path below the bank, the planting changes from dark acanthus, viburnum and *Cistus laurifolius* to the softer green of rosemary and grey of yucca, euphorbia, othonna and *Cistus* 'Silver Pink'. The original idea had been to continue this soft colouring with *Bergenia ciliata* emerging from the dusky drift of buglossoides, but Miss Jekyll changed her mind and substituted the large-leaved form of *B. cordifolia*, adding weight and sharp contrast to this central part of the planting, fading again with santolina, senecio, phlomis, and the misty twiggery of Scotch briars. In contrast to this eventful and finely adjusted arrangement of plants along the main path, the gently jostling growth of whortleberry and Scotch briars enfolds the other two sides of the triangle in a grey-green blanket of deceptive simplicity.

Yucca flaccida 'Ivory'. For Miss Jekyll the yuccas' handsome spiky rosettes of glaucous foliage and towering creamy white flower spires epitomized the dramatic potential for planting on rocky hillsides.

To complete the picture, two other plants need some explanation. On the northern point at the top of the bank is a long group of kerria, its bright green leaves and stems and egg-yolk pom-pom flowers an odd choice for this Mediterranean hillside. However, its position is such that it would be visible only from the top of the bank, where the straight path and open lawn beyond create quite a different character from the lower garden. In this context, and with a background of dark green *Viburnum tinus*, the kerria becomes an understandable choice for creating a temporary splash of colour in what would appear, from the upper level, as a large-scale shrub border seen from a distance across a large lawn. Next to the kerria is a solitary amelanchier, a tree in position before Miss Jekyll's scheme was designed, but one which was retained as entirely appropriate. From above it provides a small point of soft whiteness among the dark evergreens in its brief flowering season; from below its elegant dome of grey-green foliage creates a sense of depth behind the phormiums and yuccas and between the advancing wings of stronger foliage, while in autumn the brilliant colouring of the leaves has a telling effect from both above and below.

While Grayswood Hill is an obvious choice to illustrate picturesque planting in a border setting, it is difficult to pick out one example of picturesque effect on a larger scale. Carefully drawn patterns of winding walks defined by scattered groups of holly, birch, oak and thorn occur frequently among the Reef Point plans. Stilemans deserves mention for its numerous paths curving like a gigantic embroidery pattern, and Drayton Wood is remarkable for its strands of native trees and rambling roses interwoven like so many coloured silks. At Hollington trees were planted in free groups in the pasture, while graceful rides were carved through the wood, unifying the previously hard-edged blocks of woodland and grass into a single composition of great charm. An old monkey puzzle near the edge of the wood was taken as a suitably exotic prompt for the development of a small gold garden, strategically placed at the intersection of two paths.

The number and diversity of these wild gardens is such that they merit and will receive a chapter to themselves, but for the impression of wilderness on a small scale one cannot do better than to look at the plan for the nut walk at Newchapel House in Lingfield, Surrey.

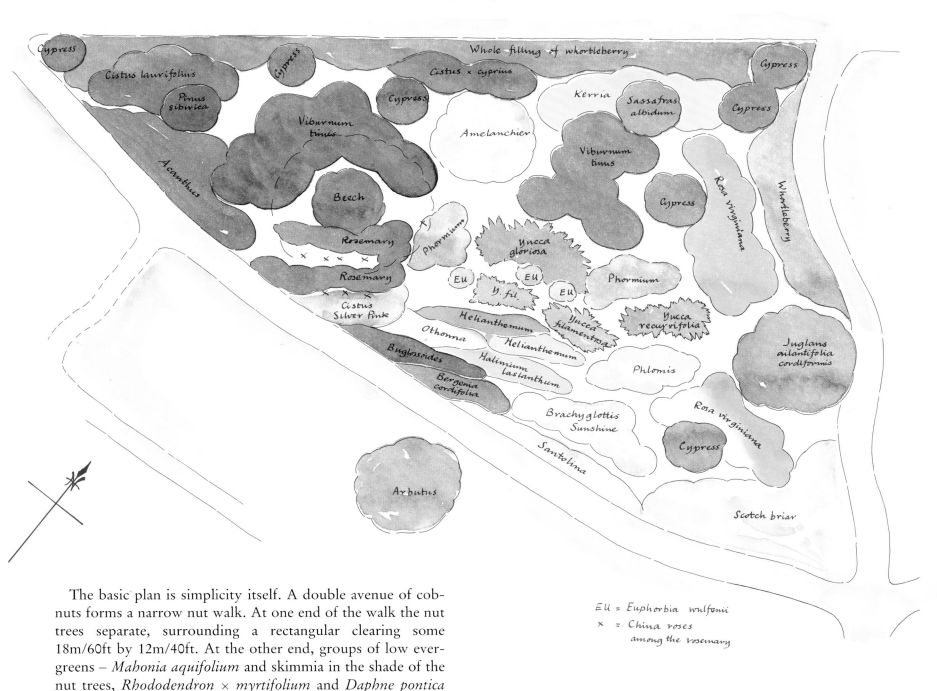

Cypress

Cistus laurifolius

Cypress

Pinus sibirica

Viburnum tinus

Whole filling of whortleberry

Cistus × cyprius

Cypress

Kerria

Sassafras albidum

Cypress

Amelanchier

Acanthus

Viburnum tinus

Beech

Phormium

Yucca gloriosa

Cypress

Rosa virginiana

Whortleberry

Rosemary

× × ×

EU

EU

Phormium

Rosemary

Y. fil.

EU

Cistus Silver Pink

× ×

Yucca filamentosa

Yucca recurvifolia

Juglans ailantifolia cordiformis

Othonna

Helianthemum

Buglossoides

Helianthemum

Halimium lasianthum

Phlomis

Bergenia cordifolia

Brachyglottis Sunshine

Rosa virginiana

Cypress

Santolina

Arbutus

Scotch briar

EU = Euphorbia wulfenii
× = China roses
among the rosemary

The basic plan is simplicity itself. A double avenue of cobnuts forms a narrow nut walk. At one end of the walk the nut trees separate, surrounding a rectangular clearing some 18m/60ft by 12m/40ft. At the other end, groups of low evergreens – *Mahonia aquifolium* and skimmia in the shade of the nut trees, *Rhododendron × myrtifolium* and *Daphne pontica* in the open – provide a firm stop to the planting. Cloudy heads of *Aster divaricatus* drooped over clumps of bergenia offer a delightfully misty contrast at the edge of the path.

Beneath the nuts, and for the entire length of the garden,

The lower garden, Grayswood Hill, Surrey

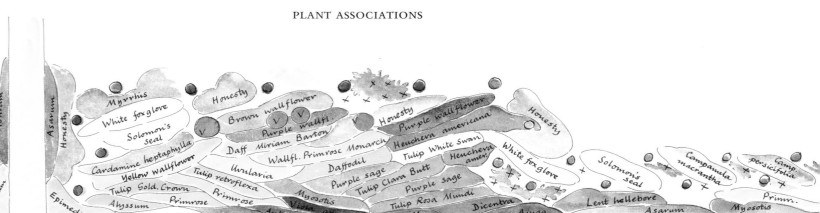

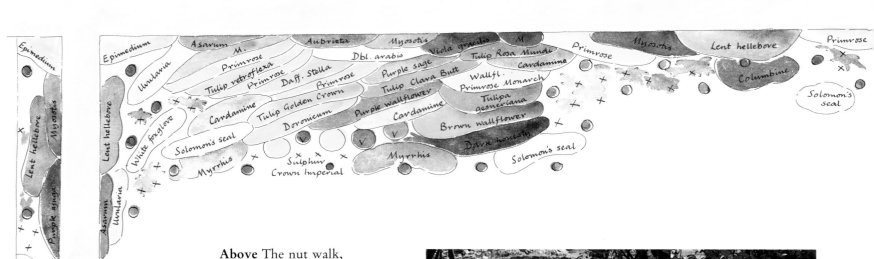

Above The nut walk, Newchapel House, Lingfield, Surrey

Right Delicate fern fronds interspersed here and there with bold-textured hellebores create the groundwork of a planting scheme beneath a nut walk. The planting here is supplemented by euphorbias – rosettes of dark, sombre foliage concealed in spring by clouds of fresh yellow-green bracts and flowers.

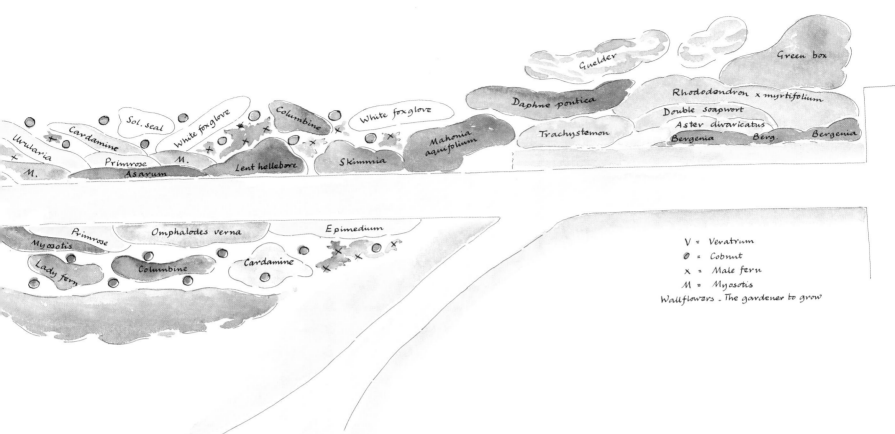

are loose groups of male fern and an occasional small patch of lady fern, the pale green groundwork of the picture. Long drifts of pale yellow primroses, blue omphalodes and forget-me-nots carpet the ground in front of the ferns, interspersed here and there with bold-textured hellebores and a neat edging of *Asarum europaeum* for a darker but glossily cheerful note. Behind and between the ferns are other plants of cool, pale elegance: columbines and stately white foxgloves, gracefully arching Solomon's seal and demure uvularia, cardamine and campanulas picking up the blue, pale yellow and white colouring of the lowlier plants.

In the nut walk itself there is only room for one or two drifts at a time, thin streams of gentle colour among the soft greenery of young ferns, but as the cobnuts separate, the drifts are ranged one against another and the palette widens to create a charming and colourful spring garden. Foxgloves and Solomon's seal, cardamine and uvularia are interwoven with purple sage and *Heuchera americana*, their bronzed foliage an

ideal foil for white and pink tulips, while wallflowers of yellow, primrose, brown and purple partner yellow tulips and daffodils and clumps of stately crown imperials.

The steady trickle of male ferns continues into the clearing, but here they are massed in opposite corners of the rectangle, thus playing down the strong parallel lines characteristic of the narrower section of the walk. The pale greenery of the ferns is supplemented, in the more colourful and more open part of the garden, by the bold, pleated leaves of veratrum. Along the edge of the path blue-spiked ajuga, pale aubrieta and snowy white double arabis, dicentra and violas are added to emphasize the sunnier and more positively colourful character of the little clearing, while epimediums (semi-evergreen plants of the greatest elegance), bold hellebores, an edging of glossy asarum and casual groups of *Rhododendron × myrtifolium* reiterate the planting at the start of the nut walk, bringing to a close this wonderful impressionist vision of woodland grace and spring freshness.

This small sketch of translucent freshness was developed into a major picture in the remarkable Japanese Water Garden at Field House, Clent, in Clwyd. Forbes and Tate were the architects for the garden and, as might be expected from so traditional an office, the water garden was far removed from the normal conception of Japanese. The plan is quite difficult to interpret without the architects' additional notes and sketches, but what look like two straight rows of pergola posts on the east side of the plan are in fact the uprights of a vaguely Japanese bridge spanning a ha-ha. The bridge rests on a small semicircular landing, from which the path continues to right and left before curving back to enclose a semicircular pond. On the opposite side of the garden the existing brook is

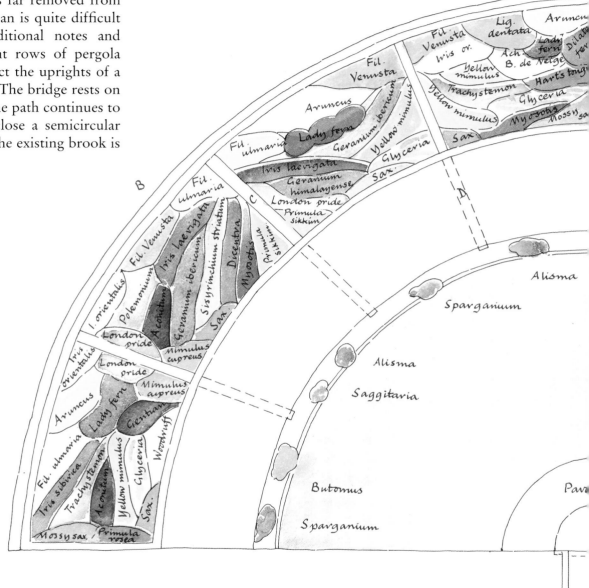

Above The creamy white plumes of *Aruncus dioicus* help establish a mood of waterside luxuriance.

Opposite *Iris sibirica*: clear blue butterfly flowers poised elegantly among arching sheaves of pale green foliage.

The Japanese Water Garden, Field House, Clent, Clwyd

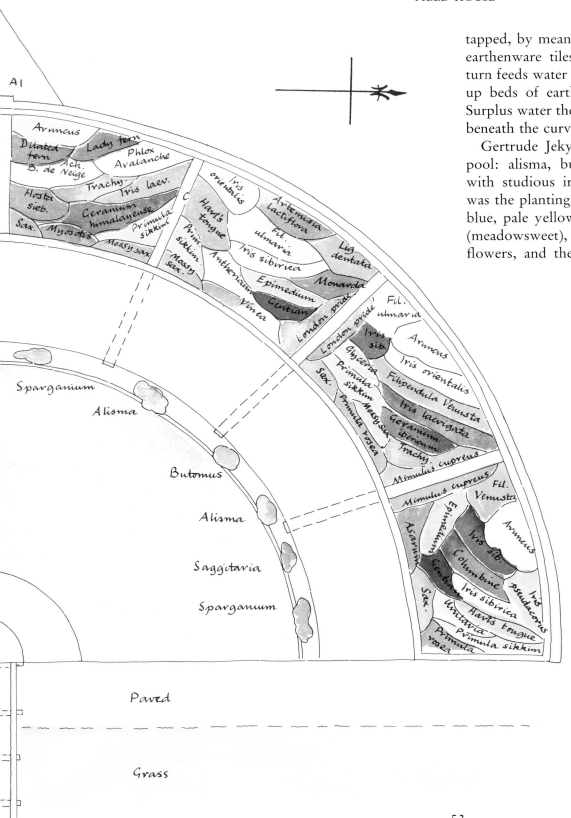

tapped, by means of a sluice, to feed a channel of half-round earthenware tiles, repeating the semicircle. This channel in turn feeds water through secondary channels into the banked-up beds of earth, forming a bog garden of eight sections. Surplus water then filters through smaller tile drains and is led beneath the curved path into the pond.

Gertrude Jekyll suggested a few waterside plants for the pool: alisma, butomus, sagittaria and sparganium, planted with studious irregularity. Her main contribution, though, was the planting of the damp border in a wonderful blend of blue, pale yellow, white and pale green. *Filipendula ulmaria* (meadowsweet), with its milky white heads of fragrant flowers, and the taller plumes of *Aruncus dioicus* form the

A: Existing brook
A1: Sluice
B: Earthenware channel
C: Rough channel, cement with boulders
D: Drains half round

backbone of the scheme, being repeated throughout the border. *Iris sibirica* (blue and white), *I. laevigata* and *I. orientalis* between and in front of these anchor plants provide the repetitive rhythm of sword-like leaves, and more solid but beautifully moulded butterfly flowers of blue and white. A single patch of the yellow *I. pseudacorus* at one end of the border continues the rhythm while providing a lively contrast in colour.

The other principal components, though less freely used, are *Trachystemon orientalis*, geraniums (both *Geranium himalayense* and *G. ibericum*) and mimulus. Trachystemon offers its pale pink-tinged blue flowers early in the year, combining with the few evergreen and semi-evergreen plants to provide interest when the ground would otherwise be bare, but the main reason for its inclusion lies in its impressive colonies of huge, bristly, pale green leaves. The geraniums follow with their generous display of brighter purple-blue flowers over soft mounds of more elegant fingered leaves, overlapping in season with mimulus, whose sharp yellow trumpets and fresh green foliage epitomize the luxuriant but graceful vigour of waterside planting.

With these few plants setting the mood and covering rather more than half the border in total, variations upon the theme then commence: lady fern, blue spikes of aconitum and the later-flowering willow gentian in the first section of the border, with the grassy foliage of white-striped glyceria and an edging of sweet woodruff; aconitum again in the second section, emerging from a carpet of geranium this time, with sisyrinchium providing a narrow-leaved contrast and feathery dicentra, blue forget-me-nots and mossy green hummocks of saxifrage a charming edge. Thus the composition develops through the full sweep of the border; glossy London pride, asarum and hart's tongue for their cheerful winter greenery, a group of hosta matching the trachystemon in boldness of leaf, slender anthericum, frail uvularia and occasional groups of columbine and epimedium. Distributed unevenly though this sea of harmonious planting are groups of *Primula sikkimensis*, its clear yellow flowers rising above its surroundings in late spring and early summer, when the foliage of the border is at the peak of its late spring freshness.

In complete contrast, and clearly pencilled in as an afterthought, are three small patches of *Primula rosea*. In the main period of the border's full beauty, from late spring to midsummer if one counts only the beauty of flowers, *Primula rosea* would contribute its neat rosettes of pale green to the edge of the border; but its flowering season is much earlier – it produces its bright, shining rose-pink flowers over newly emerging foliage in the first days of spring. Why such a bright and early flower? One basic principle of Miss Jekyll's planting was that each border should be planned primarily *but not solely* for a limited season. If *Primula rosea* could justify its place in the main scheme as a neat foliage plant for edging, then its flowers, deliberately placed at conspicuous corners of the garden, could be allowed to provide an unexpected incident of bright cheer, bringing out a warmth of colouring barely hinted at in the purple-blue trachystemon flowers then pushing on naked stems through the bare ground.

Each of these schemes, distillations of misty softness and of

The Manor House, Upton Grey, Hampshire, overall plan

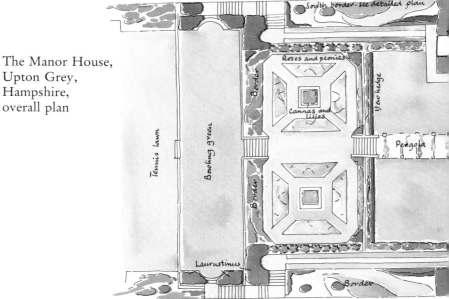

■ Cistus laurifolius
o Birch
White broom
+ Transplanted laburnum
R Climbing roses

Mediterranean warmth, woodland and luxuriant waterside, has been chosen to indicate the breadth of character, the atmosphere and impressions which Miss Jekyll was able to conjure up by her careful selection and arrangement of plants. But the greatest appeal of her work lies in the way in which many, sometimes all, of these strikingly different strands could be woven into a wonderfully harmonious, unified garden picture.

The Manor House at Upton Grey, in Hampshire, is a perfect example of this versatility of expression: a leafy drive bordered by hollies and tree peonies ending in dark masses of yew; a forecourt, fringed with handsome evergreens and delicate ferns, leading to a tranquil wild garden with winding walks down to a secret pool; a pergola embroidered with carefully chosen climbing plants; colourful flower borders surrounding smooth green lawns, then discreet side openings

Left The pergola at Upton Grey supports climbing and rambling roses alternating with other plants. The result is a tantalizing balance of symmetry and irregularity. Each plant contributes its own character – sweetly scented jasmine, the curious flowers and huge leaves of aristolochia, the brilliance of Virginia creeper – while they combine in a picture of unrestrained growth.

Right Beyond the pergola, the drystone walls are generously planted with mounds of low plants that link the borders above and below. While the flowers of the irises and peonies in the foreground contribute only briefly to the summer garden, their foliage provides interest for months.

– flights of steps between dark mounds of laurustinus – descending to larger compartments such as the rose garden and tennis lawn.

In large gardens the elaborate and colourful flower gardens would merge into a different world of green woodland walks among irregular masses of rhododendrons. Finally, perhaps, there might be a surprise – a secret garden bright with flowers, or a rose arbour, as a reminder that this informal setting is indeed a garden, a work of art, not a fortuitously charming piece of natural woodland.

Upton Grey, though, is not a large property. The sixteenth-century farm house was enlarged by Charles Holme in about 1890, when he retired from industry to devote himself to his Arts and Crafts interests. Its tile-hung exterior, half-timbered on the central bay, created an ideal backdrop for Miss Jekyll's garden scheme.

The house is set well back from the road, with a long drive running close to one boundary before turning at right angles to enter the forecourt. Miss Jekyll uses hollies in a long,

irregular line to conceal the drive from the garden proper, adding more hollies on the outer side to reduce the hard line of the boundary hedge. Long, slender drifts of tree peonies floating over rounded masses of centranthus line the drive, making the approach a garden in itself. Dark masses of yew separate this graceful peony garden from the forecourt, which is low-walled and simply planted with dark greens to under-score the more elaborate charms of the house. Once in the forecourt, the full extent of the garden behind the hollies is revealed, shaped by Miss Jekyll into a long ride, sweeping down to a small pond, then returning by branching subordinate paths to the circular steps connecting wild garden and forecourt.

Massed yews and free-growing roses fill the south side of the garden, screening the less than picturesque church and graveyard, with laburnums transplanted among the dark ever-greens, where their early colour and fresh greenery can be appreciated to the full. Roses continue across to the north side, the taller ones flinging long trails of blossom into the

Left In the rose garden at Upton Grey, enclosed on three sides by the drystone walls, there is much to enjoy both before and after the roses' flowering season. The stone centrepieces contain fragrant *Lilium regale*, with bold-leaved cannas to take over later in the summer. The rose beds, edged with woolly stachys and with glossy-leaved peonies interspersed among the roses, are surrounded by narrow borders of lavender, rosemary, pinks and other grey foliage.

Opposite Laurustinus and bergenia line the steps which lead from one garden compartment to another. In summer their dark, handsome foliage forms the backbone of the flower garden, while discreetly tempering the architectural lines of the garden. In winter and early spring, when most of the garden lies dormant, the two important evergreens come to the fore, their dusky pink flowers and the bronze leaves of the bergenia harmonizing with the subtle colours of mossy stonework.

hollies lining the drive, the lower ones interplanted with *Cistus laurifolius* and (on the south side) white broom for the sake of their contrasting greenery, domed and spiky respectively, and for their abundant succession of white flowers.

Nearer the pond the planting takes on a more flowing character, with long drifts of herbaceous plants – spiky kniphofia, dusky red polygonums, statuesque heracleum – among bolder groups of bamboo, with generous masses of fresh green water elder (*Viburnum opulus*) and dark yew.

On the other side of the house, the original garden dropped away in formal terraces to a tennis lawn on the lowest level, the levels being separated by grass embankments. Miss Jekyll did not much like grass embankments (the type of terracing scornfully dismissed by William Robinson as 'railway embankment gardening'). Because the banks tapered in width as they diminished in height down the natural slope, they left awkward shapes of grass on each level. Under her influence, drystone walls replaced the banks, and rectangular gardens were thus shaped from the odd trapezoids of grass.

From the house springs a short pergola, alternate piers planted with roses, the remainder with bold-leaved aristolochia, delicate-fingered Virginia creeper and sweetly fragrant jasmine. Ahead, the new drystone walls are planted with drifts of aubrieta, arenaria, pinks and campanula, cascades of cerastium and spires of white snapdragons, and below them lies the rose garden. Here, the formal pattern of roses and peonies edged with stachys frames twin central squares planted with cannas and pots of white lilies, the cannas more lasting in their decorative effect than any of the 'perpetual' flowering roses then available, and more weighty.

To the left and right of the pergola lawn, narrow paths parallel the rose garden below, eventually descending by zig-zag flights of steps to reach the bowling green on the next lower level. These lateral paths and the central rose garden are separated by narrow borders of blue, white and yellow. In the border shown in the detailed plan, *Campanula latifolia alba*, blue *Clematis heracleifolia* var. *davidiana* and *Aster sedifolius* wreathed with white *Clematis recta* flow into drifts of white snapdragons, thence to bolder groups of yuccas and the thistle heads of *Eryngium* × *oliverianum*. Beyond, pink snapdragons and *Fuchsia gracilis* add a warmer note. In the wall below, the same colour themes are continued. Long drifts of

blue veronica, palest pink London pride, foamy white tiarella and lavender phlox flow over the wall from the border, meeting the carefully woven strands of arenaria, aubrieta and *Phlox stellaria* in the wall itself. White foxgloves, snapdragons and *Campanula pyramidalis* provide vertical emphasis, with the loosely rounded heads of cardamine intermediate in shape between mat-formers and spikes. Near the base of the wall, cushions of *Campanula carpatica*, blue and white, extend the colour scheme into summer.

Across the path from each of the narrow borders a much wider bed takes up the theme and develops it into a scheme of increasing intensity of colour. At either end, the colouring is of pale yellow spiked with clear blue – marigolds of palest

Upton Grey, detailed planting plan for one of the double borders above the rose garden

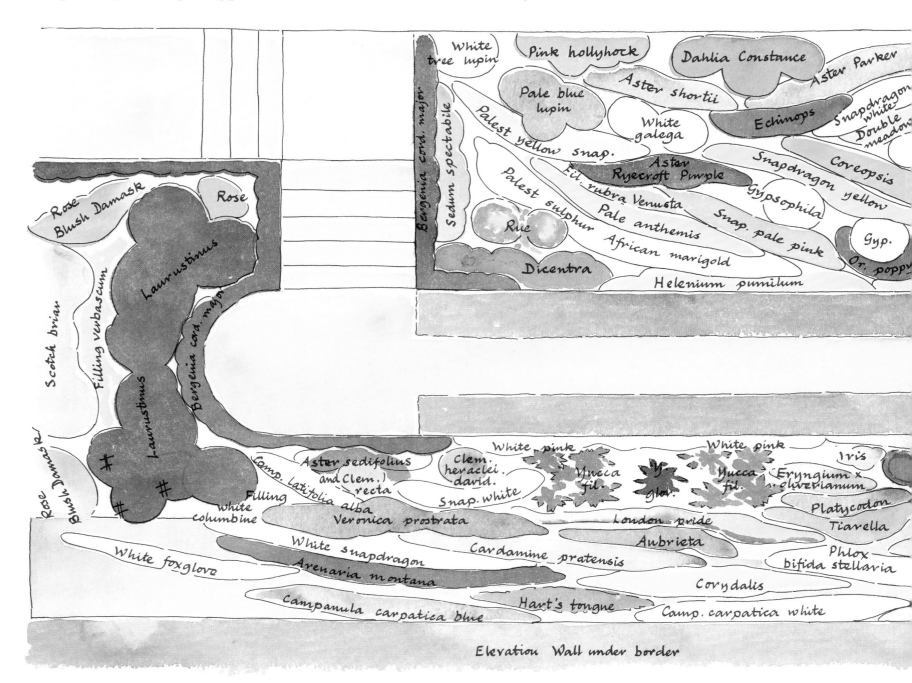

Elevation Wall under border

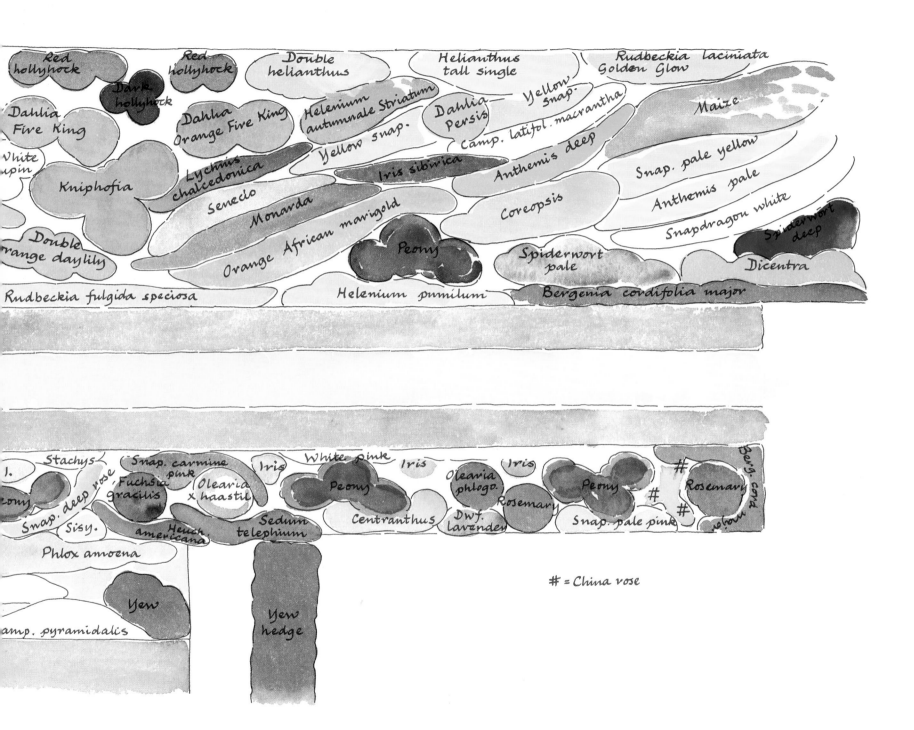

= China rose

yellow, striped maize, blue spiderwort, blue and white lupins. Towards the centre the colouring changes through yellow rudbeckias, helianthus and helenium, orange marigolds and scarlet monarda to spires of kniphofia and groups of orange and scarlet dahlias and deep red hollyhocks. These changes in the colour scheme are emphasized by groups of white, yellow, pink and rose snapdragons.

Finally, in the lowest part of the garden (not shown on these plans), are twin rose borders. Here the charm of their softer colouring is supplemented in no small measure by their intriguing display of three-dimensional geometry: the vertical outlines of roses and *Clematis flammula* on hoops and chain swags at the back of the borders are repeated in the ground plan of the scalloped front edges. Within each panel of the three-part borders the basic pattern is identical. Four groups of roses have peonies between the front pair and deep blue anchusa behind, while short drifts of Madonna lilies and gladioli (the latter in front to take over from the earlier-flowering lilies) occupy the very centre of each panel. Around these are ranged in turn white anemones at the back (for late summer and autumn), delphiniums to take over from anchusa in high summer, long-flowering antirrhinums to each side, and pots of *Lilium longiflorum* along the front.

Superimposed upon this regularity is a secondary rhythm. In the outer panels of each border the roses are red, the gladioli scarlet and the antirrhinums pink, and the whole is interplanted with chamois *Phlox drummondii* – a rich blend of strong, warm colours; in the inner portion are white roses, salmon gladioli and white antirrhinums interplanted with pale lilac heliotrope, for a cooler, softer effect.

Upton Grey is remarkable in that much of the garden is now restored to its former beauty. The wonderful richness and subtlety of planting which can only be mentally reconstructed from the plans of over two hundred other gardens can here be appreciated in every detail of colour, texture and scent. In other respects it is not remarkable at all: it captures just that balance of complexity and simplicity, the studied inevitability, which is characteristic of Miss Jekyll's gardens, albeit here on a particularly charming and relatively modest scale.

Left Scarlet lychnis and spiky kniphofias weave through the centre of the outer border above the rose garden, with yellow heleniums bordering the path. At the ends of the border these strong colours merge into the blues and whites of delphiniums, lupins and spiderwort, with dark clumps of bergenia and laurustinus providing an emphatic full stop.

Right Handsome mounds of laurustinus are used again to enclose and partially conceal steps from one level to another. Here, a battalion of stachys advances over the wall, its woolly pink flower spikes and grey foliage sharply silhouetted against the dark background.

HARDY
FLOWER
BORDERS

Lessons in planting design

Brackenbrough, Cumbria

Presaddfed, Gwynedd

Marshes, Willowbrook, Berkshire

In all the diversity of plans discussed so far, the most important and most characteristic feature of Gertrude Jekyll's garden plans, the hardy flower border, has been carefully avoided, partly to emphasize that there were other aspects to her prolific output, partly because it is quite impossible to pick out one typical example. The flower border justifies a chapter to itself.

The hardy flower border at Munstead Wood is, of course, the best known and most notable of all, because it was there, building on her earlier experiments at Munstead House, that Miss Jekyll developed her ideas and techniques of planting with 'a distinct scheme of colour arrangement'. The results she obtained, described at length in *Colour Schemes for the Flower Garden*, formed the starting point for all her later schemes in other gardens.

The Munstead Wood border was 60m/200ft long and 4.3m/14ft deep, backed by a 3.3m/11ft high stone wall. A wide stretch of grass to the fore enabled the eye to roam the whole length of the border, a broad sweep of colour contained by wall shrubs on one side and the quiet green of the woodland garden on the other. The border could be appreciated at four levels. From a distance it appeared as a single colourful episode within the leafy frame of the woodland garden and wall shrubs. Seen across the grass, it occupied the whole field of vision, 'one picture, the cool colouring at the ends enhancing the brilliant warmth of the middle'. As one walked slowly along the border, its various sections were seen in turn and in greater detail: 'each portion now becomes a picture in itself, every one of such a colouring that it best prepares the eye, in accordance with natural law, for what is to follow.' Finally, one might stop to contemplate particular details – the yellow flowers of rue shining as a point of contrast in the blue-grey part of the border, the harmonious blend of glaucous seakale foliage with the felted white leaves of *Senecio bicolor* ssp. *cineraria*, or the trails of scarlet nasturtium woven over the buff mist of the gypsophila's fading flower stems.

For Miss Jekyll herself, there was a fifth level of appreciation: a deep satisfaction derived from the work which had gone into the border, both the intellectual effort of watching and planning year by year, and the physical effort of skilful gardening to ensure that everything was just right. In order to maintain the colour scheme over several months it was necessary to train late-flowering plants over earlier ones (the nasturtium over gypsophila, for example), and to drop pot-grown plants into the border. Pale pink hydrangeas were among the plants used in this way. 'Their own leafage is a rather bright green, but we get them so well bloomed that but few leaves are seen, and we arrange as cleverly as we can that the rest shall be more or less hidden by the surrounding bluish foliage': a perfect example of art and garden craft!

The Munstead border was designed to be at its best in late summer, while the little hidden garden nearby was at its peak about a month earlier, and the border of asters through the kitchen garden on the other side of the wall was planned for early autumn show. However, a late summer peak did not preclude interest in the border at other times of year. Its setting alone, contained within yew hedges and a handsome

Pages 64–5 At Kemerton, Worcester, waves of yellow and copper heleniums, red nicotianas and dahlias and yellow achilleas build up to a fiery crescendo with spikes of kniphofia and arching crocosmia. Purple heliotrope, copper-leaved beet and paler *Sedum spectabile* introduce the next phrases of the border.

Two paintings of Miss Jekyll's garden capture contrasting moods of her planting. In *Munstead Wood*, **opposite**, by Helen Allingham, yuccas, hollyhocks and gladioli strike an emphatic note among yellow helianthus, while in George Elgood's *Michaelmas Daisies, Munstead Wood*, **above**, asters create a misty picture.

wall, and set in what was effectively a woodland clearing, was satisfying enough in itself. There were also many picturesque incidents throughout the year from the wall plants trained as a backcloth to the border – bold loquats, dark bays and laurus-tinus, cheerful piptanthus and choisya (the latter accompanied by trails of *Clematis montana* spilling over the wall) and the early flowers of wintersweet, quince and magnolia.

Within the border proper, many of the plants contributing to the main scheme in the summer months were hardly less beautiful at other times of year. It is worth noting, on the plan of the border in *Colour Schemes for the Flower Garden* (Frances Lincoln, 1988), the distribution of statuesque yuccas and euphorbias, the trails of dark bergenia and perennial candytuft (*Iberis sempervirens*) spreading from their feet, the groups of ever-grey rue and cineraria, santolina and stachys (especially at the end of the border nearer the house), and *Iris pallida* ssp. *pallida* with its durable, sword-like leaves of matching glaucous grey. Together they combine to paint a carefully planned picture of harmonious colouring.

Brighter focal points, from the solitary golden privet, early clumps of pale, lime-green daylily foliage and Oriental poppies (not shown on the plan but planted around the gypsophila to be concealed by the latter's spreading cloud of fine stems), are distributed sparingly but with telling effect, not isolated daubs

of colour but part of a carefully balanced scheme.

By early summer the grey foliage of the iris was topped by sweetly scented pale blue flowers heralding the start of the border's main season, accompanied by soft mounds of geranium and the delicate spikes of dictamnus over clumps of dark, aromatic foliage. By this time, too, the young foliage of herbaceous plants was in full growth and any spaces between had been filled with annuals: pale yellow and orange marigolds (both French and African), scarlet salvias and yellow and white antirrhinums, dahlias of white, yellow, orange and red, and tropical cannas. Many of these, with generous cultivation, would last well beyond high summer until the first frosts.

The main flowering season of the border was further

Right This grey, white and mauve-pink border at Polesden Lacey, in Surrey, shows the variety of globes, spires and flatter heads which can diversify an apparently simple scheme. The bergenias and the arching daylily foliage beneath the spheres of *Allium giganteum* play an important role.

Left Miss Jekyll often used clematis to conceal the remains of early-flowering delphiniums and anchusa. In this modern border at Powis Castle, cascades of *Clematis × jackmanii* echo both the silhouettes and the misty colouring of the trees in the background. The same colouring is repeated in aconitums and feathery-leaved polemoniums, with pale yellow daylilies and anthemis as complements.

extended by dropping in pots of lilies, *Campanula pyramidalis*, hostas and those solidly flowering hydrangeas. Plants from the main season which threatened to detract from the border's appearance later in the year were carefully concealed. Delphiniums served as supports for white everlasting pea in late summer and for *Clematis × jackmanii* in early autumn; and, in later years, also for frothy white *Clematis flammula*. As the summer progressed, the tallest sunflowers, rudbeckias, dahlias and Michaelmas daisies, even African marigolds or ageratum which had grown unexpectedly tall, were pulled down over bare spaces, the sudden change in orientation weakening their apical dominance and stimulating them to produce dozens of short side-shoots and hundreds of flowers, broad swathes of colour to refresh the border in its final weeks.

At the end of the year came the frosts. Blackened dahlia tops and the remains of annuals were carted away to provide cool humus for giant lilies in the woods or to replenish the great compost heaps for future years, and the border assumed its quieter – but not unattractive – winter dress.

The hardy flower border at Munstead Wood was a masterpiece of artistic imagination and technical skill, perhaps one of the most impressive fruits of the Arts and Crafts period. In gardens designed for other people there would be less control over events: staking and training, dropping in pots and pulling down late perennials over earlier-flowering ones might well defeat gardeners who were less able or less closely supervised. A more predictable and safer effect was called for. Nevertheless, plans for flower borders were produced, many of them memorable, and the occasional 'W.E.P.' or 'C.J.' (white everlasting pea and *Clematis × jackmanii*) on the plans showed that Miss Jekyll thought some people, at least, would take the trouble to disguise the remains of their melodramatically dying delphiniums.

The border at Brackenbrough, Cumbria

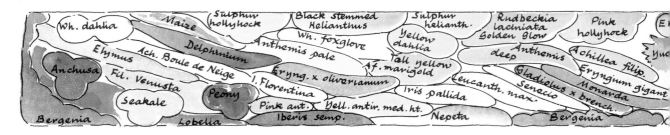

Below Miss Jekyll often used pot marigolds, for their strong colour and cottage garden simplicity. Here, the glowing colours of the marigolds are matched in intensity by spiky crocosmia, golden anthemis and the dark-leaved dahlias beyond.

The Brackenbrough border, in Cumbria, makes an interesting comparison with Munstead Wood. As at Munstead, the border is in two sections, one much longer than the other. Over 90m/300ft long, the scheme begins, as at Munstead, with blue and grey, builds up to a crescendo of orange, crimson and scarlet, then fades again to blue. It is quite unlike Munstead, however, in that the soft colouring at either end is divorced from the bold shapes of yucca and euphorbia. At Brackenbrough these strong forms are reserved for the centre of the longer section of border, where they are combined with cannas and orange marigolds, red dahlias and hollyhocks. In front of the yuccas, sword-like scarlet gladioli contrast with the cloudy forms of gypsophila, the latter bedecked with scarlet nasturtiums to make a bold and brilliant centrepiece.

A gravel path past the end of the house, some 45m/150ft away, aligns with the centre of the border: hence the concentration of bold forms and colours to create a focal point effective at a distance.

Perhaps because of the northern situation, or perhaps because of the central role of the yuccas, fewer grey plants are used at Brackenbrough than at Munstead and the effect is thus clearer and brighter. The planting starts, at the far end of the shorter section, with a bold group of bergenia. There is no dark yew hedge to enclose the border as there is at Munstead Wood, so the bergenia provides the necessary firm underpinning for the generous drifts of blue and white which

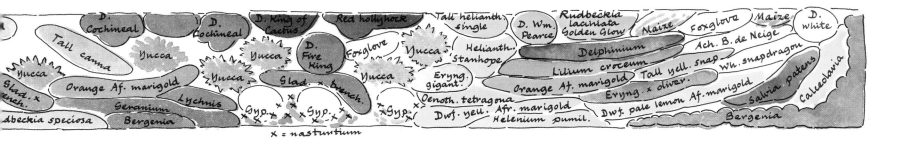

follow. Anchusa and spiderwort occupy the corner, with white phlox and the handsome foliage of *Elymus arenarius*; geraniums, asters, eryngium and echinops form longer drifts of blue, interspersed with white peonies, white foxgloves, *Achillea* 'Boule de Neige' and white-striped maize. The edging is of stachys, santolina, nepeta and, where a heavier note is called for, more bergenia. Thin bands of yellow snapdragons and pale yellow marigolds highlight the fresh blue and white of the main planting, and the first section of border ends, as it began, with anchusa and bergenia, here enlivened by the sharp yellow flowers of calceolaria.

This first section, a third of the length of the whole border, forms a complete scheme in itself, a scheme of cool, clear blue, white and yellow. The plants flanking the dividing path between the two sections of border also make up a scheme that is complete in itself, because the groups of bergenia and calceolaria which end the first section are mirrored at the beginning of the second, in a balanced but not quite symmetrical composition.

From this point on, however, drifts of eryngium, delphinium and brilliant blue *Salvia patens*, white achillea, foxglove and striped maize and pale yellow African marigolds merge in rapid succession into deeper yellow heleniums and helianthus, orange marigolds, red hollyhocks and dahlias and the central crescendo of yucca, euphorbia, canna and nasturtium-draped gypsophila. For 23m/75ft, a quarter of the total length of the whole border, crests of yucca and canna erupt from the border like white-peaked waves in a stormy sea, before subsiding again into less turbulent drifts of golden rudbeckia and anthemis, scarlet monarda and blue *Eryngium × oliverianum*, until only the spiky silhouettes of hollyhocks, scarlet gladioli and ripples of grey *Iris pallida* echo the intensity of the storm.

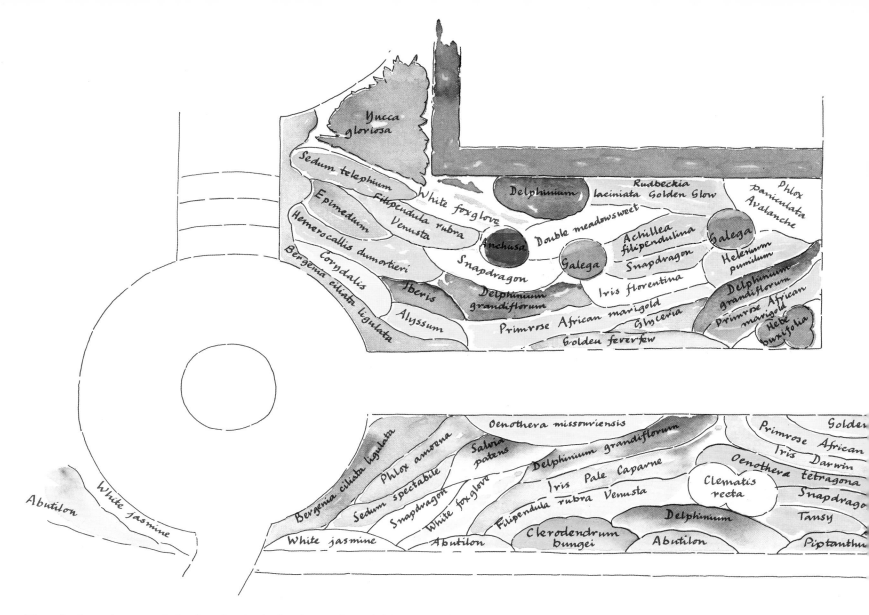

The closing phrases of the border include clear white dahlias, *Leucanthemum maximum* and achillea, and pale pink *Filipendula rubra* 'Venusta' between elymus and seakale, pale yellow anthemis, and sparkling blue anchusa. The clear blue of the anchusa is followed, later in the summer, by tall delphiniums at the back of the border and lobelia at the front, the latter interrupting briefly a long group of bergenia, an unmistakable full stop.

The scale of the Brackenbrough border is impressive – it is over 90m/300ft from end to end, with many of the drifts 6–7.5m/20–25ft in length – but even more remarkable is the way in which each section creates a picture that is complete in itself, while at the same time it merges imperceptibly into neighbouring sections. It is also of particular interest to the modern gardener as a clear example of how the many constituent themes within a border can provide inspiration for gardening on a much smaller scale.

Presaddfed, in the furthest corner of Gwynedd in North Wales, was an elaborate garden of many parts, including a whole series of one-colour and colour-graded borders. Miss Jekyll supplied ten plans for a total of fifteen different areas of the garden, including the formal gardens described on pages 84–6 and the zigzag steps and spring garden referred to in passing on page 145. Perhaps the finest of the borders were

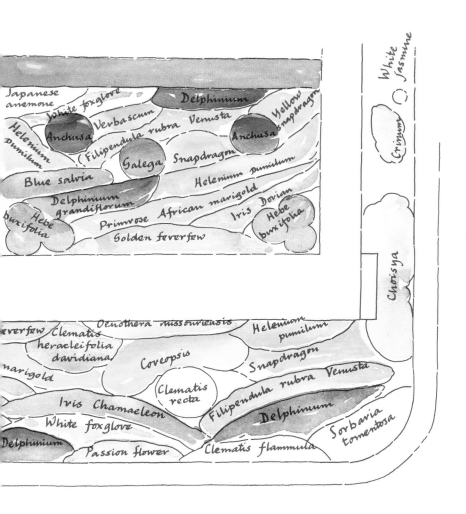

Above Whether trimmed hard to maintain the freshness of its bright yellow-green foliage, or left, later in the season, to produce its innumerable white flowers, golden feverfew provides an ideal edging to a blue, yellow and white colour scheme. The sharply aromatic scent, released in the air as passers-by brush against the leaves, is an extra delight.

The blue, yellow and white border at Presaddfed, Gwynedd

the double orange borders. (Interestingly, when Miss Jekyll used a limited number of colour schemes in her gardens, she usually turned to the stronger yellows and oranges, rather than to the pale pinks and lavenders with which she is most often associated.) However, as the stronger colours have been discussed quite fully in relation to the borders at Munstead Wood and Brackenbrough, I have singled out a smaller border in one corner of the garden for the sake of its lighter scheme of blue, yellow and white.

The scheme, an even balance of clear blue and strong yellow with only occasional points of white, is somewhat reminiscent of the two ends of the Brackenbrough border but rather different in its effect. There are no flowing edges of grey foliage, no mounds of catmint; even the stalwart geraniums have been omitted. Instead the edging is of golden feverfew (*Tanacetum parthenium aureum*) and trailing mats of lemon-yellow *Oenothera missouriensis*, with *Hebe buxifolia* providing solid dark green support at the corners of the borders in a more compact and rather more formal way than bergenia would have done. The Presaddfed borders are double borders enclosed within a dark yew hedge on one side and a wall clad with mainly dark green and yellow-green climbers and wall shrubs on the other. The whole effect is therefore distinctly darker and sharper than the pale and misty schemes of

Brackenbrough and Munstead Wood, sparkling rather than creamily rich.

The entrance to this colourful garden begins on a quiet note. Twin groups of yucca underplanted with *Sedum telephium* flank a short flight of steps down to a circle of paving ringed with soft green *Bergenia ciliata ligulata*, a subtle variation on the more usual glossy splendour of *B. cordifolia*. Epimediums, the long-flowering but diminutive *Hemerocallis dumortieri*, fern-like masses of *Corydalis lutea* and a darker mat of *Iberis sempervirens* (perennial candytuft) cover the bank around the circle, rising through white snapdragons (antirrhinums) and pale pink *Filipendula rubra* 'Venusta' to the tall white spires of the foxgloves that are dramatically silhouetted against the dark green yew hedge.

The main colours of the border are then introduced: repeated drifts of tall delphiniums, lower *Delphinium grandiflorum* and the equally brilliant blue *Salvia patens*; African marigolds, yellow snapdragons, heleniums and the flat, brassy yellow plates of *Achillea filipendulina*. Tucked in between the longest drift of marigolds and the edging of golden feverfew is a smaller drift of *Glyceria maxima* 'Variegata', its clean white stripes injecting a contrast of form and lightness of colour similar to that of striped maize in larger schemes. Occasional groups of bearded iris add their stiff fans of sword-like leaves, topped in early summer by elegant flowers of pale blue and white. Double meadowsweet (*Filipendula ulmaria* 'Flore Pleno'), white phlox and white Japanese anemones add brighter white accents in succession throughout the summer and into autumn. At the end of the border, the spires of foxgloves repeat an opening theme, their form echoed late in the year by tall yellow spikes of verbascums interweaving with delphiniums above a long drift of pale pink *Filipendula rubra* 'Venusta'.

Most of these plants are repeated in subtly varying juxtapositions in the opposite border. *Iris* 'Pale Caparne' – described by Miss Jekyll as the loveliest of the pale blues – and other cultivars alternate with the iris in the deeper border opposite, their stiff leaves threading through the middle of the border among more rounded plants. Marigolds, golden feverfew and others repeat this alternating rhythm. Because this border is slightly longer and narrower, and without the interruption of a cross path, the other drifts, too, are long and narrow. However, the narrower border is backed by a wall, and this situation is exploited by drawing wall shrubs and climbers into the main theme.

White jasmine and pale lavender abutilons begin the wall planting, forming a symmetrical arrangement with plants on the other side of the main through path. The abutilons' delicate flowers would be finished, of course, before their soft grey-green foliage was called upon to provide a background for clear blue delphiniums and *Salvia patens*. Between the two abutilons is a good group of *Clerodendrum bungei*, an interesting plant clearly placed to exploit the warmth of the wall but not immediately obvious as part of the colour scheme. Only with the recollection of that first group of *Sedum telephium* under the yuccas and the answering group of *S. spectabile* on the side of the path below the wall, with their flat heads of dusky pink flowers fading to rusty brown, does the true purpose of the clerodendrum become apparent. What better plant for injecting a note of rich, dark warmth into the background of the border than this handsome, dusky subshrub with its maroon-purple flowers opening when most of the border would be beginning to look rather tired?

Beyond the abutilons the leaf colour becomes both brighter and deeper: *Piptanthus nepalensis* with its bright yellow pea-flowers overtopping a patch of fine-textured tansy in front of it, passion flower with its more glaucous leaves and lavender-blue flowers (and the added bonus in the border of its yellow/ orange fruits after a warm summer), and *Clematis flammula*, trained on the wall but near enough to the corner group of delphiniums to be draped over them *à la* Munstead. The first group of delphiniums have as their companions grey-leaved abutilons and the pale pink plumes of *Filipendula rubra* 'Venusta', and the border closes with another group of delphiniums backed by the feathery pale green foliage of *Sorbaria*

Blue edged with yellow is one of the most refreshing colour schemes. In this border, at Clare College, Cambridge, spires of yellow verbascum and blue delphiniums are balanced by butter-yellow heleniums and flat heads of achillea, while French marigolds and *Alchemilla mollis* provide the edging. Scabious and erigerons, with their lavender-blue flowers, are beginning to take over from the delphiniums, and *Clematis heracleifolia* var. *davidiana* is just starting to produce its sweet-scented blue-grey flowers.

times very long, drifts. Even the wall shrubs, planted individually, are trained to cover long stretches of wall. To anchor the scheme and to prevent harmony degenerating into monotony, Miss Jekyll broke this flowing rhythm at appropriate intervals, interjecting an occasional point of emphasis, a dab of colour rather than a drift. It is noticeable, though, that, for this gentle scheme of cool refinement at Presaddfed, she chose anchusa (of course, for its brilliant, wide branching myriads of clear blue flowers), galega (a lavender-blue scrambling pea) and foaming masses of *Clematis recta*, rather than the bolder, more striking yuccas or cannas. Each rounded clump was carefully placed to underscore the gentle rhythm of the planting and to draw out the special qualities of its immediate surroundings, brightly coloured, or open and sunny, or deliciously pale.

The low-lying Thames-side garden of Marshes, Willowbrook, in Berkshire, offers one of the most interesting of all Miss Jekyll's colour borders. What could be more different in character than an orange border and a fern walk? Yet each has its own particular brilliance, the translucent greenery of young ferns matching, in its own way, the bold, burning orange spikes of red-hot pokers. At Marshes the two are combined in one scheme, with delightful results. The borders are doubly interesting in that all the plants in the scheme are reliably perennial. There is no filling with antirrhinums or ageratum or even with orange marigolds.

Once more, the setting is important. A short, steep flight of steps descends between high laurel hedges from a simple bridge over a stream to enter, in effect, a cool, green valley. The hedges recede on either side as the double borders widen from 1.5m/5ft to nearly 6m/20ft before opening on to a wide, circular lawn with a circular pool in the centre.

The borders begin in a quiet way: long groups of *Matteuccia struthiopteris*, the elegant shuttlecock fern, backed in summer by the greenish white plumes of *Aruncus dioicus* and edged in spring, before the ferns emerge, with the delicately coloured sprays of London pride and forget-me-not. *Artemisia lactiflora* (the one artemisia with dark green foliage), mid-green *Filipendula rubra* 'Venusta', and pale, glaucous green *Thalictrum flavum*, each with its own variation on flower heads of feathery lightness, extend the idea of a green fern walk almost half-way along the diminutive valley, where a cross path edged with heuchera and corner clumps of dark

tomentosa and supported by more filipendula, so the blue spikes are set in a sea of greenish and ivory-white flowers. In front of this delicate composition are drifts of yellow snapdragons and coreopsis and, at the border's edge, helenium and oenothera, clear bright yellows contrasting with the delphiniums but cleverly setting the tone for the bright pale green domes of *Choisya ternata* that are ranged around the seat at the end of the garden – primarily for the sake of the choisya's intensely fragrant white 'orange blossom' flowers.

All the plants thus far mentioned are ranged in long, some-

bergenia bisects the garden.

Before the path, however, brighter colours already begin to appear – *Iris sibirica* in blue and white, *Geranium ibericum* and *Helenium pumilum*, a bright but greenish gold that is, despite its strong colour, capable of merging into pale greenery in dappled shade. Generous drifts of striped glyceria and lady fern, marbled heuchera foliage and the dark green of bergenia are more than enough to absorb these occasional strokes of bright colour.

Over beyond the cross path the border widens steadily and

Opposite Greenish white plumes of *Aruncus dioicus* and elegant fern fronds establish the cool character of this lush plant association. The white-splashed leaves of *Lamium maculatum*, between arching stems of Solomon's seal, provide a lighter note, while violas introduce brighter colour.

Above In this vibrant border at Hidcote Manor, Gloucester-shire, as at Marshes, Willowbrook, red and orange are set against a cool green background. Crimson dahlias and orange daylilies are framed by heuchera, purple hazel and other bronzy foliage, merging into the pale, fresh green of tall, arching grasses.

the colour intensifies, though still with a broad, generous framework of *Filipendula ulmaria* and *F. rubra* 'Venusta', artemisia and heuchera, striped glyceria and a single bold patch of *Hosta sieboldiana* to contain the gorgeous colouring. Tall kniphofias provide the centrepieces of each border, with scarlet monarda flowing around its bold clumps of orange pokers and tall gold and crimson rayed heleniums behind. In the foreground are lower heleniums of coppery colouring, orange daylilies (with that wonderful sharp lime-green foliage vying with the freshness of ferns early in the year), and *Ligularia dentata*, one of the most spectacular waterside plants, with ragged mops of deep chrome-yellow, almost orange, flowers over large purple-green foliage.

From this main mass of glowing colour, an outlying drift of *Helenium pumilum* harks back to the earlier use of the plant in its quieter context; a long drift of *Geranium ibericum* inserts its soft note of contrast, a note answered by the delicate cloud of purple thalictrum flowers against the hedge. With these few deft touches, the whole scheme is unified into a single picture, cool green and ivory gradually building up to a fiery crescendo of orange and red flanking the view out across the pool and lawn.

Looking the other way, of course, the borders present a different and perhaps even more enchanting picture, for the false perspective created by tapering borders and grass verges enhances the impression of brilliant colour fading into the distant depths of a green woodland tunnel.

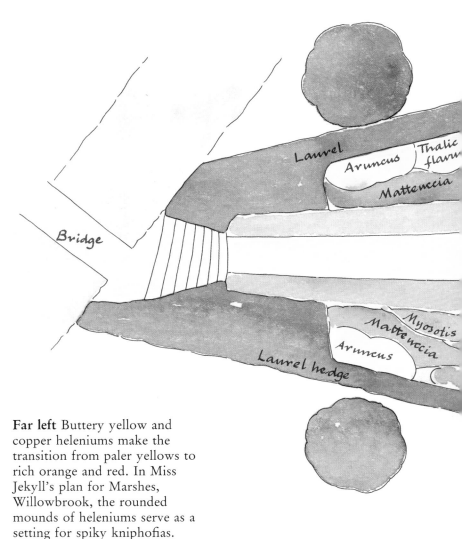

Double borders at Marshes, Willowbrook, Berkshire

Far left Buttery yellow and copper heleniums make the transition from paler yellows to rich orange and red. In Miss Jekyll's plan for Marshes, Willowbrook, the rounded mounds of heleniums serve as a setting for spiky kniphofias.

Left *Ligularia dentata*, with deep yellow flowers over bold purple-green foliage, provides a striking and colourful focal point in this moist border.

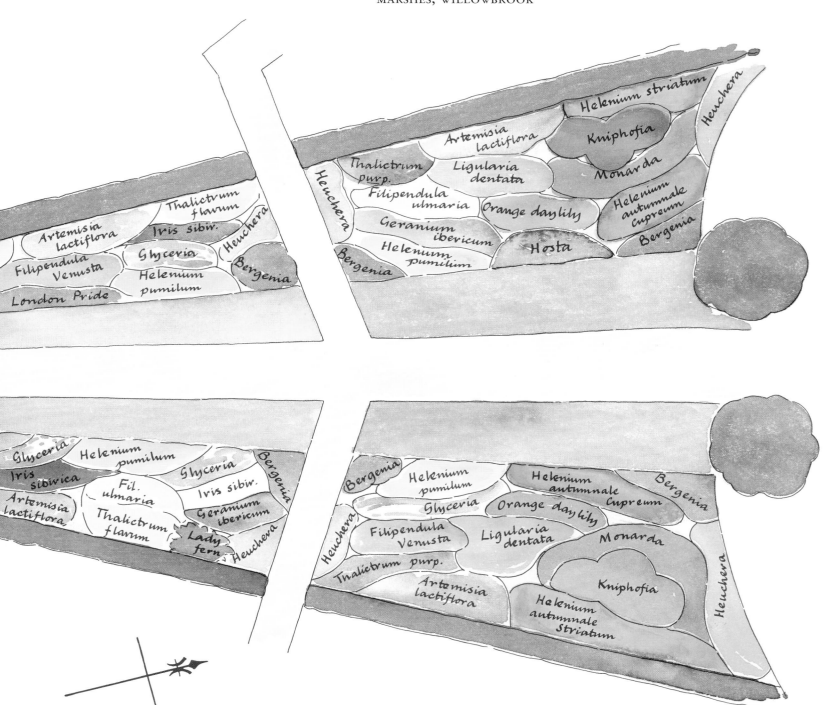

Artemisia lactiflora
Thalictrum flavum
Iris sibir.
Glyceria
Filipendula Venusta
Helenium pumilum
London Pride
Heuchera
Bergenia

Heuchera
Helenium striatum
Artemisia lactiflora
Kniphofia
Heuchera
Thalictrum purp.
Ligularia dentata
Monarda
Filipendula ulmaria
Orange daylily
Helenium autumnale Cupreum
Geranium ibericum
Hosta
Bergenia
Helenium pumilum
Bergenia

Glyceria
Helenium pumilum
Glyceria
Bergenia
Iris sibivica
Fil. ulmaria
Iris sibir.
Artemisia lactiflora
Thalictrum flavum
Geranium ibericum
Lady fern
Heuchera

Bergenia
Helenium pumilum
Helenium autumnale Cupreum
Bergenia
Heuchera
Glyceria
Orange daylily
Filipendula Venusta
Ligularia dentata
Monarda
Thalictrum purp.
Artemisia lactiflora
Kniphofia
Helenium autumnale Striatum
Heuchera

79

FORMAL GARDENS

Pattern and planting

Busbridge Park, Surrey

Presaddfed, Gwynedd

Little Cumbrae, Strathclyde

Hascombe Court, Surrey

Hestercombe, Somerset

The very phrase 'formal garden' poses a problem when discussing Gertrude Jekyll's gardens – it was, after all, under the opposing banners of formal garden and landscape garden that factions fought so belligerently, and it was as arbitrators between the formal and the natural that Christopher Hussey considered Miss Jekyll and Edwin Lutyens to have made their contribution to garden design. The problematical aspect of the word 'formal' is compounded when one looks at Jekyll/Lutyens gardens as a whole, clusters of compartments which are geometrical in themselves but arranged with deliberate asymmetry, growing out of the site and in response to local traditions, charmingly irregular in their overall effect. Were such gardens formal or informal? The clue to the dilemma lies, perhaps surprisingly, with William Robinson himself, in his proclamation that 'it is only where the plants of a garden are rigidly set out in geometrical design, as in carpet-bedding and bedding-out, that the term "formal" is rightly applied.' Had the terminology employed by the protagonists been changed from 'formal gardens' to 'formal planting', perhaps that fruitless debate would never have arisen.

The gardens designed by Gertrude Jekyll, and even more the gardens planted by her for architects, always contained

Pages 80–81 As a counterpoint to the finely detailed geometry of Edwin Lutyens's formal garden at Hestercombe, Gertrude Jekyll designed a planting scheme that is at once bold and flowing. An edging of glossy bergenia encloses panels of roses and dark-leaved peonies, the three plants together providing a long succession of pink flowers. Bold clumps of miscanthus and towering spikes of delphiniums provide the height necessary on such a grand scale.

Left Stately white lily-flowered tulips shine out against Lutyens's dark walls of clipped yew in the garden at Les Moutiers, in Normandy. In the background can be seen the greenish white balls of Miss Jekyll's favourite guelder rose, here trained as a standard.

and often largely consisted of geometrical compartments – squares, rectangles, octagons and circles – but they were never planted with regimented masses of bedding plants in rigidly geometrical patterns. Miss Jekyll enjoyed annuals and 'bedding plants'. She used them with great skill in a variety of situations. But to raise them by the thousand and to plant them out in mindless blocks of uniform (and often strident) colour represented the horticultural equivalent of that industrial mass production to which she was so averse. Moreover, she would have agreed with Robinson on the weaknesses of 'in and out gardening' near the house: the twice-yearly turmoil of cultivation and the bare ground which followed, wide spaces between fledgling plants for weeks in early summer and the starkness of effect in schemes where there was no time for plants to become established, to flow over hard edges, before the next round of planting was due. Just as Lutyens's vernacular houses and their gardens were altogether more humane, softer in character, than the Victorian gothic villa of polychrome brick and tile, so Miss Jekyll chose to temper the architectural structure of her gardens with permanent plants in soft, flowing groups.

Among the plans for Busbridge Park (only a mile or so from Munstead) is a rare example of complex geometry in a Jekyll garden: a quartered parterre. The architect for the garden was Ernest George (to whom Lutyens was briefly apprenticed) but the sketchy character of the lines attempting to establish the fine details of the scrollwork suggest that the plan was the work of Miss Jekyll and did not emanate from the architect's office. Certainly the same pattern was used seven years later, at Woodcott in Hampshire, where Miss Jekyll worked with Crickman and Sons, local architects. Annoyingly, in neither case was the planting for the parterre indicated.

There was an octagonal verbena garden in another Surrey garden, Bramley Park, but the beds were simply filled with trailing verbenas around statuesque groups of canna and maize in alternate beds. One other remarkable example of formal planting which came near to bedding out was drawn up for Sir George Sitwell at Renishaw. Lutyens was working at Renishaw but under some difficulty, as Sitwell, author of a book on Italian gardens of the Renaissance, had his own very definite ideas on architecture (and gardens), allied to a naturally

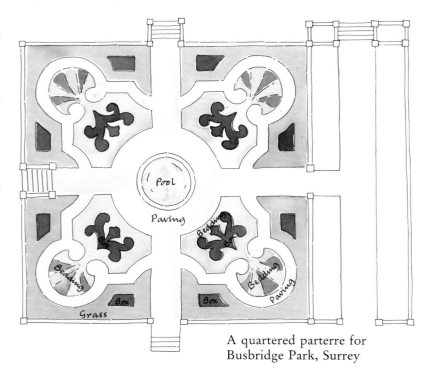

A quartered parterre for
Busbridge Park, Surrey

argumentative character. The plan of the Green Walk at Renishaw is almost certainly Sitwell's, but Miss Jekyll made suggestions for planting the alternating pattern of long rectangular and small round beds. The rectangles were planted, again alternately, with cannas and dahlias, edged with African marigolds, penstemons and *Salvia patens*, bold blocks of yellow, red and blue. Each circular bed was divided into six spiralling segments. *Stachys byzantina* filled three segments in each of the beds; ageratum, *Phlox drummondii* and *Dianthus chinensis* 'Heddewigii' – one to each bed – filled the other three in a spiralling pattern like a child's windmill.

Where the geometry of the architect's design was more complex, Miss Jekyll let the pattern speak for itself and adopted the simplest of planting. In Lutyens's circular sunken garden at Folly Farm, in Berkshire, for example, an extravaganza of interlocking circles, the central island was planted with lavender and the beds around the sculpted pool with low roses. In the main plat at Hestercombe, a much larger, elegantly detailed but rather simpler plan, she produced a more complex scheme with clumps of peony, delphinium, canna and striped maize, rising from a carpet of *Phlox drummondii* in harmonious colours.

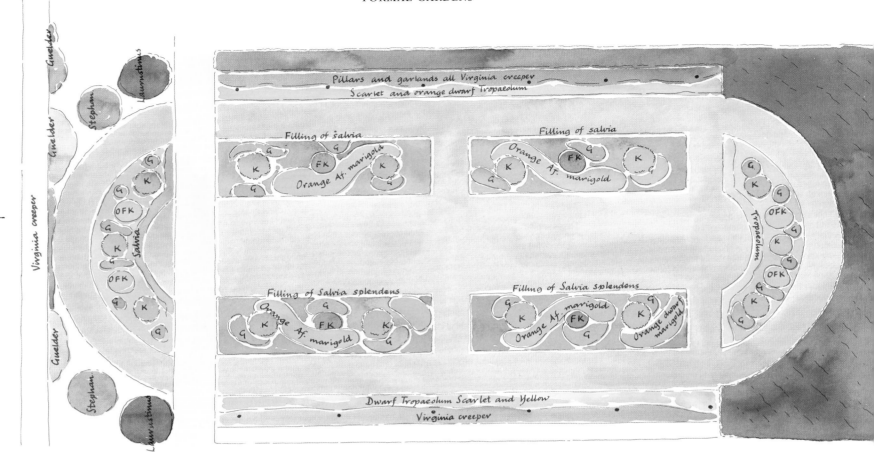

The formal gardens at Presaddfed, Gwynedd

It is plans like that for the intriguing formal gardens at Presaddfed, though, which are altogether more typical of Miss Jekyll's approach. Presaddfed is characteristic of her work in more ways than one. Two gardens of simple geometrical lines are juxtaposed, the two forming part of a much larger whole in this extensive and complex garden. The smaller compartment, primarily for early summer, is a garden of irises and peonies, with China roses interwoven between the drifts of iris. The dark surround of yew hedge and dark edgings – of London pride with its neat rosettes, particularly charming when rimmed with frost, and of asarum, forming close mats of semi-evergreen kidney-shaped leaves of remarkably elegant freshness – define the pattern of the garden throughout the year. In spring this dark combination is supplemented by the rich red of young peony foliage and the matching translucent leaves of China roses, the perfect setting for new grey fans of iris foliage. By early summer the garden has reached its peak of loveliness, blowzy peonies of white, blush and pink, their carefully staked stems arching beneath the weight of huge flowers that harmonize in colour with the very different flowers of iris – statuesque flowers of pale blue, pale yellow and white unfurling from pointed buds on stiffly straight stems. Around the central bed of milk-white *Paeonia* 'Duchesse de Nemours' and pale blue *Iris* 'Pale Caparne', the glossy rosettes of London pride are hidden by thousands of flower stems bearing their hundreds of thousands of delicately veined pink flowers. For two or three weeks the little garden presents a picture of incomparable beauty, a distillation of early summer, before the peony petals fall and the last flowers of the irises crumple into dry brown spirals. Now, however, the delicate flowers of the roses begin to appear on thin branches spreading harmlessly but effectively among

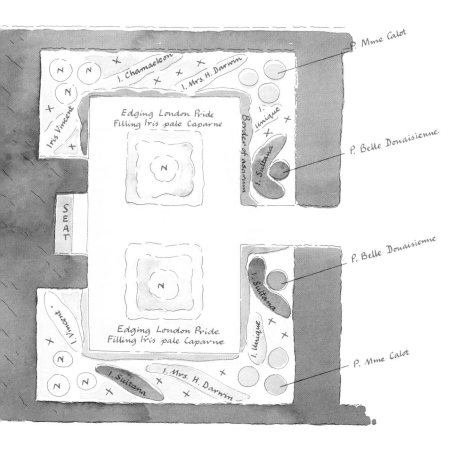

Edging London Pride
Filling Iris pale Caparne

Edging London Pride
Filling Iris pale Caparne

Note X = China Rose

 N = P. Duchesse de Nemours

 K = Kniphofia
 FK = Dahlia 'Fire King'
 OFK = Dahlia 'Orange Fire King'
 G = Gladiolus brenchleyensis

Above Battalions of pale iris, fragile and translucent against dark yew hedges at Polesden Lacey. Even after their brief flowering is over, the fans of grey-green foliage have a quiet charm.

their carefully deadheaded neighbours. Those distinguished mounds of dark peony foliage and the paler spear-like leaves of the iris take on a new role. The peony leaves highlight the presence of the frail pink roses, and the grey iris leaves harmonize with them in the changing light conditions of an English summer. Later in the year, the peony foliage takes on rich autumn tints before the whole garden has to be cut down and tidied, to assume its quiet winter appearance.

The second and larger compartment is utterly characteristic of Miss Jekyll's approach to summer bedding. Two large kniphofias (red-hot pokers) in each of the four long beds and three in the curved beds at either end provide the regular rhythm and permanent anchor for the scheme, and between the kniphofias are well-grown plants of reliable and prolific dahlias, scarlet-red 'Fire King' in the rectangular panels, paler 'Orange Fire King' in the curved end beds. Weaving between these

large anchor points come orange African marigolds, long drifts in each of the four rectangular beds, all matching in carefully drawn grace but not quite symmetrical in arrangement. Answering these long groups of rounded plants are shorter, firmer strokes of gladioli, the scarlet-red *Gladiolus × brenchleyensis* which Miss Jekyll used more than any other. Around and among the whole are scarlet salvias, the archetype of abused bedding plants here contributing its long-lasting fiery spikes to a scheme of varied but harmonious richness of colour and form.

Complex, colourful and satisfying though the planting in the central beds may be, it does not stand in isolation. On the outer edges of the garden are narrow borders filled with scarlet and yellow nasturtiums, simple bands of colour repeating and, in the yellow, lightening the colouring of the central beds. Over the nasturtiums are swags of Virginia creeper, climbing up and trailing gracefully down from regularly spaced pillars. This is an intriguing combination, because, in the summer, with trails of light fresh yellow-green foliage from every pillar, the Virginia creeper harmonizes with the sharp yellow of the paler nasturtiums below and the curtain of green – the complementary colour to red – accentuates the central scheme. As autumn approaches, the Virginia creeper assumes a darker green, matching the dahlias' foliage, and finally a rich crimson, enveloping the whole garden in fiery colour. At the end of the garden the picture is repeated with more Virginia creeper and guelder rose on the wall: pale fresh green in the summer to enhance the red of the central borders,

and glowing colour (of leaf and berry) in the autumn. On either side laurustinus stands as an unchanging baseline of dark green against which the seasonal spectacle of colour can be truly measured.

A further example of near-formal plant arrangement in a simple plan, and a wonderful variation on gardening with strong colour, can be seen in the quartered garden at Little Cumbrae, situated on a small island off the Strathclyde coast. The immediate impression from the plan is of redness – dahlias and penstemons, dark cannas and scarlet gladioli, and red begonias. Following closely on this first impression is a sense of orderly arrangement, a pattern within the many

patches of bright colour. The trio of *Dahlia* 'Cochineal' in the centre of each quarter is linked by three arms to the outer corners of the bed, arms of bronze-leaved ricinus (castor oil), dark acanthus and bergenia on two sides, cannas, acanthus and bergenia on the third. This three-winged spine is strengthened by more dahlias (the scarlet 'Fire King') and more cannas, creating two bays which are filled with columns of red penstemons and the sharper spikes of gladioli over low domes of *Sedum telephium* and red begonias.

The use of *Sedum telephium*, its 'broad heads of chocolate red bloom' echoing in early autumn the almost brown-red of canna, ricinus and dahlia foliage, is characteristic of the way in which Miss Jekyll would frequently underscore bright flowers with a deeper tone, strengthening the whole effect and immeasurably enriching the colour harmony. The use of bergenias, with their huge, dark but glossy leaves to anchor flowering plants (and often, as here, to emphasize a rhythm), is also typical.

At Little Cumbrae the bergenias are accompanied by acanthus, similar in leaf colour, bolder still in their deeply cut

outlines, intermediate in stature between bergenia and the castor oil with its own handsome bronze foliage. By late summer the acanthus contributes a further attraction to the beds, strong spikes of hooded white flowers in purple calyces, a rich accompaniment to the main colour scheme, and here a particularly ingenious use of bicoloured flowers.

The inner edge of the four beds departs from the rich orange and red scheme to create a refreshing picture of white and yellow. As on the periphery, so along this inner edge, bergenias punctuate the lighter planting, but now they separate groups of white begonias and fresh green and white apple mint (with instructions to pinch back the mint to keep it

Left Bronze-leaved ricinus, the banana-like foliage of canna and brilliant red dahlias formed a glowing harmony in the spectacular formal garden at Little Cumbrae. As annuals or tender perennials, the effect of their rich colours would have lasted from early summer until the first frosts. In this planting, at Kemerton, they are supplemented by monarda and crocosmia, both reliably perennial but with a shorter flowering season.

Right One quarter of the formal garden at Little Cumbrae, Strathclyde

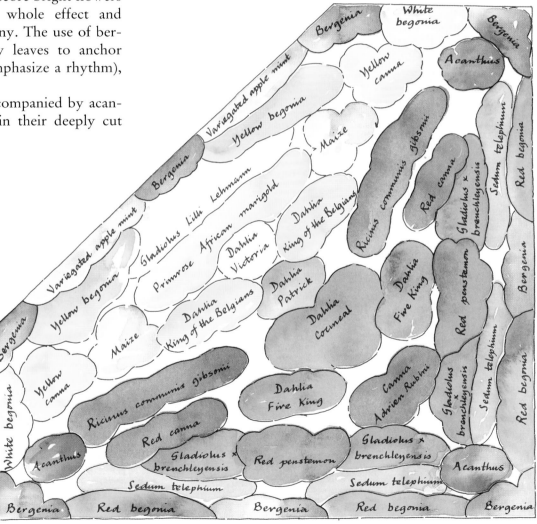

compact and bright). Yellow begonias, white gladioli, pale yellow African marigolds and white and yellow dahlias build up to the central point of each quarter, with striped maize and pale-leaved yellow cannas at the corners completing a picture of exquisite freshness, a freshness accentuated by the contrast of dark castor oil and dark, hooded acanthus behind. Suddenly the ingenuity of using acanthus becomes apparent: at the junction of two apparently contrasting schemes, the acanthus, with its dark, hooded calyces and white tubular flowers, belongs to both camps.

The little quartered garden of Little Cumbrae illustrates a very important aspect of Miss Jekyll's planting, an enigmatic, tantalizing depth of experience often below the conscious. It derives from her understanding (with its roots in her training as a painter) that colour is relative, that any colour can only be seen in relation to the colours around it.

It was this understanding that enabled her to use certain plants – yucca for example, and rosemary – in quite different contexts. In the border at Munstead Wood, surrounded by grey and blue plants, or among the cistus and euphorbias on the Grayswood Hill bank, yucca and rosemary acquire a softness of colouring in harmony with their surroundings, yet in the Brackenbrough border yucca is at home among cannas, scarlet dahlias and gladioli, a picture of dark magnificence. In many plans the rosemary is simultaneously dark and light, its small hard leaves harmonizing, for example, with laurustinus at one end of a border and grey-leaved irises at the other.

This gentle brain-teasing does much to explain the lasting, indeed the growing, fascination of Miss Jekyll's designs. An understanding of her art of paradox also explains the enigmatic quality of her near-formal designs. Pure symmetry is

quickly comprehended and quickly palls. Near-symmetry, including of course the near-symmetry of the human body and face, provokes curiosity; viewed from different directions it may take on a new character, and interest is maintained.

At Little Cumbrae, a rare example of complete symmetry (although about one axis only), the puzzle is one of colour. Are there two contrasting colour schemes, fiery orange-red outside and icy yellow-white within? Or is the use of yellow and white in fact a logical extension of a scheme ranging from dull red and glowing orange to intense white heat, as in the core of a fire? There is no answer, and the equivocation provides a never-failing source of delight.

The formal gardens at Presaddfed and Little Cumbrae are both quite elaborate, sumptuous schemes in which the planting is more important than the surroundings, but there is a second type of formal gardening much in evidence among Miss Jekyll's plans, a type usually seen in small, rectangular beds set in large expanses of paving near the house. Here

Right Fuchsias occupy an important role in many of Miss Jekyll's planting plans. Elegant pendant flowers of rich red and purple weigh down the dark-leaved branches into graceful curves throughout the summer and autumn. Their simple charm is equally suited to the wild garden or to formal gardens such as those at

Hascombe Court. 'Mrs Popple', a lower and more sturdy form than *F. magellanica gracilis*, and equally hardy, remains a popular cultivar today.

Far right Two plans for Hascombe Court, Surrey

simplicity of effect and year-round presence are of the greatest importance, and schemes such as these offer invaluable ideas for gardens of year-round interest: for the central panel of a small front garden, or for low-maintenance beds breaking up an expanse of paving around a formal swimming pool, for example.

Two small plans for Hascombe Court in Surrey are typical of such schemes. In the first, a tall, arching bush of *Fuchsia* 'Delight' forms a centrepoint between four L-shaped beds. The larger part of each 'L' has its own centrepiece, a rounded grey dome of lavender flanked symmetrically by four paler grey santolinas. Two more santolinas fill the stem of each 'L', defining the view through the little garden and surrounding the fuchsia with an octagonal grouping of soft grey hummocks. In this way, even with the shearing necessary each spring to keep the santolina compact and to remove its rank yellow button flowers, the perennial plants will grow and merge into a relaxed framework of varied grey, harmonizing

with the graceful pendants of the fuchsia, especially when the lavender is also in flower. To fill the outer parts of the bed and to complete the harmonious and long-lasting scheme, Miss Jekyll recommends pink and rose antirrhinums. She might have added, perhaps, pale yellow or purple wallflowers or pale blue forget-me-nots for spring colour.

Fuchsia 'Delight' also forms the centrepoint for the second small garden, probably because the gardens were arranged on a common axis so the two fuchsias would be seen together on the centre line. In this second instance, though, fuchsias also form the centrepieces of the quarters. The cultivar is not named but Miss Jekyll would normally have used *F. magellanica gracilis* in such a situation, unless the owner had indicated that other cultivars were already available. The dark foliage and deep purple-red flowers of the fuchsias have a stronger presence than the misty grey foliage surrounding them, so *Bergenia ciliata ligulata* is used at each corner of the quarters, providing foliage of an intermediate hue but of large and

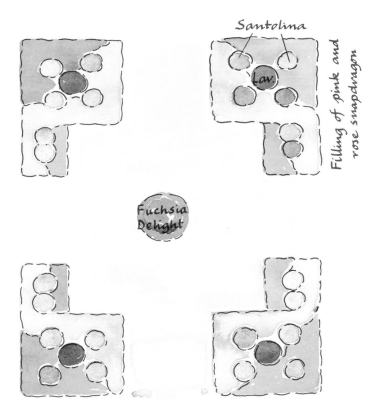

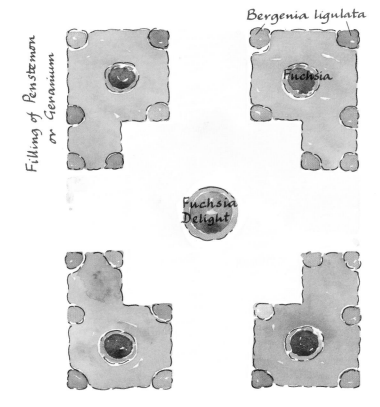

handsome outline. By emphasizing the corners, rather than the spines of the beds in this second little garden, the bergenia creates a more staccato effect than in the first garden. In addition, penstemons or geraniums are prescribed to fill the beds, red penstemons, salmon or red geraniums, no doubt, to complete the bright colour scheme.

In other small formal gardens, at the King Edward VII Sanatorium in Midhurst, Surrey, for example, yuccas and santolina, lavender and *Magnolia stellata*, kniphofia and catmint are used in innumerable simple, formal configurations of bold and soft outlines to create permanently satisfying schemes, either complete in themselves or as the frame and backbone for colourful annuals. In the shrub walk at Dyke Nook Lodge, in Accrington, Lancashire, columnar Irish yews and rounded *Magnolia stellata* march rhythmically through long twin borders, imparting a sense of order to the sea of herbaceous plants spilling around their feet. A similar feature occurs at Presaddfed, with magnolias and *Choisya ternata* alternating in the rectangular spurs of the shrub walk, each spur edged with some variation of *Euonymus fortunei radicans* 'Variegatus', *Rhododendron ferrugineum* and *Hebe buxifolia*.

Clearly, formality and informality were not irreconcilable opposites in the gardens of Gertrude Jekyll, but ends of a spectrum – and a spectrum which could be curved full circle to bring the two together, at that.

Nowhere is this marriage better displayed than in the East Garden at Hestercombe in Somerset, above the 'Wrennaissance' orangery. The geometry of the garden is Lutyens at his most playful, a small but complex scheme of circles, squares and diamonds. While the paving through the garden is meticulously regular, the four main beds which result from the geometric interplay are asymmetrical. However, the planting, ranging from ordered to casual, succeeds in furnishing the garden in a way which completely satisfies its geometric requirements.

The small circular beds, with stachys and santolina around China roses, and the larger central diamond of rosemary and dwarf lavender, are impeccably symmetrical, as their key positions in the pattern dictate. The inner bays of the main beds, with small yuccas ranged around vases encircled with nepeta, are orderly but not symmetrical: they differ in their planting from the remaining arms of the beds, filled with the

Above Hestercombe is a fine illustration of the success of the partnership between Gertrude Jekyll and Edwin Lutyens. The geometry of Lutyens's 'Wrennaissance' orangery, paying homage to Sir Christopher Wren, is echoed in the panels of grass and paving and continued in the walls and steps which form the backbone of the garden, while Miss Jekyll's restrained planting mellows the architectural lines.

Right The East Garden, Hestercombe, Somerset

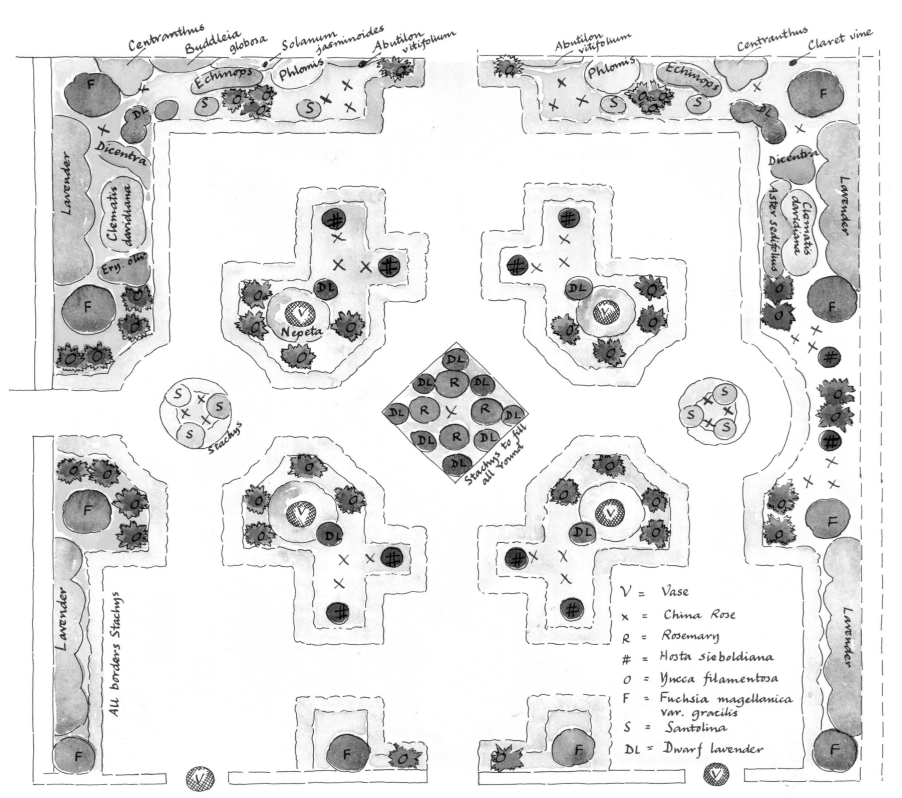

Centranthus · Buddleia · globosa · Solanum jasminoides · Abutilon vitifolium · Echinops · Phlomis

Abutilon vitifolium · Phlomis · Echinops · Centranthus · Claret vine

Dicentra · Clematis davidiana · Ery. olw. · F · S

Lavender

Aster sediflius · Dicentra · Clematis davidiana · Lavender · F

Nepeta

Stachys

Stachys to fill all round

S · Santolina

All borders Stachys

Lavender

F

F

F

Lavender

F

V = Vase

x = China Rose

R = Rosemary

= Hosta sieboldiana

O = Yucca filamentosa

F = Fuchsia magellanica var. gracilis

S = Santolina

DL = Dwarf lavender

The gardener please grow Ageratum houstonianum tall and dwarf Trachelium caeruleum for filling
and sow where marked red Suttons double rose Godetia
Snapdragons white, pale yellow and pale pink to fill

softer shapes of China roses and hostas, but are related to them by subtlety of colouring. The two parts are also connected by a single dwarf lavender in each bed, and by a continuous edging of stachys.

Each segment of the central beds is then connected to the surrounding border, in which alternating trios or pairs of yuccas and roses appear to establish their own rhythm yet infallibly answer their kind in the central beds. Lavenders and fuchsias, eryngiums and echinops, all of blue-purple colouring, and dicentras and centranthus (valerian) of dusky pink are intermingled with the two main contributors, together with *Clematis heracleifolia* var. *davidiana* with grey-blue flowers, and hostas of matching blue-grey leaf.

Broad bushes of *Phlomis fruticosa* flank one entrance to the garden, their soft yellow flowers contrasting with the generally grey-blue scheme, but not so strongly as to injure the colouring of pale pink China roses on all sides. The nearby wall supports a spreading fan of *Buddleja globosa*, often a rather coarse plant but here ideally situated to display its grey leaves and bright orange-yellow balls of flowers against the warm grey-brown stonework. Also on the wall, revelling in its warm aspect, are *Solanum jasminoides*, *Abutilon vitifolium* (a wonder of soft grey and pale lavender) and dusky claret vine. The darker leaves of the vine, changing through the year from subdued bronze in summer (toning with the centranthus at its feet) to rich purple-crimson in autumn, challenge nearby fuchsias in brilliance of colouring.

This lovely scheme of soft but varied planting, never too strictly regimented but with regularity never far removed, would have satisfied most discerning gardeners, but it was not quite enough for Miss Jekyll. A hundred snapdragons in white, pale yellow and pale pink were prescribed 'to fill', and for the same purpose the gardener was asked to grow supplies of soft blue ageratum (tall and dwarf) and *Trachelium caeruleum* (a purple-blue equivalent of valerian), and to sow Sutton's double rose godetia *in situ* in any remaining spaces. Clearly, in this delightful garden not a scrap of ground was to be wasted!

Right Generous quantities of the globe thistle *Echinops ritro* 'Veitch's Blue' complement the sophisticated geometry of Lutyens's balustrade at Hestercombe. The white-felted undersides of the echinops's jagged dark green leaves pick up the soft colouring of lavender and other grey-leaved plants nearby.

Left A sea of grey foliage and lavender flowers near the orangery at Hestercombe washes over paving of harmonious colouring. Stachys edges the beds with a woolly silver band, while the contrapuntal foliage of spiky yuccas gives the clue to a subtle regularity in the scheme.

ROSE
GARDENS

Variety within simplicity

Little Aston, near Birmingham

Sandbourne, Worcestershire

Pages 94–5 On the pillars and beams of the pergola at Hestercombe, roses offer garlands of fragrant flowers, harmonizing with the pale stone and woodwork.

Above Modern Floribunda roses – low, disease-resistant and free-flowering – have replaced the original Jekyll planting in Lutyens's circular garden at Folly Farm, but Miss Jekyll's principle of simple planting in gardens of elaborate geometry remains unaltered.

Opposite The vivid crimson-scarlet flowers of the polyantha rose 'Frensham', in a setting of purple-leaved atriplex, cotinus and berberis, form the fiery core of a border at Kiftsgate Court, Gloucestershire.

Gardens devoted to the highly cultivated Hybrid Perpetual, Hybrid Tea and, in the late twentieth century, Floribunda roses occupy a niche in garden making somewhere between formal bedding schemes of tender perennials and more permanent, more substantial shrub borders. These rose gardens present special problems to the gardener: their occupants have neither the concentrated flowering qualities of tender bedding plants nor the substance and permanent form of shrubs. Nevertheless, the special charms of roses, their elegant buds, their wide colour range, their fragrance, their romantic connotations and their very long flowering season earn for them a special place in the garden. That place has usually been a formal garden planted almost entirely with roses, the plants closely massed to ensure that there are sufficient flowers at any one time to create the desired effect of concentrated colour. This specialization also simplifies the management of plants which respond to good cultivation and seem singularly prone to aphids, sawfly and a range of debilitating fungal diseases.

Perhaps the greatest problem in the planning of rose gardens lies in the choice which must be made between variety and simplicity. The search for novelty in roses has resulted in the availability, at any one time, of an enormous number of cultivars. The constraints of a formal layout, though, demand symmetry and therefore simplicity of effect. The conventional approach, to devote each bed to one cultivar, might in some degree fulfil the requirement for simplicity, but it only accentuates any asymmetry resulting from differences in colour and pattern of growth from cultivar to cultivar.

Miss Jekyll did not face the problem presented by multitudes of bright yellow, pink, amber and multicoloured roses. To some extent she avoided such difficulties as did exist by using mainly the older and proven roses of softer colouring. Of her own garden, on light sand, she confessed 'After many years of fruitless effort I have to allow that I am beaten in the attempt to grow the grand Roses in the Hybrid Perpetual class ... The rich loam that they love has to come many miles from the Weald by hilly roads in four-horse waggons, and the haulage is so costly that when it arrives I feel like distributing it with a teaspoon rather than with the spade.' Even a generous application of loam seemed like a dusting in comparison with the 60m/200ft of dry sand underlying the rose beds.

However, in many of the gardens she planned for others, a rose garden was considered essential, and no doubt the stables of the rather larger households of her clients produced quantities of manure to offset any deficiencies in the soil. Miss Jekyll's handling of these rose gardens offers many hints appropriate to the modern garden.

A major problem with massed roses is that, while they may have wonderful flowers, they do not usually make wonderful plants. Most are essentially beautiful flowers on rather ugly sticks. Miss Jekyll overcame this problem by weaving together

Two roses of Miss Jekyll's time, **above**, the China rose 'Irène Watts', with *Lychnis coronaria alba*, and, **opposite**, the Hybrid Perpetual 'Directeur Alphand'. At Little Aston roses are blended with yuccas and peonies.

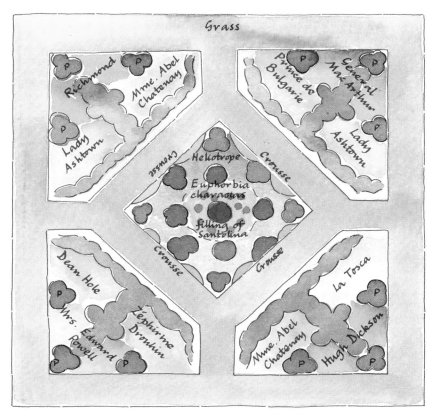

several cultivars of rose in each bed and leavening the scheme with plants other than roses, in particular grey-leaved plants and sumptuous Chinese peonies.

Peonies have the merit of flowering earlier than roses, extending the season of interest of the garden. Their magnificent, if short-lived, flowers also exhibit a colour range similar to that of the roses themselves. What is even more important, peonies have wonderful bold and glossy foliage, echoing the colour and texture of rose foliage but in more massive, dense, leafy mounds, many cultivars assuming crimson and purple tints in autumn before dying away. Even without the considerable asset of their flowers, peonies would still make perfect companions for roses.

Grey-leaved plants, in contrast, offer fineness of texture and a softness of colouring which harmonizes with the whole colour range of rose flowers, and if those grey leaves support similarly harmonious flower spikes of purple lavender, pale catmint or dusky pink stachys, the gain is doubled. Further-

more, many of the grey-leaved plants retain their foliage throughout the year, furnishing the garden when the roses are reduced to bare sticks. The rose garden may be designed to display roses, but that should not prevent its being attractive at other times of year.

The parterre at Little Aston, near Birmingham, is an excellent example of these principles in practice. Its pattern alone is quietly satisfying: three panels of grass set in a paved surround. Five beds are cut out of each outer panel, reducing the grass there to narrow paths. In the central panel the grass remains intact, save for a central paved diamond which repeats the shape of the central beds on either side. On the paving would stand a sundial or other substantial ornament.

The central diamonds of the two flower panels have identical planting (on the plan the labelling of the plants is divided between the two panels). Each is filled, not with roses, but with a pyramid of yuccas – *Yucca gloriosa* in the middle, ringed with *Y. recurvifolia* towards the four corners and

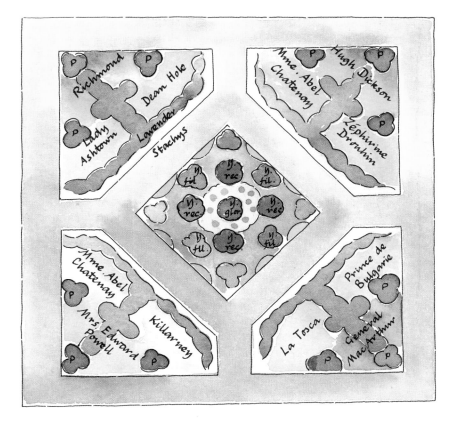

y. fil = Yucca filamentosa
y. rec = Yucca recurvifolia
y. glor = Yucca gloriosa
P = Peony

The rose garden at Little
Aston, near Birmingham

groups of the low *Y. filamentosa* around the margin. The ground between these spiky forms is filled with santolina and pale heliotrope to provide flowing masses of soft colour and the beds are edged by the ivy-leaved pelargonium 'Madame Crousse'. The rose beds themselves, on the four corners of each outer panel, have stachys and lavender lining the inner paths and more lavender extending back as a central spine to each bed. Even in midwinter, therefore, the pattern of the garden is outlined in soft grey, with the yuccas providing a focus of interest equivalent, among living forms, to the sundial in the centre of the garden.

Three clumps, of three peonies each, emphasize the outer corners of the rose beds, combining with the lavender to divide each bed into four compartments. The outer two (on the corners of the panel) are planted with one rose cultivar and the inner two with a different cultivar in each. Three groups in each of four quarters imply a maximum of twelve cultivars in all. Miss Jekyll used ten in one panel, repeating 'Madame Abel

Chatenay' and 'Lady Ashtown', and the same ten plus 'Killarney' ('Madame Abel Chatenay' being again repeated) in the other panel, using different combinations each time. Thus, although the pattern and planting give a strong sense of symmetry, the two halves are subtly different. Even the uniformity of complete variety – twelve cultivars in twelve allotted patches – is interrupted by repetition, and it is interrupted differently in the two halves – an example of the enigmatic variation from complete symmetry so characteristic of Miss Jekyll's formal designs.

At Sandbourne, near Bewdley in Worcestershire, the rose garden was much larger, 15m/50ft wide and over 90m/300ft long, so a somewhat simpler treatment was called for. The plan shows the garden ringed with pillar roses underplanted with lavender. 'Eleanor Berkeley' is placed at each end of the four long side beds and the two curved end beds to frame the entrances, and in the curved borders 'The Garland' and 'Euphrosyne' alternate in a regular pattern, with pairs of

Three of the roses used by Miss Jekyll in her plan, **below,** for the rose garden at Sandbourne, Worcestershire. **From left to right,** 'Blanc Double de Coubert', its wrinkled apple-green foliage liberally sprinkled with cold white flowers; 'Zéphirine Drouhin', which would be pegged down to encourage free flowering; 'Hugh Dickson', one of the richest red roses then known.

'Blush Rambler' on the haunches of the end beds to reinforce the sense of symmetry. In each of the side beds about half a dozen climbing roses are used – the same plants in each case, but with the pattern varied slightly to tease the observant spectator.

Each of the three circular medallions within the formal pattern has at its centre a group of five 'Blanc Double de Coubert', one of Miss Jekyll's favourite shrub roses, and then quite a new rose. 'Blanc Double de Coubert' is very different from the Hybrid Teas and Hybrid Perpetual roses in the garden as a whole, by virtue of its dense masses of bright apple-green foliage and its enormous profusion of snowy

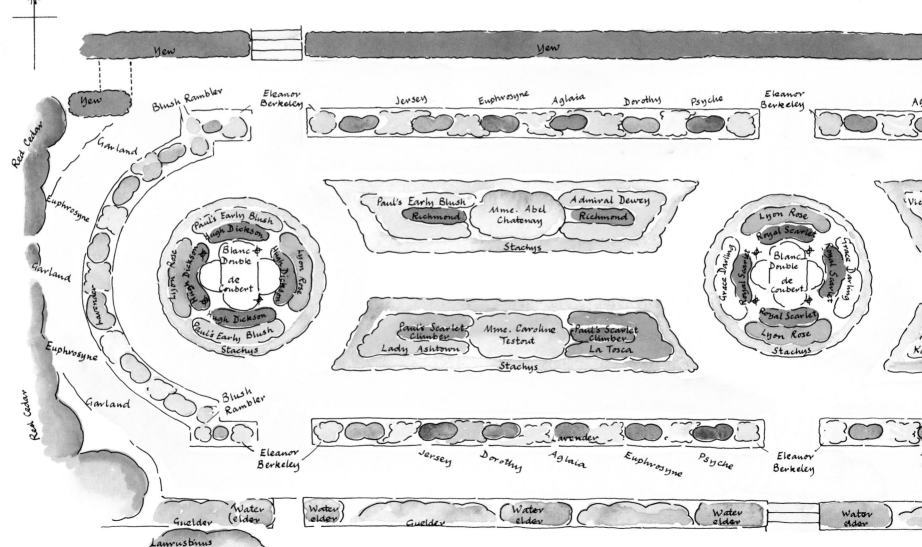

white flowers (deadheaded by the gardeners, of course, before they turn to an unsightly brown). Around these central groups are two circles of smaller, less substantial roses in various combinations of pink and red, then a generous edging of woolly-leaved stachys. The twelve plants encircling the 'Blanc Double de Coubert' in each medallion are divided into four groups of three by a symbol which is not identified on the plan but was commonly used by Miss Jekyll to represent yuccas or pots of white lilies. The latter would be highly appropriate in this position, their upright stems and narrow, dark leaves contrasting with the pale green domes of 'Blanc Double de Coubert' and arching out over the lower roses to

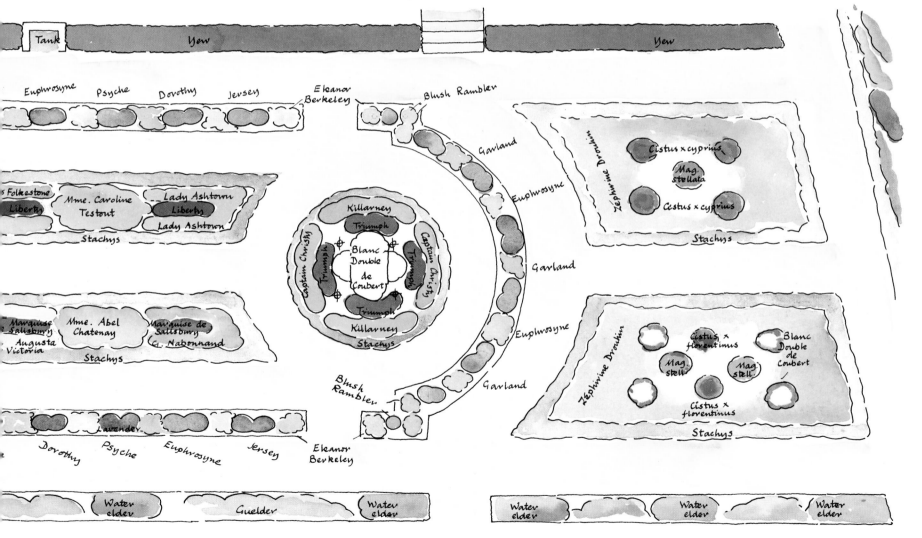

bring their intensely fragrant funnels nearer to the passer-by.

The four main central beds are planted quite simply: a large group of one rose in the centre ('Madame Caroline Testout' and 'Madame Abel Chatenay' in alternate beds), a line of a second rose completing the spine of the bed, and two other cultivars surrounding this spine (with one or two cultivars repeated about the garden as at Little Aston). Again, there is a generous edging of stachys flowing out over the edge of the path to soften the rigid geometry.

The rose garden at Sandbourne is also interesting for reasons other than its roses; its apparent symmetry conceals a charming irregularity of design. The steps in the north-west corner do not align with the centre of the circular medallion, as one might suppose they should, so the curved border of climbing roses ends with rectangular shoulders to align with the path and the steps. The central steps on the south side are indeed central to the main panel of the rose garden, while the north-east steps arrive outside this panel, in a little garden 'anteroom' that is slightly irregular in shape, because one of its paths runs at an angle to the general pattern of parallels and perpendiculars.

This little anteroom, connected to the main part of the rose garden by windows between the pillar roses and by its continuous broad edging of stachys, accommodates its asymmetry by simple mass planting. In the centre of the northern (smaller) bed is a single specimen of *Magnolia stellata*, providing delicate white flowers before the roses are even in leaf, and then compact, but eventually large, domes of pale apple-green foliage. Around the magnolia are *Cistus × cyprius*, with rather darker foliage in handsome evergreen mounds, and a mass of 'Zéphirine Drouhin', a tall rose which lends itself particularly well to pegging down, stimulating its otherwise gaunt thornless shoots to produce myriads of short laterals laden with fragrant, rose-pink flowers.

The second bed has two magnolias to fill out the centre, interplanted with cistus again but supplemented in turn towards the corners of the beds with 'Blanc Double de Coubert' (its foliage nearly identical in colouring to that of the magnolia). This extra planting is just sufficient to ensure that the main groundwork of 'Zéphirine Drouhin' is almost identical in the two beds: twenty-nine plants in the north bed, thirty-one in the south.

While the more formal end of the rose garden, the main west panel, is formally enclosed with red cedars (*Thuja plicata*), the simpler pattern of the eastern end continues, with theme and variations, into an informal border (not shown on the plan here), planted with grey-leaved shrubs and pale roses and backed by a wall on which are trained, with a mild degree of symmetry, claret vine, *Magnolia denudata* and bold dark-leaved loquat.

Of course, Miss Jekyll also used roses in many, many other ways, several of which are described in other chapters of this book. Her plans show, for example, China roses emerging delicately from a setting of rosemary, lavender or other grey foliage; *Rosa virginiana* and other vigorous species roses and shrub roses taking their place in the informal shrub garden; climbing and rambling roses flinging themselves into holly or yew or creating wide mounds of arching beauty in the wilder parts of the garden. These and other uses were explored by Miss Jekyll in *Roses for English Gardens*. However, the rose gardens at Little Aston and Sandbourne summarize admirably the main lessons to be learned from her on the planning of gardens devoted primarily to the rose.

Right In her many gardens, Miss Jekyll exploited to the full the versatility of roses. Here, in a planting at Lime Kiln Rosarium in Suffolk, the large pink flowers of 'Madame Isaac Pereire' and foaming masses of climbing roses glow against a dark background of yew.

Opposite A broad edging of felt-leaved stachys makes an ideal setting for soft pink roses, carpeting the bare ground beneath the often gaunt rose stems while providing a harmonious background for the flowers. Pulling down the rose stems encourages the buds to break freely along their whole length, forming cascades of fragrant flowers.

DESIGN
WITH
SHRUBS

Durable planting

Hydon Ridge, Surrey

Bowerbank, London

Elmhurst, Ohio

Fox Hill, Surrey

Walsham House, Surrey

Shrubs usually form the backbone of a garden, or soften the outline of more architectural 'bones'. Shrubs provide height, density, spatial definition, often good ground cover, sometimes neutrality of background for brighter flowers, as well as having their own decorative virtues of flower, leaf and twig.

Despite their importance in most gardens, shrub planting tends to be the least thoroughly considered aspect of the garden. In large gardens there is so much to think about that one is tempted to resort to random assortments of favourite plants. In small gardens individual shrubs occupy such an important place that each is included on its own merits with little thought for the overall effect. It is especially useful, therefore, to study Miss Jekyll's use of shrubs, her choice of a few indicator plants to set the scene, of accents to underline that theme and provide variations on it, her use of edging plants and fillers to extend the season and to accelerate the pace at which the border matures in the early years of a new garden. Most important of all, we learn that she seldom used shrubs in isolation; they have their merits but they also have their limitations. Lighter herbaceous plants and ferns, bolder foliage plants such as iris and kniphofia, softening trails of climbers were all incorporated to varying degrees in her shrub plantings to compensate for the generally rounded form, the somewhat diffuse flowering, the slowness of growth in the early years and the inexorable spread over the edges of borders in later years that characterize the majority of shrubs.

The full range of character possible in predominantly shrub plantings can be clearly seen in the plans for the garden at Hydon Ridge, Hambledon, Surrey. The entrance drive passes through a deep cutting fringed with irregular groups of holly interplanted with *Clematis vitalba*, the latter trailing its festoons of green-white flowers and silky seedheads down the bank and up into the dark hollies in a perfect example of a designed scheme – 'learning from nature that quality which, in painting, is known as "breadth"', to use Miss Jekyll's words.

Pages 104–5 Simple drifts of azaleas in the wilder parts of the gardens at Les Moutiers capture the sense of freedom and informality which Miss Jekyll sought to create with her shrub planting. The skilled arrangement of shrubs carefully selected for good form and foliage ensures the continuing beauty of the garden long after the relatively brief flowering season is over.

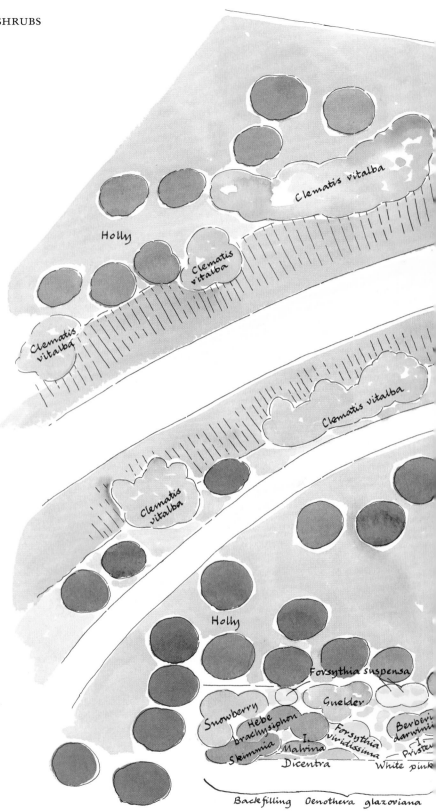

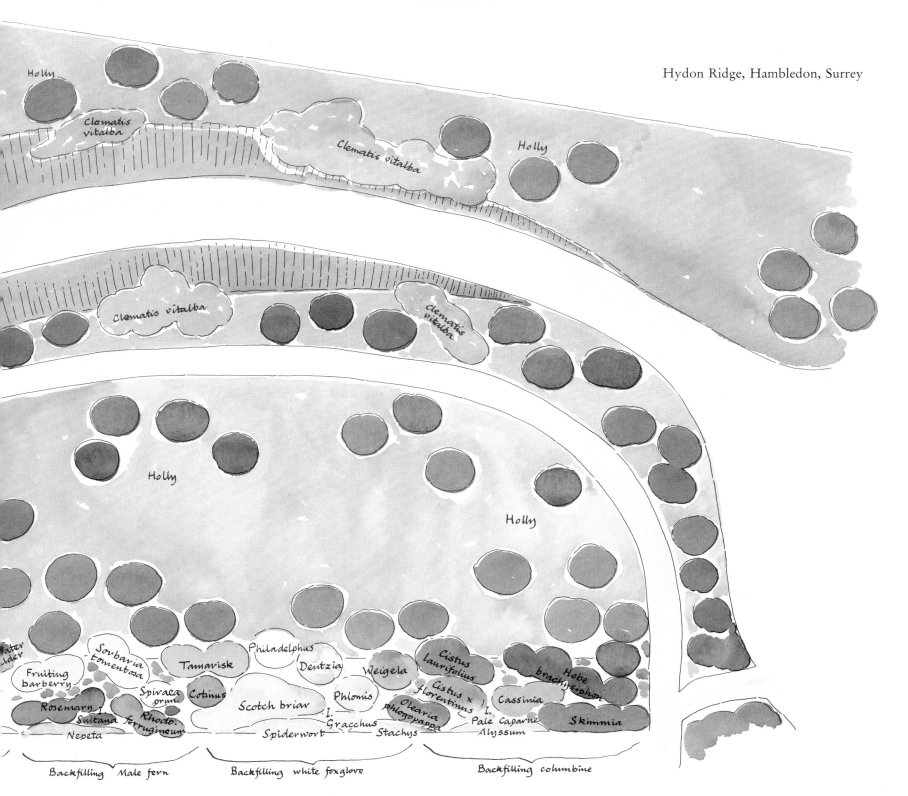

Hydon Ridge, Hambledon, Surrey

Holly

Clematis vitalba

Clematis vitalba

Holly

Clematis vitalba

Clematis vitalba

Holly

Holly

Water alder

Sorbaria tomentosa

Philadelphus

Tamarisk

Deutzia

Weigela

Cistus laurifolius

Hebe brachysiphon

Fruiting barberry

Spiraea orum

Cotinus

Scotch briar

Phlomis

Cistus x florentinus

Olearia phlogopappa

I. Pale

Cassinia

Rosemary

Rhodo. ferrugineum

I. Gracchus

Caparne Alyssum

Skimmia

Sultana

Nepeta

Spiderwort

Stachys

Backfilling Male fern

Backfilling white foxglove

Backfilling columbine

107

On the level above the drive and fringing the forecourt, the hollies thicken into a near-continuous but loosely margined mass, creating, on one side, a charming informal glade opening on to a footpath and, on the other, a dark green background for the more obviously decorative border enclosing the formal tennis lawn at one end of the house.

Within this border, lower evergreen shrubs form the same sort of irregular, loose but unified drifts that enclose the footpath from the drive and glade. Dark-leaved skimmia and *Hebe brachysiphon* begin the border. These are followed by brighter green *Berberis darwinii*, rosemary and low *Rhododendron*

ferrugineum (alpenrose), greyer phlomis, olearia and cistus, and the fine-textured yellow-green mass of *Cassinia leptophylla fulvida*, with a second group of hebe to end the border more or less as it began. Notice how the foliage colour changes from dark to mid-green and grey (with phlomis at the lightest point), then more rapidly back to dark in the large concentration of evergreens reinforcing the border at that point where the footpath and forecourt come closest to the lawn.

Around and among the evergreens are grouped deciduous flowering shrubs: grey-green snowberry enclosed by hollies at

one end of the border, brighter green forsythias and water elder, feathery *Sorbaria tomentosa* and still lighter tamarisk above a broad mass of pale, fine-textured Scotch briar leading up to the phlomis, then darker philadelphus, deutzia and weigela connecting with the evergreens near the house. At the middle point of the border are solitary plants of *Spiraea prunifolia* and *Cotinus coggygria*, perfect choices to blend together the grey-green plants on all sides and beautiful in themselves. The spiraea is at its best in spring, when its slender branches are weighed down by festoons of snow-white blossom. The cotinus is impeccably presentable in and out of leaf but spectacular when its brilliant autumn foliage develops amidst its soft-coloured surroundings, outshining but complementing the not inconsiderable autumn tints of *Viburnum opulus* at the farther end of the border.

The border shows what can be achieved by careful planning with shrubs, and presents an attractive picture in leaf alone, but it has a second level of beauty in the carefully considered arrangement of its flowers. Forsythias help to begin the season: trails of pale yellow *Forsythia suspensa* where it can climb into the hollies or fall forward over dark mounds of hebe; the sharper yellow of *F. viridissima* to the fore. Yellow barberry and bright orange *Berberis darwinii* are deeper still in colour, set in a frame of cool white *Viburnum opulus* (the single water elder on one side and double guelder rose on the other) and separated from the dusky pink heads of alpenrose, if their spring and early summer flowering seasons should chance to overlap, by the long drift of rosemary. Its pale grey-blue flowers provide the ideal intermediary.

The mainly bright yellow flowers at the farther end of the border give way to softer pink and red near the house. Rosemary and alpenrose start this second theme, merging into delicate pink Scotch briars and tamarisk, heavily scented white philadelphus, pale deutzia and darker red weigela, again set against the white and off-white flowers of the sorbaria, olearias, hebe and handsome, aromatic cistus.

The greenish white globes of the guelder rose, or snowball tree, *Viburnum opulus* 'Roseum', introduce a cool note into the shrub border. Its vigorous boughs of bright green foliage deepen to bronze in the autumn, while the foliage of the fragrant lilac in the background remains a light grey-green until it falls.

The shrubs at the back of the border are visible at intervals from the footpath, through the intervening hollies: pale green water elder with its greenish white flowers and the soft yellow trails of forsythia at one end, tall philadelphus festooned with later white flowers near the middle, and dark green hebe at the other end, nearly indistinguishable from the holly from a distance until its own spikes of white cover the dark foliage in midsummer.

At the front of the border, long drifts of compact herbaceous plants are used to define the straight edge of the tennis lawn. Pink dicentra and white pinks at the farther end extend the summer colour scheme established by the weigela and other shrubs flowering at this time. Yellow alyssum brings the spring colouring into the foreground, with grey-pink-purple nepeta (catmint), stachys and spiderwort (tradescantia) near the middle of the border to continue the conciliatory role of the rosemary between yellow and pink. Behind the front line of low, rounded mat-formers, groups of iris interpose their strong sword-like leaves at regular intervals and any spaces between the shrubs, particularly important in the early years of the border, are filled with yellow oenothera (evening primrose), pale green male ferns, white foxgloves and soft pink and purple columbines.

Next to this part of the garden 'above the entrance road' is the forecourt, with narrow borders of predominantly dark green low shrubs against the house. The plan of its planting is included in the chapter on sun and shade (see page 153) because of the other qualities it displays, but it is worth looking at the two together. They encompass with remarkable completeness the whole breadth of opportunity and expression which can be achieved in shrub planting.

One of the most valuable lessons in using shrubs lies in Miss Jekyll's use of good plain dark green foliage: yew, Portugal laurel, laurustinus and holly especially, together with lower plants such as skimmia, *Daphne pontica* and *D. laureola*, *Danaë racemosa* and of course *Hebe brachysiphon*, the plant used to such good effect at Hydon Ridge. With their quiet dignity and the cheeriness of countenance created by the bright polish of their leaves, these neat, glossy plants lend an air of distinction to the garden. Used in combination they provide subtle variations of hue and texture, and because so many of these evergreens are tolerant of dry, shady and rooty places, they are a considerable asset to those parts of the garden which would otherwise be dusty liabilities.

At Bowerbank, a relatively small, rectangular garden in Wimbledon, the looped front drive is separated from the road by close masses of *Rhododendron ponticum*, paler-flowered Ponticum hybrids ('Album Grandiflorum' and 'Everestianum') and holly, edged with *Mahonia aquifolium*. The subtle interplay of long rhododendron leaves in rounded masses and the more upright growth of holly, each leaf spined and curving to reflect light from its black-green surface, is continued in the paler, leaden hue of the mahonia. Miss Jekyll described mahonia as having 'every leaf a marvel of beautiful drawing and construction', with flowers 'fuller of bee music than any other plant then in flower'. With generous feeding and regular pruning to maintain its handsome appearance, it would lap elegantly around the base of rhododendrons and holly, sending the occasional taller shoot up to display its soft yellow flowers against the darker background of the other shrubs.

On each corner of the front garden, white birch trunks spear through the dark masses of holly and rhododendron, the fruits of a lesson learned at Munstead Wood, where Miss Jekyll wrote of her wild garden, 'Now we pass on through the dark masses of Rhododendron and the Birches that shoot up among them. How the silver stems, blotched and banded with varied browns and greys so deep in tone that they show like a luminous black, tell among the glossy Rhododendron green; and how strangely different is the way of growth of the two kinds of tree; the tall white trunks spearing up through the dense, dark, leathery leaf-masses of solid, roundish outline, with their delicate network of reddish branch and spray gently swaying far overhead!' At Bowerbank, these lovely contrasts of woodland grace are distilled, represented by a few plants only. Where the drive branches to enter the service court there are paler guelder rose and *Spiraea prunifolia*, each with its own white flowers to add a more transient freshness to the scene.

The borders against the house, on either side of the front door, are too narrow to admit large shrubs. Instead, *Chaenomeles japonica* (flowering quince) is trained on the walls for the sake of its bright flowers on bare spring branches, giving way to summer foliage of a cheerful glossy green. Duller green laurustinus rounds out the corners of the borders and flanks the doorway, with mahonia filling many of the remaining spaces, to create a sense of unity and restrained dignity in the front garden as a whole. The remaining planting takes full advantage of the south-facing aspect of the borders: *Berberis darwinii*, with orange flowers lining its upright branches in a sunny situation, springs out of the largest group of mahonia, with its own miniature holly leaves hinting at its close relationship to the mahonia; dull grey-green domes of *Olearia × haastii* and bold clumps of acanthus emphasize the southern aspect; in the continuum of generally dark but dull greens thus created, long groups of grey lavender are planted to catch the eye of visitors and passers-by through the dark wings of rhododendron by the road. Finally, in recesses on either side of the front door, are two climbers: pale green *Clematis montana* on the short east-facing wall, echoing the colouring of guelder rose both in leaf and in the cool white of its fragrant spring flowers; *Jasminum officinale* repeating the dark green of holly, and producing its scented white summer flowers in the warm west-facing corner.

This theme of mainly solid greens, relieved by lighter deciduous greens and white flowers, is seen in many of Miss Jekyll's plans. For the source of inspiration for such schemes, one does not have to look beyond Munstead Wood – to the point where the garden merged imperceptibly into woodland, with picturesque groups of birch and holly and rhododendrons, or to the cool north court, where swags of *Clematis montana* were draped to meet the upright stems of *Viburnum opulus*, while pots of ferns, campanulas, lilies and hostas repeated the pale green and white colouring at a lower level. For the smallest spaces, asarum and London pride replaced mahonias or skimmias. In larger schemes hollies might be intermingled with other dark evergreens: their strong sense of enclosure would protect the illusion of woodland grace created by the lighter greens from the realities of the outer world. There might be room, too, for frothier ferns (male fern, especially, being invaluable for capturing the essence of moist woodland even in a dry border), guelder rose and other pale greens epitomizing the cool, translucent loveliness of a woodland in spring.

At Bowerbank, as at Hydon Ridge, the main structure of the garden derives from the shrubs themselves. The backdrop of varied but neutral greens is important as a setting for lighter

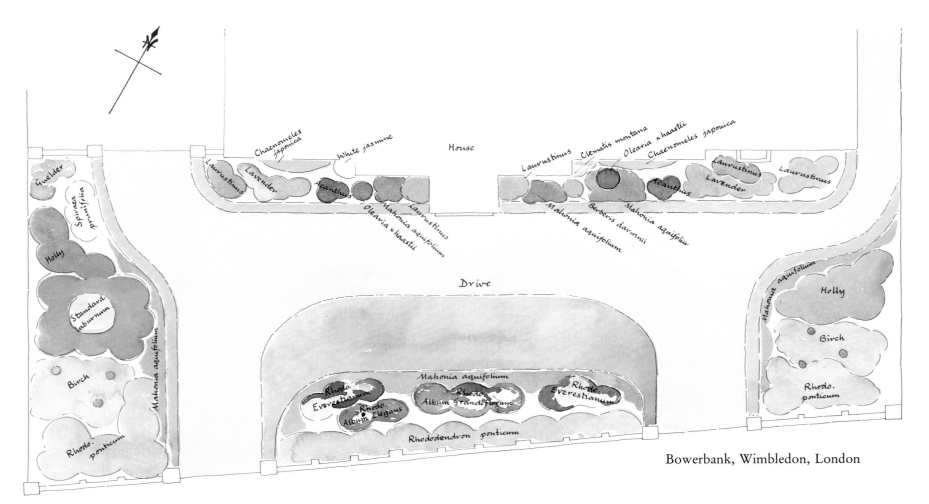

Bowerbank, Wimbledon, London

foliage and flowers. In other instances, where walls provided any necessary neutrality and solidity of background, shrubs could be used for their more colourfully decorative attributes, to blend foreground with background and thus to enhance the apparent depth of the planting.

Again, Munstead Wood provides a precedent, with robinia and abutilon behind the grey-blue end of the flower border, yellow-green magnolia and choisya foliage accentuating the clearer blue of delphiniums, and fuchsias and claret vine enriching the red and orange section of the border.

What is perhaps the peak of subtlety in the relationship between foreground flowers and background shrubs was reached at Barrington Court in Somerset. In a plan of one of its many long borders, the ordinary, rather dull green and softly hairy *Viburnum tinus* is used at the ends, behind the

rich reds of antirrhinums, kniphofias, penstemons, *Lobelia cardinalis* and *Sedum telephium*, while the glossier, brighter green *Viburnum tinus* 'Lucidum' is substituted in the central section to tone more effectively with striped maize, white and yellow antirrhinums, yellow heleniums and rudbeckias and an edging of bright, cheery green tansy.

In the Groesbeck garden near Cincinnati, Ohio (discussed on pages 24–6), purple-leaved *Prunus cerasifera* 'Pissardii', 'cut down every year', is used behind the stronger-coloured section of the flower border, adding the crimson-purple richness of its vigorous young foliage to scarlet monarda and lychnis, kniphofia (red-hot pokers) and heleniums rayed with crimson and yellow. Behind the opposite border, golden privet, golden elder and the heath-like, yellow-tinged branches of cassinia combine with white antirrhinums and phlox, pale

Elmhurst, Cincinnati, Ohio

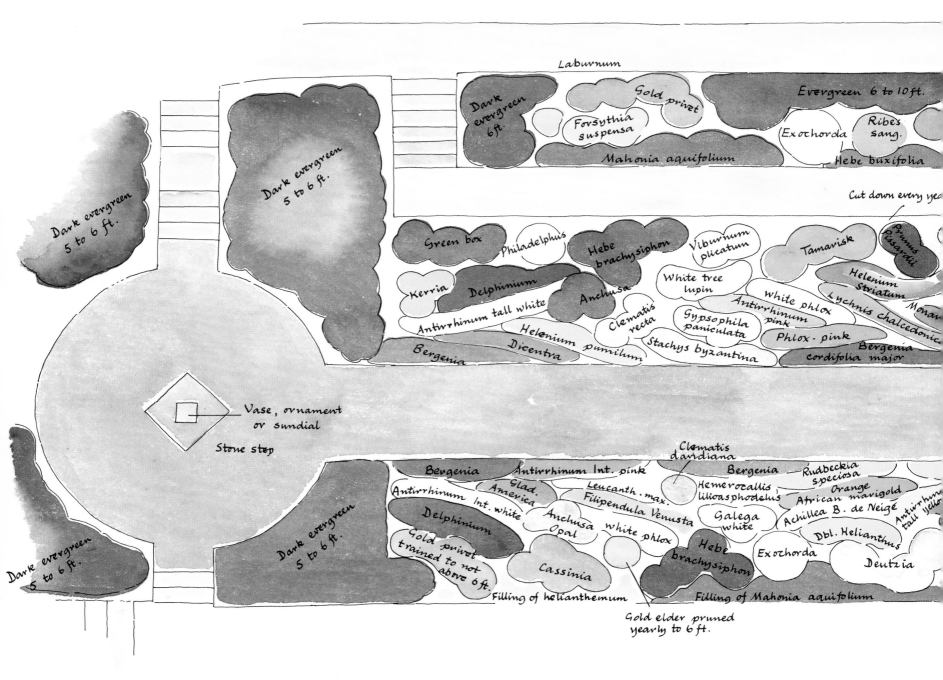

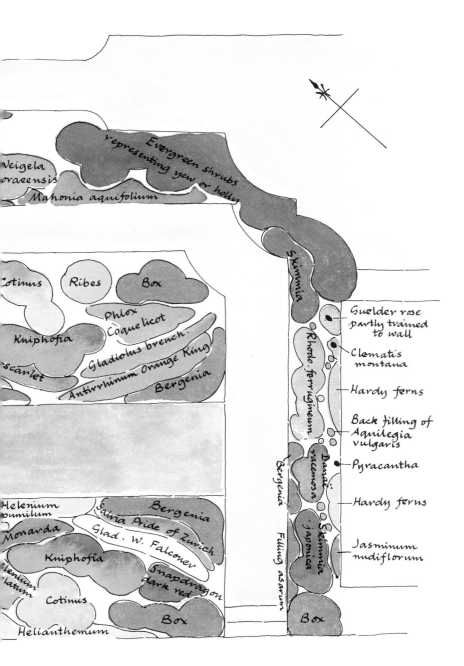

Veigela
oraeensis
Mahonia aquifolium
Evergreen shrubs
representing yew or holly
Skimmia
Cotinus
Ribes
Box
Phlox
Coquelicot
Kniphofia
Gladiolus brench.
Antirrhinum Orange King
scarlet
Bergenia
Rhodo. ferrugineum
Guelder rose
partly trained
to wall
Clematis
montana
Hardy ferns
Back filling of
Aquilegia
vulgaris
Danaë racemosa
Bergenia
Pyracantha
Hardy ferns
Helenium
pumilum
Bergenia
Salvia Pride of Zurich
Monarda
Glad. W. Falconer
Kniphofia
Skimmia japonica
latum
Snapdragon
dark red
Bergenia Filling asarum
Jasminum
nudiflorum
Cotinus
Box
Box
Helianthemum

pink *Filipendula rubra* 'Venusta' and white *Leucanthemum maximum* (Shasta daisies) to create a picture of perfect freshness and an ideal frame for pale blue anchusa and the later spikes of clear blue delphiniums.

Notice, incidentally, how the flower borders in this plan are contained within repeated groups of bergenia, harmonizing with box and *Hebe brachysiphon* in the background. And notice, too, the wonderful small border against the house, a cool display of guelder rose, *Clematis montana*, ferns and skimmia, dark pyracantha and bergenia, hummocky *Rhododendron ferrugineum* and spiky *Danaë racemosa*, with winter jasmine on the corner of the house providing a fountain of bright yellow flowers in the winter months and arching sprays of dark foliage on lighter green stems through the summer.

At Fox Hill, Elstead, in Surrey, shrubs move from the subordinate position of 'useful background' to take centre stage as the focus of attention in a remarkable design in which formal stonework – flights of steps ascending from the house in alternating arcs and direct flights – is heavily enclosed, almost engulfed, in the type of plants one would normally expect to see reserved for the wild garden: heaths and azaleas, cistus and sea-buckthorn, merging into large masses of ferns, with birch trunks on the skyline. The scheme is essentially a distillation of the extensive rolling heaths and cistus-covered hills which Miss Jekyll would have loved to orchestrate, and which she partially created on a modest scale at Munstead Wood. At Fox Hill, the spirit of wild heath is invoked in a manner entirely appropriate to its situation between house and wood, and in keeping with the sophisticated border of white, yellow and orange flowers at the foot of the slope.

The scheme begins on the terrace by the house with a low dry wall draped in cerastium, sedum and pterocephalus. A spreading carpet of *Ceratostigma plumbaginoides* and spiky-leaved *Iris unguicularis* spring from the base of the wall, while pinks, nepeta, lavender and helianthemums flow over its top in a study of soft grey colouring.

This grey theme continues on the hillside above the wall, with mounds of santolina and fine-textured masses of Scotch briar, the bold silhouettes of *Euphorbia characias* ssp. *wulfenii*, the repeated spikes of pale tree lupins and dark but soft grey-green domes of *Cistus laurifolius*. Behind the cistus are groups of yellow broom, hidden from below as the cistus

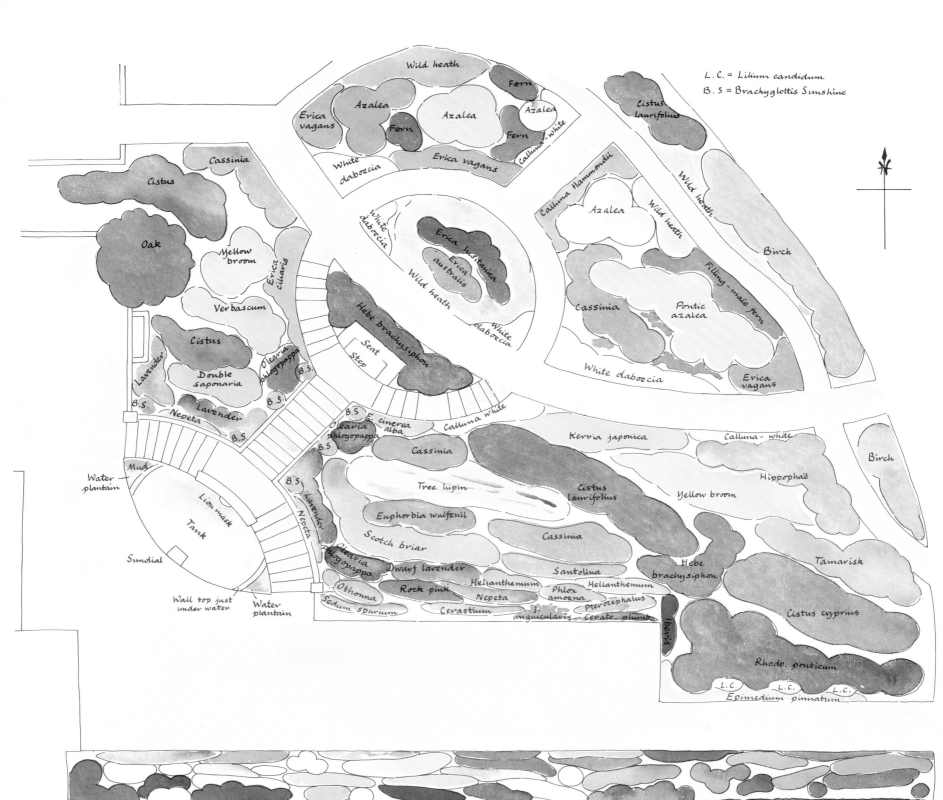

Wild heath

Fern

Azalea

Erica vagans

Azalea

Fern

Azalea

Fern

Calluna - white

Cistus laurifolius

L.C. = Lilium candidum
B.S = Brachyglottis Sunshine

White daboecia

Erica vagans

Cassinia

Cistus

Oak

Yellow broom

Erica ciliaris

Verbascum

Cistus

Olearia phlogopappa

B.S.

Double saponaria

B.S.

Lavender

B.S.

Lavender

Nepeta

B.S.

White daboecia

Erica lusitanica

Erica australis

Wild heath

White daboecia

Hebe brachysiphon

Seat

Step

Calluna Hammondii

Azalea

Wild heath

Wild heath

Birch

Cassinia

Pontic azalea

Filling - male fern

White daboecia

Erica vagans

Olearia phlogopappa

B.S.

E. cinerea alba

Calluna white

Cassinia

Kerria japonica

Calluna - white

Birch

B.S.

Water plantain

Mud

Lion mask

Tank

Sundial

Wall top just under water

Water plantain

Lavender

Nepeta

Olearia phlogopappa

Othonna

Sedum spurium

Tree lupin

Euphorbia wulfenii

Scotch briar

Dwarf lavender

Rock pink

Cerastium

Nepeta

Cassinia

Santolina

Helianthemum

Phlox amoena

Helianthemum

I. anguicularis

Pterocephalus

Cerato. plumb.

Hebe brachysiphon

Iberis

Cistus laurifolius

Yellow broom

Hippophaë

Tamarisk

Cistus cyprius

Rhodo. ponticum

L.C.

L.C.

L.C.

Epimedium pinnatum

matures. Nearby are grey-leaved hippophaë (sea-buckthorn) and equally narrow-leaved kerria. While most of the plants are distinctly grey or grey-green in leaf, the kerria is bright green and the broom an indeterminate bright yet glaucous green, pale on close inspection but open enough in its fine, twiggy growth to create dark shadows within itself. Drifts of cassinia and *Hebe brachysiphon* are interleaved to develop the counterpoint of bright and soft, extending at the eastern edge of the bank into grey tamarisk, dark grey-green cistus and black-green *Rhododendron ponticum*. Notice how deftly the scale of this large mass of large-leaved rhododendron, so essential to balance the extensive planting on the bank, is incorporated into the smaller-scale garden below. A drift of dark green iberis (candytuft) over the wall, an edging of paler epimedium and three groups of Madonna lilies, and the long wall of rhododendron suddenly matches the scale of the flower border across the path.

The character of planting on the hillside continues in the smaller section of bank to the west. Nepeta and lavender, pale pink double soapwort and dark-leaved cistus are ranged in tiers below tall spikes of yellow verbascums and the lower, partially concealed, spikes of yellow broom and cassinia. Among these varied greys and greens, the shapely mounds of *Brachyglottis* (*Senecio*) 'Sunshine' are repeated at regular intervals, at each corner and at the midpoint of the steps, as a gentle reminder that there is a formal backbone to the garden and that one is still not far from the house. Formality is the note struck, too, by the crescent-shaped block of hebe at the top of the main flight of steps, but beyond this point the presence of woodland is increasingly acknowledged.

The second part of the central circle is planted in a balanced pattern of tree heaths in a carpet of wild calluna, enclosed on either side by the neat mounds of white daboecia, larger in leaf than the other heathers, bolder by virtue of its two-tone foliage (dark green above, white beneath) and welcomed for the long display of large heather bells in late summer and

Right At Stancombe Park in Gloucestershire, shapely mounds of *Brachyglottis* 'Sunshine' border a long flight of steps, enhancing the architectural backbone of the garden, as they do in the plan for Fox Hill. Although brachyglottis (Miss Jekyll's *Senecio greyii*) has suffered unwarranted abuse at the hands of botanists and landscape contractors, it remains a handsome plant, with its immaculate grey-green foliage on boldly arching stems, and crowds of white-felted buds opening to bright yellow daisy flowers.

Left Fox Hill, Elstead, Surrey

autumn. More daboecia spills less formally in long drifts bordering the paths, merging into other heaths, both grey and dark in leaf, and these in turn fill the spaces between groups of azaleas, colourful and fragrant in spring and colourful again in their autumn foliage. The azaleas are grouped in threes and fours, ranging in colour from yellow through pale to deep orange, but the overall effect when not in flower is of a broad irregular mass of soft green, merging into a continuous flowing carpet of heather and then, at the woodland edge, into ferns and the slender white trunks of the birches.

The last example of shrub planting, at Walsham House (in the same village as Fox Hill), is much simpler in character. It shows an apparently effortless scatter of shrubs and trees at the meeting of formal and natural gardens, where straight walks around the house merge into the flowing curves of a woodland garden. The planting is mainly of azaleas, beautifully graded from pink and white through pale yellow near the house to stronger yellows and deep oranges and back to the clear, bright yellow of sweetly scented pontic azalea, *Rhododendron luteum*, for the relatively brief flowering season. For the rest of the year, the azaleas form a single flowing mass of foliage, with minor variations in form and shade of green from cultivar to cultivar, intermingled with darker cistus near the house and merging into red-stemmed dogwood, the bold, dense pyramids of glossy liquidambar, deeply toothed scarlet oak and the freer, spreading canopies of wild cherry. In summer, flower interest is maintained along the upper path with bold spikes of eremurus and, later in the year, of kniphofias. Away from the house, though, the picture is a simple one of dappled light and shade, with glossy liquidambar among the duller green of wild cherries and red-stemmed dogwood. As autumn advances, variations once again appear within the broad sweep of azaleas, variations in the reds, yellows, purples

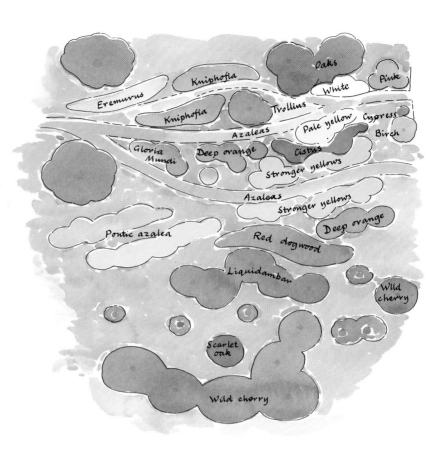

Walsham House, Elstead, Surrey

At La-Celle-les-Bordes in the forest of Rambouillet, near Paris, an apparently effortless scatter of azaleas and slender birch trees creates a sense of depth and serenity. The occasional solid column of Lawson cypress provides an unchanging baseline of solid green against which to measure the changing character of the seasons – from the fresh, translucent colours of spring to the richer golds and bronzy purples of autumn foliage.

and oranges of their autumn tints, and these differences are magnified in the rich purple of dogwood foliage, orange-crimson of the cherries, scarlet oak leaves and the multicoloured flaming tints of the liquidambars. As the leaves fall, the picture returns to one of simple harmony, the red dogwood stems, dull green cistus foliage and scattered columns of Lawson cypress providing the main points of interest among dark-stemmed oaks and the heavy cork-ridged branches of liquidambar.

There is nothing extraordinary in this plan; but in the 'drawing' of the groups, the easy flow of one group into another, and the effortless gradation from exotic red-hot pokers to graceful wild cherries, it exemplifies the pervasive influence on Miss Jekyll of her training as a painter.

WILD GARDENS

Low-maintenance gardening

Drayton Wood, Norfolk

Monkswood, Surrey

Highcroft, Hampshire

Little Aston, near Birmingham

Pages 118–19 Beeches with their smooth grey trunks, slender birches in young spring foliage, and dark, glossy masses of holly interwoven with bulb-strewn clearings were characteristic of Miss Jekyll's wild gardens. In this small corner of a woodland glade at Knightshayes Court in Devon, the darting, delicate flowers of *Narcissus cyclamineus* repeat the bright yellow of celandines among patches of larger narcissus, blurring the divide between the naturalistic and the truly natural.

Left Elegant spires of white foxgloves tower over glaucous hosta leaves in the woodland garden at Knightshayes. The foxglove is equally at home illuminating the flower border, springing from the joints of a drystone wall, or mimicking the lofty verticals of trees in a wood, and Miss Jekyll used it frequently for all three purposes. Wherever the woodland was thinned to cast its remaining trees into picturesque groups, she scattered a little foxglove seed on to the disturbed ground, to heal the scars with colonies of this beautiful flower.

One of the most fascinating aspects of Miss Jekyll's plans is her management of contrast – frail ferns among dark evergreens, or scarlet gladioli spearing through misty clouds of gypsophila. On the larger scale there was the contrast between one garden compartment and the next. Finally, the character of the garden as a whole rested ultimately on the balance between the formal core of the garden (the flower borders and rose gardens discussed in earlier chapters) and its informal setting, which was merged where possible into the surrounding countryside. Much of Miss Jekyll's enduring popularity can be attributed to her designs for this informal setting, real designs giving substance to the rather vague notions of the 'wild garden' promulgated by William Robinson.

The wild garden was a timely development in the decades following the Victorian peak of horticultural opulence. It provided a less ruinously expensive system of gardening, and one more appropriate to accommodating the wealth of new hardy plants flooding in from China and surrounding countries. It also proved a garden style that suited the majority of garden owners, people who – no matter how much they might admire and appreciate the splendid formality of Victorian bedding – actually preferred in their own gardens to indulge in plant collecting and plant cultivation.

The value of informal gardening was increasingly appreciated as the twentieth century advanced and the large armies of skilled professional gardeners diminished. Miss Jekyll's designs for wild and woodland gardens continue to present attractive possibilities today; in our present age of declining or non-existent garden staff, with those large gardens that survive largely maintained by ride-on mower and chain saw, her ability to transform shapeless tracts of characterless scrub into wild gardens with a few deft touches of thinning and regrouping of plants is an invaluable source of inspiration.

Drayton Wood, in Norfolk, is characteristic of many Jekyll wild gardens. Starting with a hard-edged paddock, sandwiched between two hard-edged blocks of woodland, she began by filling one end of the paddock and softening its edge with large groups of hazel around a small clearing of birches.

Hostas, darmera (peltiphyllum) and the contrasting vertical leaves of iris line the path that flows through the wilder part of the garden at Hidcote. The freshness of this tapestry of pale greens is accentuated by the tiny flowers of white ranunculus.

The other edge, nearer the main garden, is blurred with smaller groups of birch and Scots pine. Two long groups of oak, a dozen plants in each, fill the point of the paddock, partially enclosing a now-irregular but shapely wild garden, and the enclosure is accentuated by repeated drifts of holly, Scots pine and birch, blackthorn and whitethorn (hawthorn), with the occasional more conspicuously decorative tree such as amelanchier, mountain ash or double cherry. The whole of the area, made beautiful by these simple changes, is interlaced with gently winding paths; or perhaps the paths were planned first and the spaces infilled with planting, for paths and plants combine into a single, harmonious composition.

Near the house, the planting of predominantly native species merges into dense masses of azaleas, and the free-flowing path network winds back to meet the long green ride. The strongly architectural form of this ride is edged with dark rhododendrons and hollies at one end but fades into the softer masses of shrub roses and hazels at the other, as it narrows and enters the woodland.

Drayton Wood, Norfolk

Where paths leave the azalea garden they are edged with evergreen pernettya. Compact masses of *Polygonum molle* fringe the paths as they pass through the more densely planted woodland part of the new wild garden, the polygonum giving way to taller sweetbriars where the paths cross more open, rough grassland. The edgings are far from continuous but form long drifts at intervals, lining first one side of the path, then both, then the other, to unfold a series of discreetly planned views. As one looks across the garden, rather than along the paths, these long transverse drifts build up to form overlapping layers of low roses, taller thorns and hollies, and vigorous young oaks, pines and slender birch, capturing the

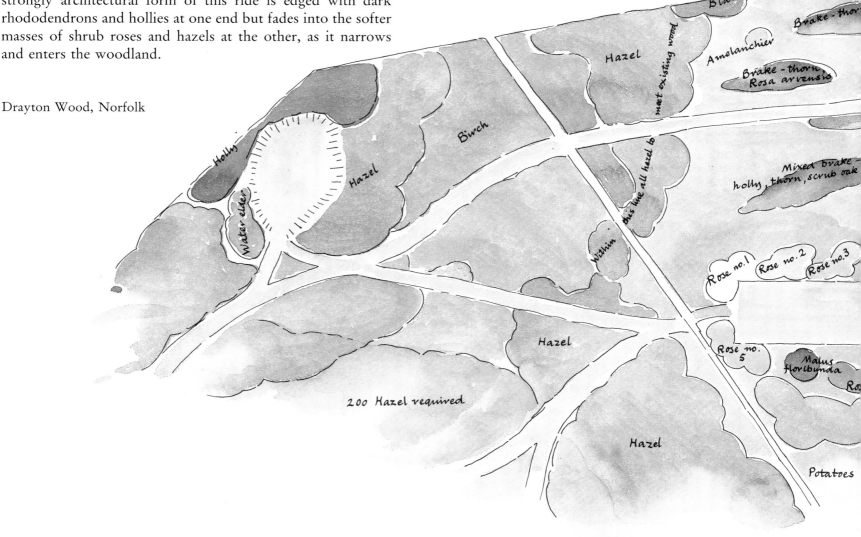

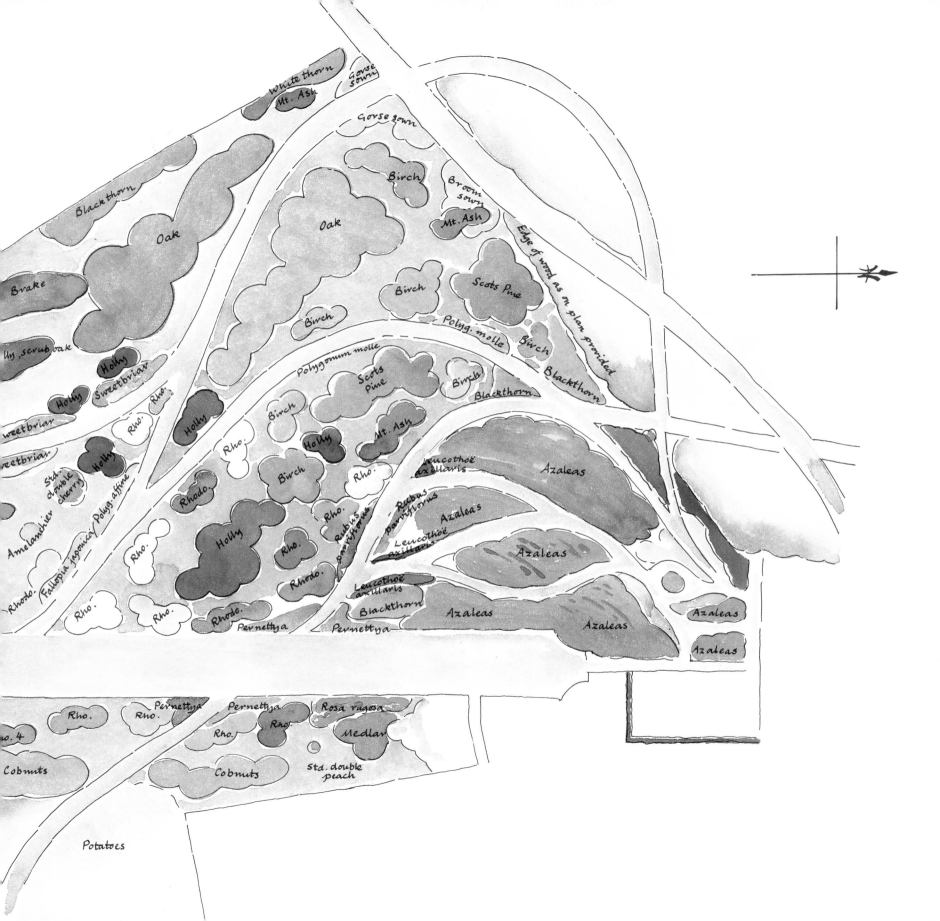

white thorn

Mt. Ash

Gorse sown

Gorse sown

Blackthorn

Oak

Birch

Broom sown

Mt. Ash

Oak

Birch

Scots Pine

Edge of wood as on plan provided

Brake

Birch

Polyg. molle

Birch

Polygonum molle

lly, scrub oak

Holly

Sweetbriar

Rho.

Scots Pine

Birch

Blackthorn

Holly

Sweetbriar

Rho.

Holly

Birch

Mt. Ash

Blackthorn

weetbriar

Rho.

Holly

Leucothoë
axillaris

Azaleas

wetbriar

Std.
double
cherry

Holly

Rho.

Birch

Rho.

Rhodo.

Rho.

Rubus
parviflorus

Azaleas

Amelanchier

Holly

Rho.

Rho.

Rubus
parviflorus

Leucothoë
axillaris

Azaleas

Fallopia japonica/ Polyg. affine

Rho.

Rhodo.

Rho.

Leucothoë
axillaris

Rhodo.

Rho.

Rhodo.

Pernettya

Pernettya

Blackthorn

Azaleas

Azaleas

Azaleas

Azaleas

Azaleas

Pernettya

Rho.

Pernettya

Rosa rugosa

o. 4

Rho.

Rho.

Rho.

Medlar

Cobnuts

Rho.

Cobnuts

Std. double
peach

Potatoes

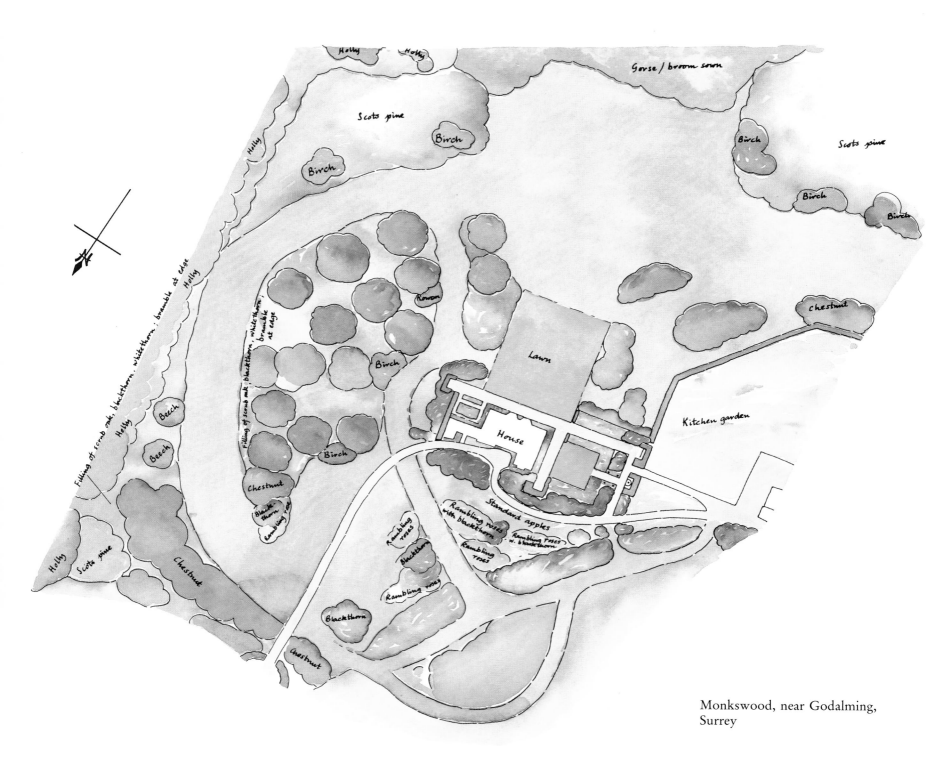

Gorse / broom sown

Holly

Holly

Scots pine

Birch

Holly

Birch

Birch

Scots pine

Birch

Birch

Filling of scrub oak, blackthorn, whitethorn, bramble at edge

Holly

Rowan

Holly

Filling of scrub oak, blackthorn, whitethorn, bramble at edge

Birch

Chestnut

Lawn

Beech

Birch

Kitchen garden

Holly

Beech

Birch

House

Chestnut

Blackthorn

Standard apples

Rambling roses

Rambling roses with blackthorn

Rambling roses w. blackthorn

Holly

Scots pine

Chestnut

Rambling roses

Blackthorn

Rambling roses

Blackthorn

Chestnut

Monkswood, near Godalming,
Surrey

sense of perspective to be found in successive lines of hedge-rows fading into the misty distance of an English landscape.

A smaller plan of Drayton Wood shows in detail the planting around the core of the azalea garden, not the azaleas themselves, which would present a fairly uniform sea of soft green foliage in rounded masses when not in flower, but the more intricate planting bordering the paths around a small pool at the heart of the garden. The pool itself, lying in a distinct hollow, is fringed with alternating masses of bold and soft: *Ligularia dentata* opposite one entrance to the clearing, feathery *Filipendula ulmaria* and lady fern to either side, and the upright sword-like foliage of irises beyond them. On the outer edge of the path, opposite this assemblage of lush but graceful planting, the ground is banked up with long lumps of stone to create an informal area half-way in character between a naturalistic rock garden and a more regularly ordered dry wall. Behind the spreading drifts of mainly grey-leaved plants on the rockwork, the planting is taller and in rather larger groups: dark pernettya and skimmia, *Pieris floribunda* and *Leucothoë axillaris* merging into duller green *Rhododendron × myrtifolium*, savin and box, all combining to form a perfect introduction to the surrounding masses of azaleas with their pale green leaves. It is interesting to note how the edges of the planting scheme are dovetailed so that the azaleas will fit in with no hard edges, just as the edges of the wood and paddock in the larger scheme are fragmented, interrupted by short stabs of planting.

Monkswood, near Godalming in Surrey, is less noticeably designed than is Drayton Wood, less complex in its planting but no less satisfying in the subtle interplay of open space and informal woodland. Again the starting point was a straight-edged field, here bounded by the road on one side and with a small patch of woodland in one corner.

In Miss Jekyll's design a long, irregular drift of hollies defines a dense boundary on one side, while a hedged kitchen garden, connected to the house by a simple formal garden and outlying shrub groups, extends the enclosure provided by the existing woodland on the other. In the outlying corners of the garden, grey-blue masses of Scots pine are added to frame a wide vista from the house. Groups of birch lighten the edges of the pine groups and create picturesque effects with their fluttering pale green foliage, or golden autumn tints, or bare

The Rambler rose 'Paul's Himalyan Musk' in an apple tree. Rambling roses flinging their long wands into small trees provide the main flower colour in Miss Jekyll's plan for the garden at Monkswood.

Their combination of natural freedom and highly cultivated flowers introduces the precise note needed at strategic points in an otherwise green woodland garden.

Slender, gracefully curved stems of silver birch set the scene for many of Miss Jekyll's wild gardens. In this private garden in Sussex, a strategically sited trio of silver birch links the shrub garden of heathers, pieris and other acid-loving plants with the quieter green recesses of the woodland, where the trees have been skilfully thinned to form open glades.

white trunks, against the unchanging solidity of the pines.

The two groups of pine are connected by a stretch of 'gorse and broom sown', straight-edged on the inner side, within the garden, to echo the more formal edge of the lawn, merging in spirit with the pines and birches on either side but low enough to permit views over the surrounding countryside with its less organized scenes of pine and birch, gorse and heather. From the lawn, flanked by large groups of shrubs, there is thus an expanding picture from mown lawn to rough grass to wood and heath. On each side of the lawn there are also lesser openings, framed by planting within the garden but winding gently out of sight around and within the trees.

The east side of the garden, enclosed by dark masses of holly, is largely filled with glossy green sweet chestnut and beech interplanted for immediate effect and variety with scrub oak, blackthorn and whitethorn – a slender margin of woodland and a larger central island enclosing two long glades of differing character. Into this simple picture are inserted picturesque details: groups of rowan and birch where they can be glimpsed from the lawn and the house; an irregular margin of bramble; and rambling roses scrambling through a blackthorn at the northern tip of the island to present a combination of the wild and the cultivated at a strategic point along the drive. At the front of the house the original bland line of the wood is varied, with rambling roses climbing into blackthorns and tumbling in tangled masses with brambles. The house itself is embedded in shrubs, leaving between it and the woodland another narrow glade, this time planted with standard apples – a fitting introduction to the kitchen garden beyond.

The result of this charming understatement is a garden which grows out of its surroundings and merges with them, never losing the combination of control and freedom and offering a never-ending series of garden pictures. From the entrance, for instance, the drive emerges through a thin belt of young trees into an irregular clearing fringed with blackthorn and rambling roses. Tantalizing glimpses of curving woodland glades, wide and narrow, are revealed before the drive finally passes through close masses of shrubs to a forecourt planted with handsome evergreens.

Monkswood is a garden which illustrates very well Miss Jekyll's use of native plants. Thorn and bramble, oak, birch and rowan, and direct seeding of gorse and broom, bear striking resemblance to the 'ecological planting' which many landscape architects might regard as an idea developed in the late twentieth century.

Miss Jekyll's many and varied plans for wild gardens on the scale of Drayton Wood and Monkswood show clearly her approach to design: broad strokes of a few key species to establish the character of the place; smaller strokes to build up the picture, to flesh out the forms, to establish contrasts of light and shade, and finally the small points of detail, unnoticed perhaps by the casual observer but creating a depth of colour and richness of incident to ensure lasting appreciation. The balance between light and shade, solid and void, is painstakingly worked at until it is just right. It is as if Miss Jekyll walked through the plan as she worked on it, studying the views in all directions and adjusting the shapes of plant groups to achieve her endless succession of garden pictures. What works as a plan also translates into a wonderful garden.

The garden at Highcroft in the New Forest bears a passing resemblance to Monkswood but is unique among the Jekyll plans in compressing the elegant curves and varied character of a wild garden into a small and regular space. The immediate impression on plan is of a rather blocky design, but the lines which are the dominant feature of the plan merely differentiate between close-mown and rougher grass and would have much less significance on the ground – especially if one were able to follow Miss Jekyll's example at Munstead Wood and send a man with a faghook after the lawnmower to remove the hard mechanical line at the edge of the path!

The lines of the paths are carefully drawn, some more or less straight, others more or less curved, branching and recombining, but all lending an atmosphere of firm but gentle control. The amelanchier in the centre of the first, nearly square panel of rough grass creates an almost formal quality, appropriate to its position near the formal gardens leading up to the house, but to this amelanchier others are added in gradually less regular arrangement, merging on one side into taller birches (which partner the birches on the edge of the garden), merging on the other into whitethorn and rambling roses where denser plants are called for, then finally into groups of water elder (*Viburnum opulus*) and the closer domes of azaleas under fine-textured mountain ash.

Azaleas also edge this corner of the garden, providing the definite enclosure required in that part of the scheme where curves are tightest and the ends of grass panels at their narrowest. However, this corner group soon merges into a patch of *Rubus parviflorus* (an American raspberry or 'salmon berry' with individual large clear white flowers over arching stems of soft green leaves), then into a darker and glossier group of cut-leaved bramble. The bramble is repeated in smaller numbers on the edge and corner across the wide mown path to create the strongest sense of enclosure near the arbour, and the arbour is covered with tea tree, *Lycium barbarum*, a straggling half-climbing shrub of more subtle colouring, with purple flowers for much of summer, followed by scarlet berries in autumn.

There is nothing particularly outstanding about this design, no glowing masses of graded colours or wide expanses of woodland, but it is a salutary reminder, in an age prone to horticultural indigestion and addicted to 'variety', of the quiet and satisfying charm that a few well-chosen plants can create throughout the year: clouds of fleeting amelanchier blossom hovering over young bronze-tinted foliage and backed by white birch stems in spring; the brighter colours of carefully grouped azaleas below the heavy-scented white domes of mountain ash and closely related whitethorn as spring merges into summer. As summer advances, there is the fresh effect of the water elder, with its white lace-cap flowers topping bright green, maple-like foliage; then come masses of white roses on dark, arching stems, white salmon berry and white-flowered bramble arching into the dull purple potato-flowers of lycium. By the time the lycium produces its first scarlet fruits, the mountain ash is laden with berries of similar hue, quickly followed by the first autumnal tints of leaf. With this signal of autumn, the pale grey-green leaves of amelanchier

At Gilles Clément's garden at La Vallée, in central France, graceful, wide-branching heads of azaleas build up slowly into undulating mounds to reinforce strategic points in the wild garden planting. Pale green summer foliage burnishing to gold or bronzy purple in the autumn extends the beauty of the plants beyond their brief but spectacular spring flowering season. The gentle meander of the grass walk flows naturally between the alternating spurs of azaleas and other plants along the woodland margin.

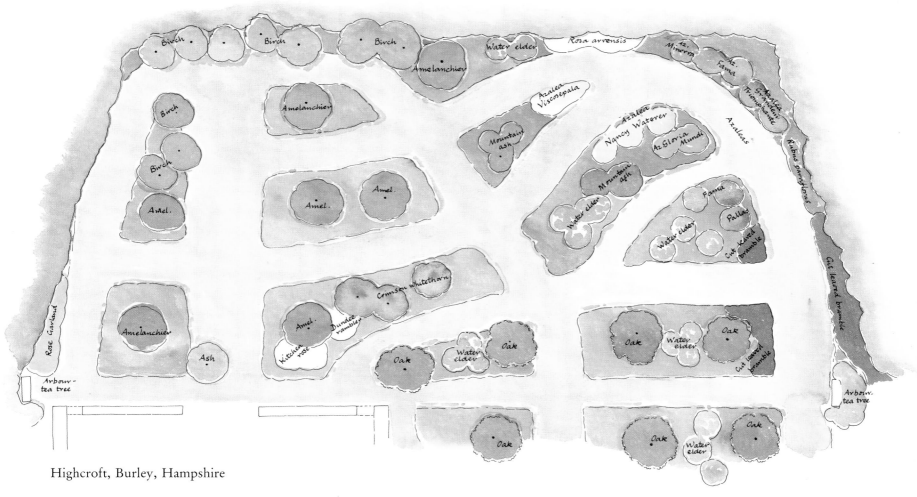

Highcroft, Burley, Hampshire

begin turning to crimson and scarlet in advance of the paler yellows and deeper purples of azalea foliage, and of birch, viburnum and bramble. Finally the leaves fall and all that remain are the quieter colours of winter: grey-brown azalea stems, silver-striped and elegant amelanchier twigs, rusty rubus and dark, polished bramble, and the near-black twigs of birch swaying above their graceful white trunks.

No bulbs are indicated on the plan, but the wild garden offered much scope for bulbs in spring and autumn and there are many clues in Miss Jekyll's writings (rather fewer in her plans) for their picturesque use in such a setting.

For anyone contemplating a garden similar in character to that at Highcroft, the capacity of birch to spring anew from the ground in multi-trunked elegance when it has grown too

large for its situation is a valuable asset – especially where space is limited. Highcroft also offers invaluable guidance for the would-be island bed enthusiast. Miss Jekyll's plan shows the merit of allowing the paths to dictate the shapes of the beds, rather than dealing out amoeboid beds at random on to an unsuspecting stretch of lawn, then trying to cope with the amorphous consequences – never quite enclosed, never truly open, and terribly wasteful of mowing effort.

At Little Aston, whose rose garden was discussed on pages 98–9, the character of the wild garden was very much dictated by the nature of the old quarry in which it was created. Instead of the long, almost languid, curves of Drayton Wood and other wild gardens created out of open pasture or cut through woodland, the paths in the Little Aston wild garden show a bolder variation of alignment. The uppermost path is almost straight on plan, but four slight curves take it from the base of a 1.2m/4ft high bank to climb gently across the slope before disappearing into dense masses of *Rosa multiflora* scrambling over dark hollies. Looking along the line of the path with the plan held at eye level will show the true effect of these apparently slight changes in alignment.

The lower path follows a graceful, sweeping curve some 1.5–1.8m/5–6ft below, parallel to the bank and separated from the upper level by flowing drifts of roses, pink soapwort (arching forward from the bank over low helianthemums), scrambling masses of rose-pink *Lathyrus grandiflorus* and greenish white *Clematis vitalba* climbing into the lower side of those same dark hollies. At this point, the lower path meets the third main path. This winds more sharply along the base of the main bank, some 4.5–6m/15–20ft high at this point, then zigzags around a spur of rock and into a short extension of the main valley. It then doubles back around a drift of dense *Cistus laurifolius* before flowing in easier curves along the base of the bank to rejoin the other paths at the upper end of the pit. One short, straight cross path connects the two

lower paths, interrupting the otherwise rather attenuated central section of the pit floor and offering sudden lateral views of the tiered planting on the banks as a change from the slowly unfolding views along the paths.

The planting in the quarry is a wonderful example of how the character of the garden can be established by repetition of a few good plants, with gentle diversification to create interest – the interest of variety rather than contrast – on a smaller scale. It is worth tracing over the plan in order to study the

The wild garden at Little Aston, near Birmingham

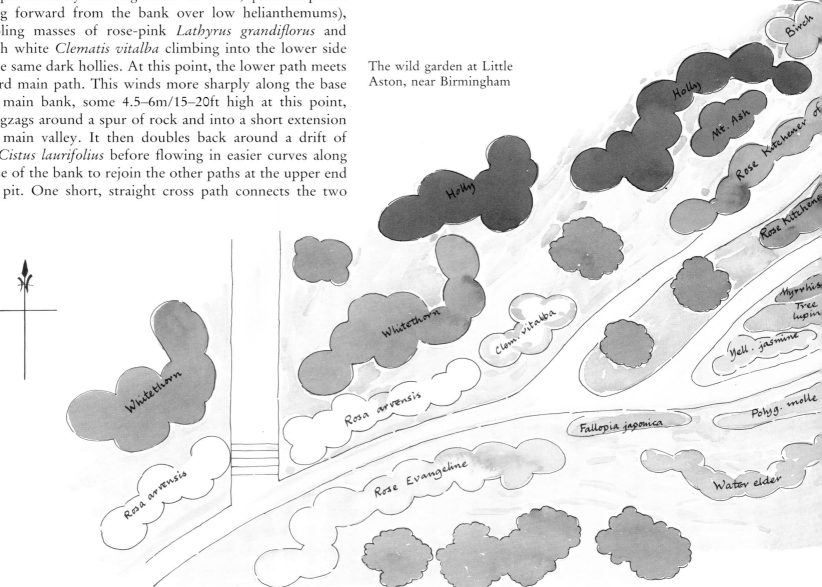

development of the scheme as plant groups are built up and skilfully woven together. This will give a much greater appreciation of Miss Jekyll's planting technique than can be obtained by simply looking – however carefully – at the finished plan.

The existing vegetation shown on the plan consists of two dozen small trees, unidentified but very probably oaks, scattered around two sides of the pit, and, on the north side, a small group of hollies with a single outlying plant. Miss Jekyll then adds more holly: long thin groups along the slopes and more compact groups on the flatter east side of the pit, finally merging into a broad mass bordering the drive. Into this framework come blackthorns, with their bare dark branches studded with white blossom against the glossy mass of holly in spring, and whitethorns (hawthorns) with their heavier wreaths of tiny white flowers over pale fresh spring foliage. Thus, with three plants only, the hollow is ringed with a mosaic of dark and glossy, dark and dull, and pale fresh green foliage, enlivened by two brief periods of contrasting white blossom, or three if one counts the less conspicuous flowers of the holly. The same pattern continues into the central hollow, with holly and blackthorn separating the two lower paths for much of their length.

Into this mosaic are inserted tall white-stemmed birches in small irregular groups among the holly, and mountain ashes for the sake especially of their harvest of orange berries and their autumn foliage among the dark permanence of the holly. Two amelanchiers, each sihouetted above the sharp curve of the path against an otherwise unrelieved mass of holly, add small accents of spring blossom, fresher but more fleeting than the hawthorn, and autumn colour to excel, for a similarly brief spell in autumn, the warm colours of mountain ash and more subdued colours of hawthorn and blackthorn.

On to this picturesque distillation of woodland charm are stitched slender wands of *Rosa arvensis*, the stronger, glossy-leaved canes of *R. multiflora* with heavy swags of fragrant white flowers, and the vigorous, scrambling trails of *Clematis vitalba*. The Rambler rose 'Evangeline' and large bushes of 'Lord Kitchener of Khartoum' add more colour and fragrance in the height of summer, reminding anyone who might have forgotten that this is a garden, albeit a garden representing the essence of natural beauty.

Three other shrubs complete the structural planting. Spreading groups of water elder (*Viburnum opulus*) and the more arching growth of *Rosa virginiana* spill over the bank on the southern edge of the pit, forming a light fringe of pale green and dark glossy foliage respectively below the oaks, in contrast to the close masses of varied foliage ringing the larger part of the pit. Lastly, the entrance to the leafy hollow is marked by a group of yellow jasmine, *Jasminum humile* 'Revolutum', a bush of dense but delicate bright green foliage, covered in clear yellow flowers in summer. Seen through a narrow defile covered in white roses and pale green-white clematis, no plant could be more effective at half-concealing the inner recesses of the old quarry from the outside world.

With containment thus assured, the inner margins of the pit, bordering the paths which wind gently but purposefully between dense clumps of holly and thorn, are embroidered with bold and elegant herbaceous plants. Tree lupins form the spine of the first long tongue of ground, the pattern of their innumerable spikes of flowers – pale blue, yellow and white – telling to full effect as they weave between the rounded shapes of jasmine, rose and thorn. The base of the lupins, never their most elegant feature, is concealed by sweet cicely (*Myrrhis odorata*), fine ferny masses of foliage and soft heads of off-white flowers to fill in below the tall lupins. After flowering, both lupins and myrrhis would be pruned hard, the former to extend their normally short life, the latter to encourage a second flush of its pale filigree foliage. Further on along the path a long drift of Solomon's seal produces a spring picture of woodland grace, made still more cool and elegant by the contrast with the helianthemum, soapwort and rosy pea on the sunny bank opposite.

The soft colouring established by this association of sun-loving plants continues at the corner of the path, where a group of *Cistus laurifolius* reinforces the sharp turn. Its dull, grey-green evergreen mounds are repeated in a lighter and lower fashion by the carpet of helianthemum at its feet. From this corner, the path runs below and a short distance away from the bank at its highest point. The shallow bays formed between path and bank are filled with the dark, bold foliage of Lent hellebores, arching Solomon's seal and pale sweet cicely. In the deeper recesses, larger patches of Solomon's seal flow between clumps of male fern, lady fern and statuesque giant

With the poise of its arching stems, the subtlety of colouring in the green-tinged flowers opening from pearl-like buds to elegantly flared bells, the veining and undulations of graceful yet surprisingly firm pale green leaves, Solomon's seal conveys an air of woodland grace. Miss Jekyll used generous drifts in the lower part of the quarry at Little Aston.

hogweed (heracleum), its huge cartwheels of flowers over vast glossy leaves declaring its somewhat surprising relationship to the low mounds of sweet cicely at its feet. From this point onwards the pattern of planting is repeated with variations: cistus guarding the second sharp corner and introducing another group of soapwort, this time speared through by the sharp, blue-grey foliage of *Elymus arenarius*; more hellebores where their dark leaves will emphasize the curve in the path – and where their nodding white and purple flowers will cheer the winter scene; a second view of that long spine of lupins, their slender spikes echoing the repeated peaks of a mountain range, or of spruce forests clinging to the mountainside. The near-evergreen foliage of the hellebores lends visual support to lighter male ferns and foamy myrrhis below the fringe of water elder, while dusky mounds of *Polygonum molle* and spreading canes of *Fallopia japonica* var. *compacta* (both with glossy foliage and pink and white spikes of flowers) add a quiet note to a picture of varied but harmonious beauty.

Reference has already been made to Miss Jekyll's use of native plants, her sowing – at Monkswood and elsewhere – of gorse and broom, thorn and oak, but it is worth stopping to consider another aspect of this 'ecological planting' exemplified at Monkswood and even more in the quarry garden at Little Aston, namely its function as a wild garden, and particularly as a haven for birds. Dense hollies, thorn and oak, and tangles of roses both wild and cultivated, support a rich insect life and offer sheltered nesting sites for many birds. Fruits from the amelanchier and mountain ash supplement those of holly, thorn, rose and viburnum, while the smaller seeds of birch and hogweed support other species of birds. Bird song and the constant movement of birds and insects would thus add a further dimension to a wild garden of great visual beauty, with its colours and fragrance held in a hollow removed from the bustling world beyond.

STEPS AND WALLS

Planting to soften hard lines

Rignalls Wood, Buckinghamshire

Barton St Mary, Sussex

Frant Court, Kent

Brambletye, Sussex

Pages 134–5 Flowing colonies of grey-leaved stachys cascading over the wall at Upton Grey, and the graceful flowers of columbines above and below, unify the different levels in the garden and soften, without concealing, the firm backbone of wall and yew hedge. The whole is woven together by *Clematis montana* var. *rubens*, trailing in elegant swags over both wall and hedge.

Left *Corydalis ochroleuca* springs from the wall and steps below a stone-arched gateway at Hestercombe, emphasizing the cool, shady character of the situation. On either side, fern-like sprays of corydalis merge into glossy mounds of *Choisya ternata* and hence into the bolder foliage of yucca and clerodendrum. Over time other plants have appeared – the odd tuft of hart's tongue, the occasional warmer patch of valerian – until it is hard to tell what is natural and what is designed.

Opposite Cascades of *Corydalis ochroleuca* are also used freely in the shaded walls at Upton Grey, with glossy green hart's tongue providing points of emphasis echoed by the yuccas above the wall. The fresh colouring of the hart's tongue is repeated in the rosettes of London pride spilling over the top of the wall, where the airy sprays of pale flowers can be studied at close range.

In 1901, following the gratifying success of *Wood and Garden* (1899) and *Home and Garden* (1900), Miss Jekyll published *Wall and Water Gardens*. The topic is interesting in itself, combining as it does two extremes of plant life – alpines and drought-tolerant plants in drystone walls, with aquatics and marginal plants in and around garden ponds. It had, however, a far wider significance in illustrating the possibilities of combining the two apparent extremes of gardening – the formal and the natural.

Miss Jekyll's ideas for gardening in dry walls evolved over many years, fuelled by her observation of plants growing in and on the rocky banks of Surrey lanes deeply incised into the sandstone, in drystone walls about the country, and in the rocky wastes in which she took such evident delight on her visits abroad.

In her garden of summer flowers at Munstead Wood, she used a wide double drystone wall, about 60cm/24in high, as a backbone to the scheme, creating, out of the irregular central panel of the garden, a long narrow border surrounding three sides of this raised spine. The raised section was planted with 'important masses of fine form', *Euphorbia characias* and its subspecies *E. characias* ssp. *wulfenii*, yuccas and othonna, as a quiet background for geraniums, cannas, gladioli, penstemons and the other summer bedding plants which occasioned such expressions of surprise from visitors to Munstead Wood.

In *Colour Schemes* she describes 'some pretty incidents' where a seedling of *Campanula pyramidalis*, a spreading sheet of thyme and wayward shoots of wild clematis combined (with some careful orchestration) to decorate the shallow steps rising up from the house to one of the walks which led from the lawn to the woodland.

It was domestic examples such as these which persuaded Edwin Lutyens to do what would have been anathema to Victorian architects, as they defended their pristine walls of elaborate diaper brickwork against the merest wisp of vegetation. He deliberately perforated his handsome retaining walls and left spaces in the joints of paving and steps in order to create homes for Miss Jekyll's planting. Thus the sophisticated geometry of Lutyens's garden architecture combined with Miss Jekyll's finely drawn drifts of flowers with the most enchanting results: cascading sheets of mat-forming alpines with their tiny flowers brought nearer to eye and nose for

easy appreciation; the repeated verticals of antirrhinums, foxgloves and verbascum, the rounded masses of valerian and lavender springing from the face of the wall, and the sprays of *Iris unguicularis* nestling below, all stimulated into greater abundance of flower by their confined circumstances.

Rignalls Wood in Buckinghamshire shows the first stage of this highly productive union of building and gardening. The long series of steps, some 3m/10ft wide and folded into the slope, connects a rose garden on the upper level with a pergola and lower lawn.

At the base of each riser, twin drifts of low plants flow out from the edge of the steps, almost meeting on the centre line of the steps and multiplying thirtyfold the half-accidental charm of that incident on the steps at Munstead Wood. Plant numbers are carefully regulated so that the steps are furnished but not obstructed. The gap between the drifts straying out from either side is near but seldom at the centre of the tread. In this way a gently meandering route between the drifts is suggested but not enforced upon the user, and the rigid lines of the architecture are mellowed but not disguised. A combination of severe cutting back of the mat-forming plants after flowering, of division and replanting of cushion plants, and of the natural regulation of plants by treading feet, serves to maintain a balance between plants and stonework.

The planting on the steps received the same careful consideration as the planning of the elaborate borders, rose

The translucent orange and lemon flowers of Welsh poppies play an important part in Miss Jekyll's planting schemes. At Rignalls Wood their bright, clear colours shine out from a setting of *Iris foetidissima* and hart's tongues.

garden, pergola and bank which they connect. The upper steps are planted with aubrieta to echo the soft colouring of grey-leaved olearias in the garden above. Then come pale pink *Sedum spurium* and grey cushions of scented rock pinks for interest later in the year. Yellow *S. reflexum* follows the pinks, while cushions of the silky grey *Achillea compacta* combine the grey foliage colouring of aubrieta and pinks with the hard yellow flowers of the sedum. At the base of this first flight of steps the colour deepens from pink *Saxifraga paniculata* 'Rosularis' to the crimson form of *Sedum spurium* with its handsome rosettes of glossy purple foliage.

After the first landing, the steps turn through 90 degrees, and the change of orientation which results is accompanied by a marked change in the pattern of planting. The general symmetry of the southward flight with its twin drifts is replaced by a distinct north/south divide. Against the sunny south-facing retaining wall are long drifts of campanulas (*Campanula cochleariifolia* and *C. carpatica* in blue and white forms), saxifrages and bright yellow mimulus; at the shadier north-facing end of the steps are hart's tongue ferns and *Iris foetidissima*, tufted plants close against the side of the steps reinforcing the natural desire of those using the steps to move away from the high retaining wall and towards the open view below the steps. Thin strands of the delicate woodlander *Oxalis articulata* spill out from the base of the hard green sprays of iris foliage to prevent the north/south divide becoming over-obvious. Their presence introduces a subtle serpentine line into the planting of this second flight of steps, again reflecting the natural movement of someone descending the steps and negotiating the 180-degree turn of the second landing. This flowing curve is gently underlined, too, by the planting on the landings, with hart's tongue and bolder male fern on the shady outer curve of the upper landing, and *Iris unguicularis* on the lower landing, its tufts of narrow, grey-green leaves revealing a succession of pale, fragrant flowers throughout the winter in this sheltered and confined corner.

Asymmetry is repeated in the third flight of steps, with blue and white *Campanula carpatica* again on the sunny side, followed by pale pink *Sedum ewersii* (used on the roof at Highmount, see page 39), spreading white mats of silene and quantities of *Ceratostigma plumbaginoides* continuing from the lower steps on to the last landing.

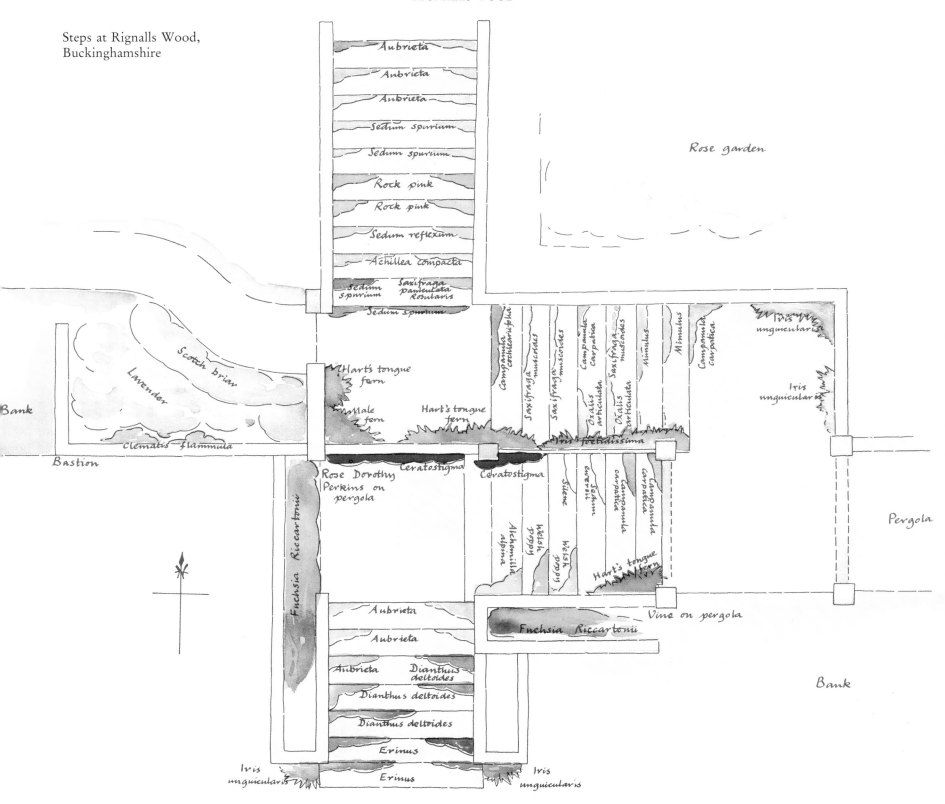

Steps at Rignalls Wood,
Buckinghamshire

Rose garden

Aubrieta

Aubrieta

Aubrieta

Sedum spurium

Sedum spurium

Rock pink

Rock pink

Sedum reflexum

Achillea compacta

Sedum spurium

Saxifraga paniculata Rosularis

Sedum spurium

Scotch briar

Lavender

Bank

Clematis flammula

Bastion

Hart's tongue fern

Male fern

Hart's tongue fern

Campanula cochlearifolia

Saxifraga muscoides

Saxifraga muscoides

Oxalis articulata

Campanula carpatica

Saxifraga muscoides

Oxalis articulata

Mimulus

Mimulus

Campanula carpatica

Iris unguicularis

Iris unguicularis

Iris foetidissima

Ceratostigma

Ceratostigma

Rose Dorothy Perkins on pergola

Fuchsia Riccartonii

Silene

Sedum ewersii

Campanula carpatica

Campanula carpatica

Alchemilla alpina

Welsh poppy

Welsh poppy

Hart's tongue fern

Pergola

Aubrieta

Aubrieta

Aubrieta

Dianthus deltoides

Dianthus deltoides

Dianthus deltoides

Erinus

Erinus

Fuchsia Riccartonii

Vine on pergola

Bank

Iris unguicularis

Iris unguicularis

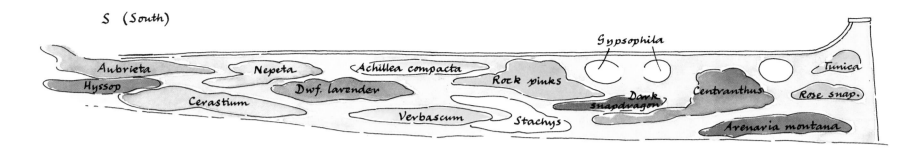

S (South)

Aubrieta · Hyssop · Cerastium · Nepeta · Dwf. lavender · Achillea compacta · Verbascum · Stachys · Rock pinks · Dark snapdragon · Gypsophila · Centranthus · Arenaria montana · Tunica · Rose snap.

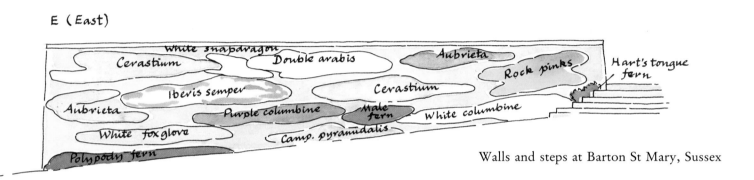

E (East)

White snapdragon · Cerastium · Double arabis · Aubrieta · Ibevis semper · Aubrieta · Purple columbine · Cerastium · Male fern · White columbine · Rock pinks · Hart's tongue fern · White foxglove · Camp. pyramidalis · Polypody fern

Walls and steps at Barton St Mary, Sussex

This low, wide-spreading ceratostigma was much admired by Miss Jekyll for its delight in hot, dry borders at the base of sunny walls. Its use at Rignalls Wood is particularly apposite. Just where the ceratostigma covers the steps, the walls flanking the steps are doubled back to enclose narrow raised beds planted with *Fuchsia* 'Riccartonii', their elegant crimson and purple flowers being borne close to eye level as a result. The ceratostigma, with its autumn harvest of clear blue flowers over foliage changing from leaden green to purplish crimson, would accompany the fuchsia in a marvellous association of brilliant colours, outlasting it in a favourable winter, to remain attractive until the first flowers of *Iris unguicularis* unfurled their delicately veined petals.

On the shaded side of the third flight of steps there are hart's tongues again in handsome clumps, then the sharp yellow of Welsh poppies extending in longer groups to repeat the serpentine curve of the flight above, and finally the neat, bright carpets of *Alchemilla alpina*, glossy green above like the hart's tongue and felted white beneath to harmonize with the

aubrieta and pinks spilling across the first few steps of the last short flight. Finally, where the steps emerge from the close confinement of retaining walls on to the open lawn, *Erinus alpinus*, one of the smallest and most charming chink-fillers, is used to clothe the lowest steps with its deep green rosettes, while twin clumps of *Iris unguicularis* mark the point at which steps, grass and border meet.

The sketch of walls and steps at Barton St Mary in Sussex shows the next stage of integration between architecture and planting. Here the walls, rather than the steps, are planted. Retaining walls gain in strength if they are built leaning back into the slope which they support, as much of their weight is transmitted on to the slope rather than vertically down on to footings. For drystone walls, built without mortared joints, this slope or batter is essential. In *Wall and Water Gardens* Miss Jekyll recommends a batter of 5cm/2in in 30cm/12in, a slope which not only provides the wall with its necessary strength but also assists infiltration of rain water into the joints and hence down to the roots of plants in the wall.

This deviation from the strictly vertical has further advantages in enhancing the visual appearance of massive strength and in easing the difficult junction between horizontal (grass or paving) and vertical surfaces in the garden. When, in addition, steps are recessed into the upper level and extend beyond the wall line out on to paving at the bottom, the horizontal/vertical break is further diffused. The effect of plants springing from the base, lapping over the summit and colonizing the face of walls and steps, also helps to dissolve the bleak geometrical break between horizontal and vertical into a picturesque continuum of stone and planting.

At Barton St Mary the distinction between horizontal and vertical is still fairly clear, but Lutyens's gently battered walls, supporting the formal south garden above a sloping lawn,

have an unassuming informality enhanced by the shallow steps opening out from the east side of the garden. Miss Jekyll's planting accentuates the informal effect.

On the south wall the planting is primarily of grey-leaved plants: aubrieta, nepeta (catmint) and lavender for a continuous succession of lavender-blue flowers, harmonizing with the soft pinks of stachys, rock pinks, centranthus and rose-pink snapdragons. A long drift of white cerastium at the west end of the south wall is answered, remarkably, by large mounds of gypsophila towards the east end, myriads of fine grey stems struggling to lift themselves to the vertical (overtopping the wall), then periodically collapsing to curtain the face of the wall before curving up once again. Domes of blush-white tunica near the gypsophila and slender trails of *Arenaria*

When early festoons of aubrieta in the sunny walls at Upton Grey have faded, their soft lilac colouring is continued in the taller swathes of grey-leaved catmint. The neat rounded domes of catmint take on quite a different character when cascading down a wall. Here, the subtle but insistent vertical line of its innumerable flower stems is repeated by antirrhinums, soon to add a bolder note with clear white snapdragon flowers over handsome columns of foliage.

montana at the base of the wall mediate between the chalky whiteness of gypsophila and the stronger pinks of snapdragon and valerian.

Into this picture of misty softness are inserted sharper notes, the brassy yellow corymbs of *Achillea compacta* (a dwarf, silvery-leaved yarrow) and the similarly coloured spires of verbascum, bright yellow in flower but the whole effect softened by grey woolliness on leaf and flower spike. Dark greens play an important part, too: glossy domes of hyssop at the west end of the wall, its blue flowers adding to the meander of lavender and catmint flowers, and a small but significant group of dark red snapdragons towards the eastern end, deepening the colour effect of the centranthus below and standing erect with enhanced richness against the trails of gypsophila.

Some of this south wall planting occurs again on the east wall: aubrieta at either end, and large groups of snowy white cerastium, and rock pinks, the softness of their flat grey-green mats echoed in the long drift of double arabis top centre. But the woolly grey character of the south wall soon gives way on this cooler east wall to a softer, glaucous grey-green, and the warm pinks and lavenders of the flower colours change to a scheme of white and purple. White snapdragons arching out from the flat sheets of arabis and cerastium set the tone for this cooler scheme, with long groups of white and purple columbines adding to it in the lower and damper section of the wall. White foxgloves on the east wall replace the spires of sun-loving verbascums on the south, and the long drift of *Campanula pyramidalis* completes the main picture with its spikes of pale blue, another reminder of that incident on the steps at Munstead Wood.

The lower part of a retaining wall is usually noticeably damper than the upper part, because of ground-water seepage from above. This characteristic is exploited at Barton St Mary by underscoring the pale greens of columbine and foxglove with the dark, glossy green fronds of common polypody fern, a plant which will tolerate dry conditions but which produces infinitely richer foliage when well supplied with water. Paler hart's tongue ferns mark the junction of wall and steps, and a bold group of male ferns arches out among the columbines with much the same graceful boldness as characterizes the gypsophila on the south wall. The combination of translucent,

Above Colonies of white and pink valerian in the walls at Upton Grey create, on a garden scale, that sense of freedom and natural abundance characteristic of valerian growing wild on rocky clifftops. The silver foliage of artemisia at the base of the wall catches the light in much the same way as the flower heads of valerian, while flat carpets of bronze-leaved *Sedum spurium* paint in the shadows of the picture.

Opposite Grey foliage, purple campanulas and soft pink thrift combine to make a wonderfully harmonious picture in the Upton Grey walls. The distinctive bold curves of flower stems springing from the dark, flat cushions of thrift add a lively note to the composition.

frail columbines, pale foliage, foxgloves and ferns creates a subtle but surprisingly distinct change of character, from the warm Mediterranean slope of the south wall to a fragment of cool woodland floor only a short distance away. The change is helped by the insertion of a dark green mass of *Iberis semper-virens* between the grey-greens in the upper part of the east wall and the more translucent soft greens towards the base, anchoring the whole scheme in much the same way as does the hyssop on the south wall and harmonizing surprisingly well with both sunny and shady extremes of planting above and below.

The coloured plan makes it easy to appreciate the colour scheme and to detect the variations upon it, but colour is only one aspect of this carefully planned association. Form plays an equally important part. Here, the essentials of the scheme are a near-continuous groundwork of low plants cascading down the face of the wall (aubrieta, cerastium, stachys, arenaria and pinks, billowing up in places to the taller domes of catmint, lavender, columbine and centranthus), and a counterpoint of vertical plants such as verbascum, foxglove, campanula and snapdragons. The shortest plants occupy the upper parts of the wall, where they can cascade within limits set by the gardener and where they will not infringe on the garden above. Vertical plants are used lower down where their flowers can be seen against a harmonious curtain of foliage or a backdrop of stone without creating a wispy silhouette of spikes above the wall.

Within this quite simple balance of carpet and spire there are many nuances of harmony and contrast. On the south wall, a long, curving group of stachys wraps around the base of the verbascums, underpinning their bold grey foliage with even whiter silkiness and adding attractive colonies of dull pink flower spikes to the loftier and equally woolly yellow columns of the verbascums. Nearby are dark rows of sentinel snapdragons, a marked contrast to the swags of gypsophila lapping from above to surround the velvety red spikes with their own mist of tiny white flowers. On the east wall, the tall white snapdragons below the coping are placed just where they will break the line of the wall when in flower, answering the more rounded outline of the gypsophila nearby, while the thin drifts of columbine provide both rounded hummocks of

elegant glaucous foliage and the repeated verticals of their slender flower stems above and through the arching sprays of male fern.

Among the many plans of Stilemans (in Godalming, Surrey), there is a charming drawing showing wall planting broadly similar to that at Barton St Mary: groups of cerastium, rock pinks, aubrieta and catmint, here supplemented by alyssum, dwarf phlox, helianthemums and *Sedum spurium*. At Stilemans, though, the intention is clearly to smudge the outline of the wall. Dwarf lavender is planted in the face of the wall and along its top, as are slender poppies and grey-leaved othonna. A large clump of *Sisyrinchium striatum* occupies a strategic point on top of the wall where its spiky fans of striped, grassy leaves can fill a step in the wall, and *Iris unguicularis* occurs repeatedly along the sunny base of the wall and at its corners, repeating the pointed outline of the sisyrinchium. One long group of *Ceratostigma plumbaginoides* breaks the rhythm of the iris clumps, its leaden green foliage harmonizing with the paler grey-green iris foliage and

Fragile mounds of daisy-flowered *Erigeron karvinskianus* and the more robust trails of fragrant honeysuckle on steps and walls at Hestercombe soften the architectural lines without obscuring the handsome proportions. The main mass of erigeron where steps and wall meet fades into small outliers in the sunny south-facing wall and in the tapestry of low plants lining the risers of the steps. On the shadier east-facing wall the cooler colouring of the honeysuckle is picked up by soft mounds of *Corydalis ochroleuca*.

its clear blue flowers providing a point of interest late in the year, safely after the grey-blue spikes of lavender have faded to pale fawny-grey.

These and many other examples of planting in, on and below walls provide a wealth of ideas for the small urban and suburban garden, and a refreshing change from the coffin-like raised beds which serve only to accentuate the harsh lines of the typical housing-estate garden. A complex mosaic of roughly hewn stone walls and steps would of course look incongruous in the back garden of a bland brick house, but repetition of horizontal and vertical lines by creating sunken areas and raised terraces, and repetition of the building materials of the house in the walls and steps connecting these elements, will unify house and garden. With this unity firmly established, pillars or breaks in alignment will reduce the scale of plain house walls and long, straight fences, while all-too architectural lines can be smudged with climbers and wall plants, transforming a typical box-like back yard into a lush and welcoming oasis.

Once the softening of the rigid divide between horizontal and vertical has begun, of course, walls and steps (and especially stone walls and steps) are amenable to any interpretation, from the crisply architectural to the ruggedly natural, merging into the naturalistic alpine scenery of the best Victorian and Edwardian rockwork.

At Presaddfed in North Wales, formal steps and terraces descend in elegant tiers from the main front of the house, while rougher steps zigzag in longer flights down the valley left between the ends of the terraces and the boundary wall. Planting at the sides of the steps flows out across the treads, merging into the colourful drifts of a charming spring garden.

At Frant Court in Kent, the scale of the steps is altogether larger and simpler: a long, serpentine series of steps organized into flights of a dozen or so, descending from the formal gardens around the house and through a small dell to meet other paths of the wild garden. The first curve (to the right as one descends) is through existing rhododendrons and other dark greens, effectively separating the formal gardens above

Gold and silver variegated ivies trained along the risers of a flight of steps provide a vibrant colour scheme throughout the year. At the top of the steps the chalky white of the ivy is intensified by the softer white of woolly-leaved stachys. In the moister conditions at the foot, pale lilac violas contrast with the sharp green-gold of the ivy, while echoing the warmer colour of the clematis scrambling from its cool root-run to clothe an unsightly wall.

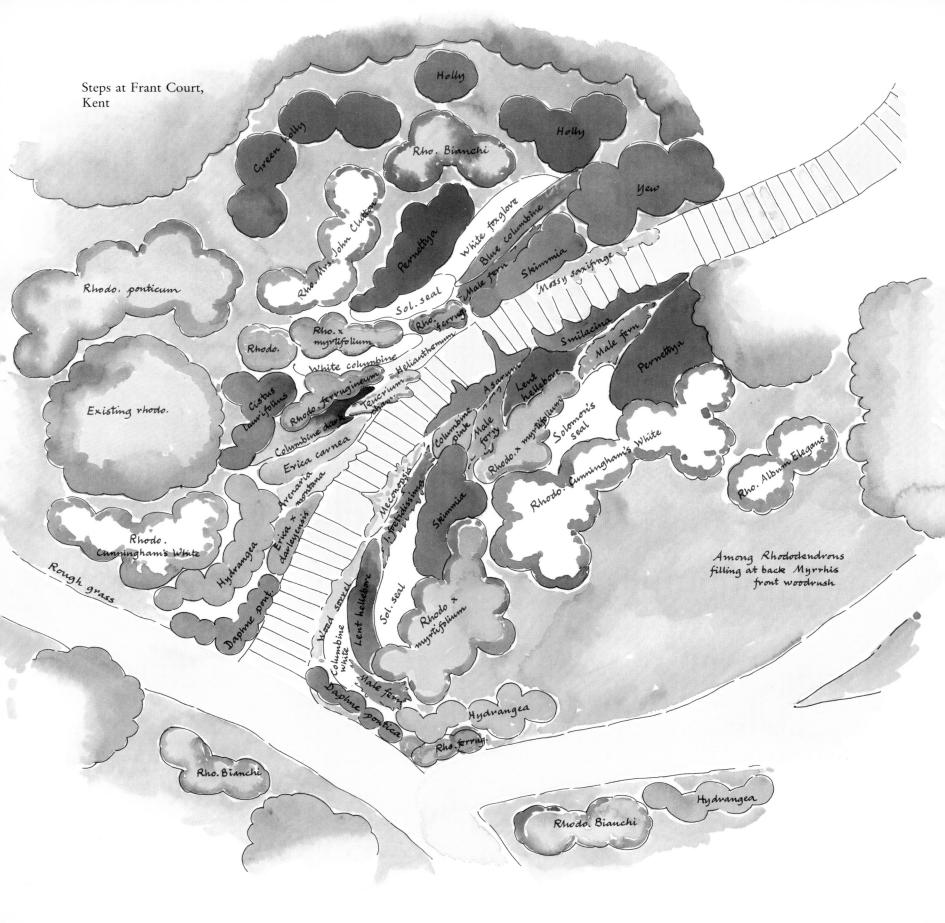

Steps at Frant Court,
Kent

Holly

Green holly

Rho. Bianchi

Holly

Yew

Rhodo. ponticum

Rho. Mrs. John Clutton

Pernettya

White foxglove

Blue columbine

Skimmia

Male fern

Mossy saxifrage

Sol. seal

Rho. ferrug.

Smilacina

Rho. x myrtifolium

Rhodo.

White columbine

Helianthemum

Male fern

Pernettya

Asarum

Lent hellebore

Cistus laurifolius

Rhodo. ferrugineum

Teucrium chaen.

Columbine pink

Rhodo. x myrtifolium

Solomon's seal

Columbine dark

Erica carnea

Male fern

Existing rhodo.

Arenaria montana

Mecanopsis M. speciosissima

Rhodo. Cunningham's White

Rho. Album Elegans

Erica x darleyensis

Skimmia

Rhodo. Cunningham's White

Hydrangea

Wind sorrel

Lent hellebore

Among Rhododendrons
filling at back Myrrhis
front woodrush

Daphne pont.

Columbine white

Sol. seal

Rhodo x myrtifolium

Rough grass

Male fern

Daphne pontica

Hydrangea

Rho. ferrug.

Rho. Bianchi

Hydrangea

Rhodo. Bianchi

from the more naturalistic wild garden. The return curve, a longer and more graceful sweep, is bordered by Miss Jekyll's planting. On the inner side of the curve the planting is simple and restrained, with large groups of *Rhododendron* 'Cunningham's White', pernettya and *R. × myrtifolium* forming the backbone. These support the curve, and their decreasing height accentuates the slope of the ground. Skimmia, *Daphne pontica* and *Rhododendron ferrugineum* form a lower middle ground of solid evergreens, while long groups of Solomon's seal, male fern, hellebores, columbines and smilacina are used as brushstrokes of woodland freshness to leaven the evergreen frame. Pale, frothy myrrhis is used as a filler among the slow-growing rhododendrons, with woodrush to the front, the grassy tufts of the latter repeated in the dark green foliage of *Iris foetidissima* nearer the path.

On the outer curve, many of the same plants are used but the drifts are shorter and they curve away from the path, drawing the eye into the planting. With existing rhododendrons already providing some height, the background is of *Rhododendron* 'Cunningham's White' and other hardy hybrids, with *R. ponticum* and hollies, taller plants than on the opposite bank, to enclose the more decorative planting in a bowl of dark green. Skimmia and pernettya, *Rhododendron × myrtifolium* and *Daphne pontica* echo the planting across the path, with the lower *R. ferrugineum*, dark rounded bushes of *Cistus laurifolius* and deciduous hydrangeas to vary the scheme. Within this matrix of rounded, mainly evergreen shrubs, thin strands of lighter planting are interwoven – columbines in blue, deep purple and white, Solomon's seal and male ferns, as on the other side of the path, but also helianthemum, heathers, teucrium and *Arenaria montana* on this sunnier slope.

In many ways this planting of the rock steps at Frant Court resembles the rock garden and wild garden planting at Grayswood Hill (pages 47–9), Fox Hill (pages 113–17) and Drayton Wood (pages 121–5), but the Frant Court plan is noticeable for the very obvious way in which the plants edging the path – meconopsis, glossy asarum and smilacina on one side, saxifrage, teucrium and arenaria on the other – are clearly intended to flow on to the steps, occasionally right across them, unifying the planting on either side and making the steps an integral part of the planting plan.

At Brambletye, in Sussex, the fusion between walls and planting is complete. The tennis lawn and summerhouse are terraced into the gentle cross slope, cutting into the ground at the eastern corner of the court and standing above the natural level to the west. Part of the spoil from the excavation is mounded beyond the tennis lawn so that what might have been a hard, mechanical scar in the garden becomes a piece of undulating scenery, with the tennis lawn below, a circular formal garden above, and a gently curving path through a shallow valley between the two. Each bank is supported with rockwork, varying with the degree of slope from a near-vertical drystone wall to more natural stratification in the flatter parts, and the whole is planted in a characteristically Jekyll manner.

On the warm slope facing south-west, grey foliage predominates – sea-buckthorn (*Hippophaë rhamnoides*) at the highest point, *Cistus laurifolius* and phlomis to either side, and yuccas, for their dramatic spiky forms, lower down, towards the tennis lawn. Edging the lawn are long drifts of flowering plants that provide a succession of soft blue-grey to harmonize with the grey foliage. *Iris pallida* ssp. *pallida*, *Eryngium × oliverianum*, dwarf lavender and *Clematis heracleifolia* var. *davidiana* between them flower from late spring until early autumn, three of the four adding delightful fragrance to their other attributes. Trailing mats of othonna, woolly hummocks of santolina and larger domes of *Brachyglottis* (*Senecio*) 'Sunshine' complete the grey scheme.

As the bank turns the corner of the tennis lawn, it becomes increasingly shaded by the hedge around the circular garden. A new theme is introduced. *Hebe brachysiphon*, *H. buxifolia*, tree ivy (the free-standing shrubby form of common ivy) and bergenia strike a much stronger, darker note of rich green, yet one which accords with perfect ease with the bold silhouettes of yucca and the dull but distinguished leaden green of *Clematis recta*, so different in its general effect from the large, glossy, palmate leaves and scattered thick-petalled flowers of the *C. heracleifolia* var. *davidiana* only a short distance away. The generally dark planting continues away from the tennis lawn, on the north side of the hedge, with savin (*Juniperus sabina*), more cistus and hebe, skimmia, bergenia and the demure but distinguished black-stemmed *Aster divaricatus*.

Dark foliage is used, too, to emphasize the difference

between the south-west and north-east slopes of the ridge extending from the summerhouse. At the summit of the ridge, grey hippophaë and phlomis give way instantly to scattered groups of dark skimmia, clumps of *Ruscus aculeatus* (butcher's broom) and long drifts of male fern and *Iris foetidissima*. Here too, though, there is that important group of *Cistus laurifolius* to serve as a link between the grey-green, sun-loving plants and the darker greens of the north-east slope. Bergenia, tolerant of full sun and of shade, is again used to edge the path, alternating with epimedium on the shadier side for lighter effect.

On the rather flatter south-west slope beyond the path, the planting is broader and simpler: groups of peony and crinum alternating against a background of *Euphorbia characias* ssp. *wulfenii*, *Cistus laurifolius* and acanthus, in a bold, free way calculated to enhance the character of the rock from which they spring. This breadth of treatment extends to the north-east slope where lady fern, male fern, hart's tongue and asarum combine to create a picture of pale green, merging the planting on the rock banks into the tree-shaded garden beyond.

It is worth noting how the various plant groups are distributed and repeated to enhance, without obliterating, the rock beneath, and how the planting thickens at strategic points: acanthus, crinum and bergenia at one end of this narrow tongue of rockwork; skimmia, *Iris foetidissima*, hart's tongue and asarum at the other, to strengthen the scheme and to reduce the visual impact of the rock as the garden returns to a blend of densely planted borders and grass.

Brambletye is a particularly useful example of Miss Jekyll's planting of drystone walls and rockwork, as her plans of the planting schemes also include charming sketches to show the three-dimensional effects which can only be imagined from flat plans. The transition from drystone wall to sloping rock strata, the studied distribution of spiky yuccas, the balance of rock and planting, and the variation in weight from solid bergenias to soft cotton lavender, are all conveyed with a few deft strokes of her pencil. The sketch shown here also illustrates how readily such apparently disparate elements as the formal level of a tennis lawn and rugged outcrops of rock can be combined if the scale, arrangement and planting of the rockwork are all carefully studied.

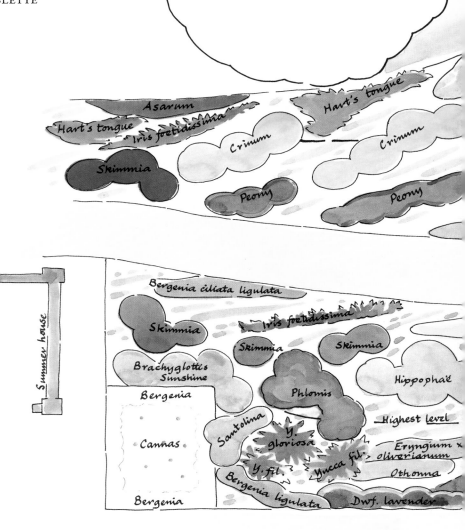

Rockwork at Brambletye, Sussex

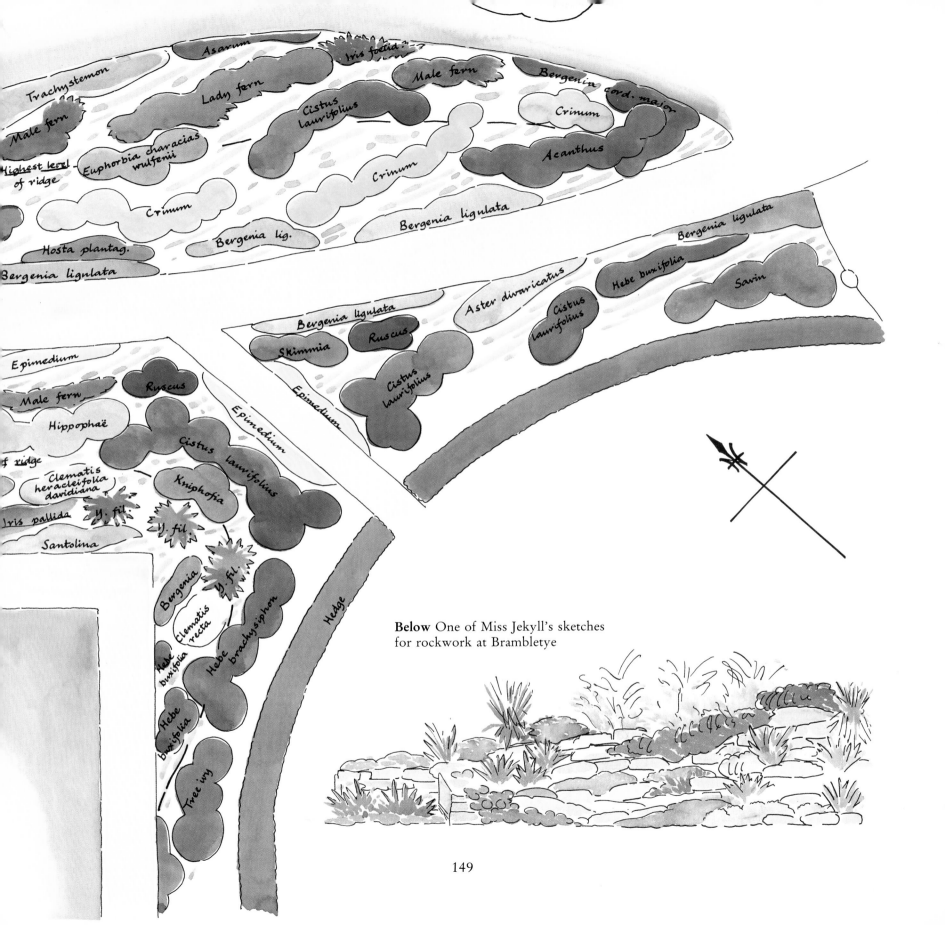

Trachystemon

Asarum

Iris foetid.

Male fern

Bergenia cord. major

Male fern

Lady fern

Cistus laurifolius

Crinum

Highest level of ridge

Euphorbia characias wulfenii

Acanthus

Crinum

Crinum

Hosta plantag.

Bergenia lig.

Bergenia ligulata

Bergenia ligulata

Bergenia ligulata

Bergenia ligulata

Savin

Hebe buxifolia

Aster divaricatus

Epimedium

Bergenia ligulata

Cistus laurifolius

Male fern

Skimmia

Ruscus

Hippophaë

Ruscus

Epimedium

Cistus laurifolius

f ridge

Epimedium

Cistus laurifolius

Clematis heracleifolia davidiana

Cistus laurifolius

Kniphofia

Y. fil.

Iris pallida

Y. fil

Santolina

Y. fil.

Bergenia

Clematis recta

Hebe brachysiphon

Hedge

Hebe buxifolia

Hebe buxifolia

Tree ivy

Below One of Miss Jekyll's sketches for rockwork at Brambletye

149

SUN AND SHADE

Exploring different aspects

Hydon Ridge, Surrey

Hawkley Hurst, Hampshire

Hestercombe, Somerset

The terraces and walls that formed the backbone of many of the gardens for which Miss Jekyll provided planting plans were designed to give a sense of order and symmetry. But their very construction created the asymmetry of opposing aspects. If one side of a formal courtyard, or one retaining wall in a levelled flower garden, faced south, the other would face north; if one faced east the other would face west. Miss Jekyll's handling of this situation is so interesting as to merit a chapter to itself.

Rather than attempting to smooth out differences of aspect in the name of symmetry, Gertrude Jekyll chose to exploit the variation, and in so doing accentuated the character of the site itself. South- and west-facing walls were clothed with grey-leaved plants to highlight their sunny aspect, while north- and east-facing walls receded into shade which was intensified in character by ferns, asarum, corydalis and other plants of a cool, woodland nature. In this way, the natural patterns of light and shade in the garden were dramatized by exaggerating the differences in plant associations.

This principle is developed, for example, in the entrance court on the south side of the house at Bowerbank, Wimbledon (see page 111). Deep green rhododendrons, hollies and mahonia form shaded masses of glossy foliage on the north-facing side of the court, to be seen from the house, while strategic patches of grey-green lavender and olearia emphasize the sunny south-facing aspect of the façade. That scheme is reversed in the garden behind the house, with dark evergreens along the foot of the north-facing house wall providing a firm base of handsome foliage, while wide beds of soft pink China roses and lavender bask on the sunnier outer edge of the terrace, facing towards the windows.

At Hydon Ridge, the holly-lined drive (also discussed on page 106) opens on to a roughly circular forecourt on the north side of the house. The planting which shapes the forecourt on either side of the front door is minimal, but it is characteristic of the plants used by Miss Jekyll for shady places. *Mahonia aquifolium* is the mainstay of the planting, more handsome in the damp shade against a building than

Pages 150–51 Dark-leaved hellebores, pale tellima and Solomon's seal and the acid-yellow flower heads of *Euphorbia ephithymoides* both tolerate and emphasize the shady aspect of the border at Barrington Court, Somerset, while wisteria flourishes overhead in full sun.

Right The pale, delicate-looking foliage and abundant ivory-white flowers of *Corydalis ochroleuca* epitomize the type of planting Miss Jekyll used on shady walls, to create a cool and refreshing effect.

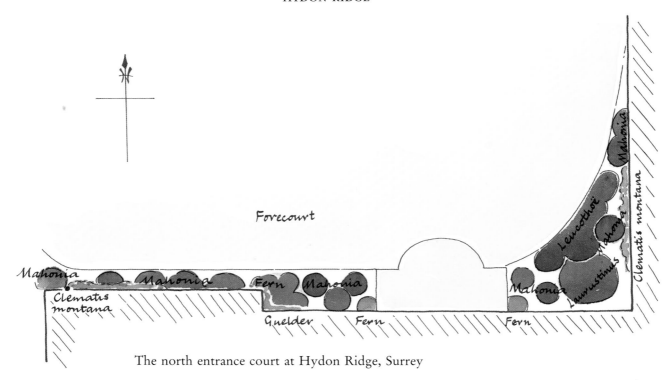

Forecourt

Mahonia

Clematis montana

Mahonia

Fern

Mahonia

Guelder

Fern

Fern

Mahonia

Laurustinus

Mahonia

Mahonia

Leucothoë

Clematis montana

The north entrance court at Hydon Ridge, Surrey

when struggling in the rooty, dry shade beneath trees, and benefiting in foliage quality from the hard pruning needed to contain its wandering tendencies in this confined situation. Laurustinus (*Viburnum tinus*) provides weight in the corner between house and porch, with a group of leucothoë arching out from the rounded mass of viburnum. Male ferns flank the door and fill one corner of the narrow border with their arching fronds of paler green, a colour repeated in the foliage of guelder rose (*Viburnum opulus*) and *Clematis montana* – an association used repeatedly by Miss Jekyll for its harmonious blend of pale foliage and greenish white flowers on plants of contrasting forms. The silky seedheads of the clematis and the berries and rich autumn colour of the viburnum follow as a bonus, marking the passing of the seasons.

In contrast to this handsome but restrained display of cool greenery in the forecourt, doors on the garden side of the house open on to a terrace planted with a soft grey-green and aromatic blend of rosemary, olearia and lavender, santolina, stachys and pinks, for year-round effect. These are inter-planted with peonies and nepeta, pale China roses and fuchsias for their seasonal wealth of red, pink and purple flowers, a warm invitation to leave the house and explore the garden.

Differences exist here not only between the north entrance court and the south terrace, but also between the warm west end of the terrace and the colder garden of darker greens east of the house. The general effect of the terrace planting is of grey and pink, deepening to red for the brief peony season and later in the delicate profusion of tiny fuchsia flowers, but the bergenias at either side of the paths from the house – repeated groups of solid dark green – establish a regular rhythm in an otherwise casual blend of soft colours. This regularity answers the formal line of the lavender hedge against the terrace wall. The bergenias also form the basis of a subtle change in the scheme from west to east.

Although the overall impression on the terrace is of soft colours, the leaves of both rosemary and olearia are quite a dark, sombre green on their upper side, while the roses and peonies inject a note of richer, glossier, bronzed green. Fuchsias, too, have rather dark green foliage as the year progresses, often burnished with bronze. Their crimson and purple pendant flowers provide an even deeper tone.

At the west end the addition of lavender and santolina, nepeta and pinks is sufficient to create a distinctly soft, grey effect, emphasized by the silky rosettes of stachys bordering

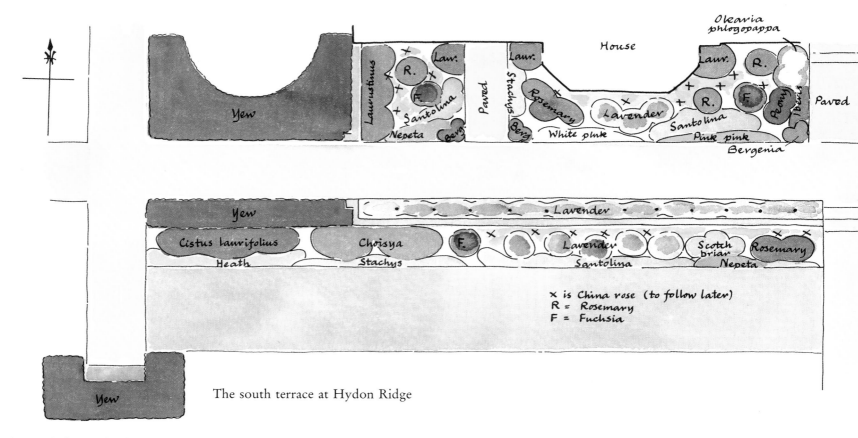

The south terrace at Hydon Ridge

Within the plan:

Olearia phlogopappa

House

Laurustinus · Laur. · R. · Laur. · Paved · Santolina · Rosemary · Lavender · R. · F. · Peony · Iberis · Paved

Yew · Santolina · F. · Nepeta · Berg. · White pink · Santolina · Pink pink · Bergenia

Yew · Lavender

Cistus laurifolius · Choisya · F. · Lavender · Scotch briar · Rosemary

Heath · Stachys · Santolina · Nepeta

x is China rose (to follow later)
R = Rosemary
F = Fuchsia

Yew

the path from the house and by the contrasting dark mass of yew enclosing the terrace walk. In this context the bergenias strike a note of distinct but not discordant contrast, their glossy, dark green leaves serving to anchor the lighter plants.

At the east end of the terrace, though, stachys is replaced by *Iberis sempervirens*, fine-textured mounds of narrow leaves even darker than the bergenias. This small change combines with the preponderance of olearia, rosemary, fuchsia, peonies and roses in this corner (all the darker components of the main scheme) to sound a deeper note, making an easy introduction to the formal garden beyond the east end of the house, where laurustinus, leucothoë, skimmia, holly and other shrubs vie with each other in their rich dark green foliage.

A similar gentle transition characterizes the planting below the terrace wall. Against the clipped mass of yew are *Cistus laurifolius*, with leaves as dark as the yew but larger and duller green, and heath (almost certainly *Calluna vulgaris*, as Miss Jekyll always named particular species when ericas were

intended). Next comes *Choisya ternata*, and then a solitary fuchsia to separate the bright, glossy green of the choisya from the planting which follows: grey lavender and pale China roses, fine-textured Scotch briars and rosemary, with a soft grey edging of santolina and nepeta. The rosemary, interplanted with China roses to continue the theme established above, is planted on either side of the main path, the one element of symmetry in an otherwise irregular scheme.

Miss Jekyll struck out the bergenia which was her first thought to edge the border in front of the choisya, and replaced it with stachys. The bergenia, though in some ways the obvious choice, might have overdone the note of symmetry introduced by the rosemary. The effect of replacing it by stachys, thus linking the main group of lavender and rosemary to the cistus at the end of the border, is to extend the grey planting on this lower level to the full width of the house above, and to highlight the softer character of this western side.

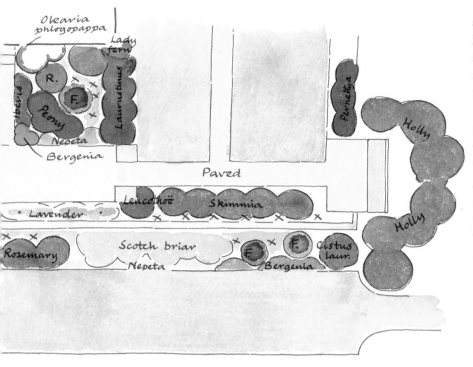

On the other side of the path the planting continues with more rosemary and nepeta, a much larger group of briars, twin fuchsias and a single *Cistus laurifolius* where the border meets the dark hollies of the east garden. At this end, bergenia has been retained to edge the border. Its bold, glossy rosettes, in conjunction with the replacement of grey lavender by greyish green briars and the use of dark-leaved fuchsias and darker cistus, underline the transition from small-scale planting on the sunny sheltered terrace – planting of a distinctly Mediterranean character – to the larger scale and more English greens of the garden beyond.

Other small-scale examples of contrasting sun and shade planting in the Reef Point drawings are numerous, but the plans for Hawkley Hurst, Hampshire – two small borders drawn on the same sheet as if to draw attention to their differences – are particularly delightful. The border facing south-west, against the wall of the house but rather to one side of it, differs from the plans already described in its

abundant use of wall plants. *Ceanothus dentatus* is squeezed into the narrow ribbon of border beneath the bay window, its stiff branches of dark but bright glossy leaves spilling out to soften the edge of the border and its smother of deep blue flowers dominating the scene in early summer. Next to it is *Ceanothus* 'Gloire de Versailles', an altogether looser and softer green plant with attractively red-tinted bare stems in winter and panicles of soft, powder-blue flowers throughout the late summer into autumn. Then comes a magnolia: *M. × soulangeana* or, more probably in this warm position, *M. denudata* – wonderful in the purity of its large snow-white flowers on bare branches but extremely frost-sensitive. The yellow-green foliage of the magnolia, becoming more glaucous as the season progresses, is an excellent intermediary between the rather grey-greens of the ceanothus on one side and the cheery light green of *Choisya ternata* and darker but yellow-green leaves of *Chaenomeles japonica* (flowering quince) which complete the wall planting on the other side. Beyond the quince a group of laurustinus ends the border on a solid note, enclosing the lesser planting and separating the small border from the steps and upper garden at the corner of the house.

These few plants create a varied tapestry of greens and between them provide some flowers for most of the year: laurustinus in winter, colourful sprays of quince in late winter and spring, followed in rapid succession by the glistening white goblets of magnolia, the blue powder-puffs of *Ceanothus dentatus* and the fragrant white 'orange blossom' of the choisya in early summer. In high summer there is a gap in the floral calendar, but a gap that is barely noticeable as the wall plants then have an equally important role to play as backcloth to the lower flowering plants in the centre of the border. The late summer flowers of *Ceanothus* 'Gloire de Versailles' and the usual second crop of choisya flowers soon pick up the sequence again, continuing in flower until the laurustinus begins the cycle once more.

The front edge of the border is defined by hummocks of dark grey-green rosemary, grey lavender and woolly white santolina, with the low rosettes of stachys disappearing behind a final and emphatic drift of bergenia, a sudden contrast in colour and form to strengthen the corner of the border and to associate with the dark mass of laurustinus behind.

Each of these foreground plants has its own season of floral beauty, soft lavender-blue to echo the ceanothus or the sharp yellow of the santolina as a perfect contrast, but the main task of providing flowers through the summer is left to herbaceous and annual plants woven into the centre of the border. China roses, peeping over the lavender and rosemary or sharply etched against the dark laurustinus, produce their delicate pink butterflies of flowers through much of the summer, rarely in great quantity but of a quality which invites close appreciation of their beauty and scent. Dusky pink centranthus follows on, its bright green hummocks of young foliage paling in imitation of the magnolia beside it until its increasingly glaucous colouring tones with that of the lavender and santolina nearby. Ever-expanding heads of tiny flowers on the centranthus echo both the form of the ceanothus and the subdued colouring of stachys spikes. They surround a single plant of *Fuchsia* 'Riccartonii', a tall plant with branches weighed down into graceful arches by the abundance of its charming red and purple flowers, brighter than the centranthus and glowing richly as the quantity of flowers increases towards the autumn. That richness of colouring is repeated in bolder fashion by the small group of red snapdragons, velvet-red spikes of flower over bronzed leaves emerging among the black-green, deeply cut foliage of acanthus.

This richness of colour – dark green laurustinus and bergenia, darker green acanthus merging into velvet-red snapdragons and crimson fuchsia flowers against a background of dark, glossy green quince foliage – is very different from the soft greys and mauves of the 'typical' Jekyll border, but is a natural extension of that same spectrum of plants. Indeed, the south-west-facing border at Hawkley Hurst is an excellent example of a technique frequently employed by Miss Jekyll, that of arranging a harmonious sequence of colour in a subtle curve so that opposite ends of the sequence end up close together in sharp contrast. In this instance, the gentle gradation is from dark green bergenia, laurustinus, and so on, through mid-green centranthus, pale lavender, and paler santolina and stachys, so arranged that the stachys and bergenia end up as immediate neighbours, dramatically different but logically related within the scheme as a whole.

The second of the Hawkley Hurst borders, in the corner between a north-east-facing wall and a summerhouse, is similar in size but completely different in character. Flowering quince is used again on this wall, but here it is joined by *Clematis montana* and *C. flammula*, producing their sweetly scented garlands of cool white flowers in late spring and autumn respectively, and by the Rambler rose 'Evangeline', its heads of small, single, light pink flowers again sweetly fragrant. Although the *Clematis montana* is planted within the border, the plan clearly shows it to be trained away from the quince, to clothe the wall beyond the border proper.

The remaining planting – mainly herbaceous plants of good foliage and pale lavender-blue flowers – is ranged in overlapping drifts running diagonally across the border. *Sorbaria tomentosa* occupies the darkest corner, its finely dissected pale green foliage and feathery plumes of off-white flowers continuing the backdrop of cool freshness established by the clematis. Next comes *Campanula lactiflora*, with its bold, rounded domes of pale flowers, and twin groups of Solomon's seal, unfolding elegantly into graceful arches of pale green leaves and green-tipped pendant flowers. In the bays between the campanula and the Solomon's seal are tucked groups of male fern, their fresh green, bold but finely cut fronds expanding through the spring and summer to conceal the dying remains of Solomon's seal.

The middle ground of the border consists of *Geranium ibericum* (two groups), columbines, a long group of Lent hellebore and another of *Trachystemon orientalis*. The columbines emerge on slender stems between arching fern fronds and the unfolding green-fingered leaves of the hellebores. Geraniums provide their own soft green mounds of foliage as a setting for their dark-veined blue cranesbill flowers, while the trachystemon produces leaves of similar softness but at an entirely different scale: huge, pale green paddles concealing the remains of its purple-pink flower heads. In the front rank of the border are epimediums, dicentra, *Campanula carpatica* (all pale green, slender plants) and, as a full stop to the border, a triangular group of the largest-leaved bergenia.

This small border at Hawkley Hurst is characteristic of Miss Jekyll's work. The plants are, in the main, quite ordinary. There is nothing rare and very little that is even uncommon. Each plant is carefully chosen to contribute to the overall effect (here a cool, translucent, 'woodland glade in springtime' look) and each is accorded neighbours which will bring out its

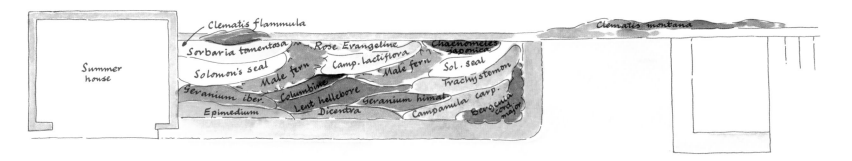

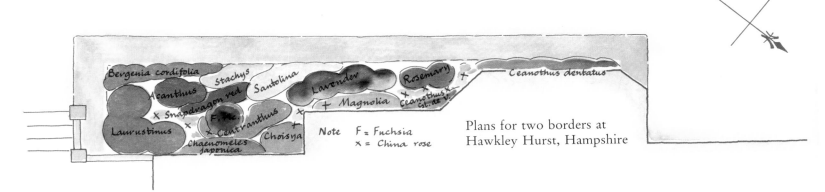

Note F = Fuchsia
      x = China rose

Plans for two borders at
Hawkley Hurst, Hampshire

particular qualities. In this instance, too, as in so many of her schemes, the plants have been chosen to provide some interest throughout the year.

The year begins with the quiet colours of hellebores, greenish white and dull purple-maroon, arising on sturdy, fleshy stems from the flattened whorls of last year's leaves, or from bare ground if the leaves have been cut away. From midwinter and for several months these handsome flowers continue to expand until their fading but still attractive cups are lost in fresh leafage.

As spring approaches the hellebores are joined by trachystemon, its murky but fascinating heads of pale purple-pink flowers pushing through the soil long before the enormous leaves. The bright orange flowers of the quince on the wall might add a ray of more brilliant colouring at almost any time in a mild season. Epimedium also starts to flower in early

The subdued flowers of Lent hellebores, maroon, blush-pink or greenish white, provide a charming start to the garden year, expanding slowly from midwinter into late spring.

Old-fashioned columbines in patchwork-quilt colours hover over mounds of fern-like, glaucous foliage in early summer.

swags of *Clematis montana*. The geranium soon follows on, with *Campanula lactiflora* adding somewhat paler but equally prolific flowers against a backdrop of pale pink roses; then, as autumn approaches, the mantle is taken up by the low cushions of *C. carpatica*, plumes of sorbaria and garlands of *Clematis flammula*, these last two forming an autumn partnership of harmonious colouring and contrasting form strikingly reminiscent of Miss Jekyll's oft-repeated spring into summer combination of *Clematis montana* and *Viburnum opulus*.

In many years, the campanulas, geraniums and dicentras would flower a second time, and the quince would produce the odd premature flower, to complete the flowering season before a combination of frost, heavy autumn rains and the ministrations of the gardeners removed the herbaceous vegetation, leaving only the handsome ferns, the darkening leaves of hellebores, the frail-looking but semi-evergreen carpet of epimedium foliage (increasingly handsome as the leaves bronze before fading to warm, beech-leaf brown), and that emphatic clump of bergenia.

By midwinter the old leaves of the hellebores would finally be cleared away. Although still handsome at this time, they become increasingly bedraggled as winter draws to a close, detracting from the freshness of their new flowers; removal of the old leaves is easier before the flower stems begin to extend. Soon after, the epimedium foliage might also be removed (only because it would otherwise conceal the first enchanting flush of spring blossom), leaving rusty ferns and glossy bergenia, carefully distributed, as the setting for a new season of hellebores, trachystemon and other harbingers of spring.

Borders such as these belie the oft-repeated criticism that Miss Jekyll's planting schemes were too fleeting to be of interest to the modern gardener. In her planning of hardy flower borders with a distinct colour theme she stressed that one could not expect the border to remain *in full beauty* for more than two or three months (in fact a not inconsiderable time), but she did not intend to imply by this that the border would look unsightly thereafter. The description of some of these borders on pages 64–79 should make it clear that most had a great deal of interest for at least half the year and often for much more. In her many other schemes, where a balanced blend of foliage and flowers created an impression or atmosphere beyond that achieved with a predominance of flower

spring, with delicate flowers of clear, soft yellow on thread-like but wiry stems disappearing eventually into its translucent new foliage. (There are white, pale yellow, orange and red forms of epimedium, too, but Miss Jekyll normally implied the yellow *E. pinnatum* if no other was specified.)

Dangling pink lockets of dicentra (*Dicentra eximea*), old-fashioned columbines and stately Solomon's seal extend the flowering season from spring into summer amid their own charming leaves, and the expanding foliage of hellebores, geraniums and epimediums, unfurling fern fronds and fragrant colour, it was not difficult at all to provide substantial interest throughout the whole year.

Having stressed repeatedly that even the largest of Miss Jekyll's garden schemes contain ideas appropriate to the small garden, one can hardly do better than to follow the two quite small borders at Hawkley Hurst with a description of the magnificent, and magnificently restored, garden at Hestercombe, as the last example of plant association to highlight differences in aspect and as a treasure trove of ideas suitable for even the smallest garden.

The Great Plat, which forms the centrepiece of the garden, is a square sunken garden intersected by diagonal grass panels. It is contained within massive drystone walls on three sides, with a lower wall and pergola on the fourth side to frame views of the open farmland to the south. Above the wall on the north side, immediately below the house, there are double borders flanking a wide terrace walk. Compartments above the east and west walls also contain double borders, but these are arranged on either side of a grass panel with a narrow central water channel.

Each of Miss Jekyll's plans for the north, the east and the west sides of the Great Plat shows as a single continuum the twin borders on the upper level, the planting in the retaining wall and the border at the foot of the wall. On the plan for the east-facing wall, *Forsythia suspensa* is shown cascading over the face of the wall from the border above, and in all the plans planting in the walls continues into the borders above and below, underlining the unity of the whole design. As the subject of the present chapter is sun and shade, only the borders immediately above and below the walls are shown on plan; the outer border on the upper level has been omitted.

There is no significant north-facing wall to the Great Plat, which meets the pergola almost on its own level. At Hestercombe it is the east-facing wall which provides a cool contrast to the greys, pinks and lavenders of the adjacent south-facing wall. The border at the top of the east-facing wall partners a long border against the outer wall of the garden. This border, not shown on the plan here, is filled with orange and yellow lilies and daylilies, yellow clematis and verbascums, blue ceanothus and white or blush-pink roses and edged with perennial candytuft, slender poppies, hostas and, at the warmer south-facing end of the border, white pinks. This colourful and rather dark-leaved theme extends into the border on top of the

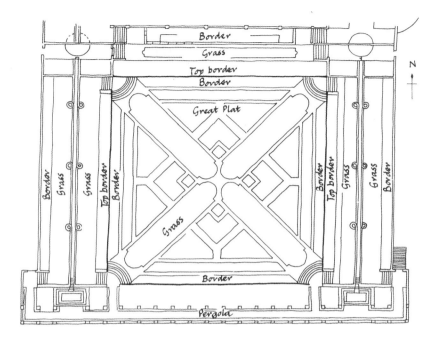

The overall layout of the Great Plat at Hestercombe, Somerset

wall, shown on the plan, but here the paler colouring of the roses prevails among an increased proportion of dark green foliage. Small groups of the bright yellow *Verbascum phlomoides* and of orange tiger lily remain to enliven the scheme, and *Forsythia suspensa* trails long wands of pale yellow flowers down over the wall in early spring, but shrub roses ('Hebe's Lip', *Rosa gallica officinalis*, damask rose, *Rosa virginiana* and its double hybrid 'Rose d'Amour') occupy more than half the length of the border, interspersed with dark-leaved, fine-textured pernettya, dark yellow-green cassinia, the pale, fresh green dome of *Spiraea thunbergii* and the trailing forsythia.

White foxgloves tower above the roses in the middle section of the border, echoing the woolly yellow columns of verbascum, while *Lilium longiflorum* and Solomon's seal arch over the front of the border, broadly edged with bergenia and *Saxifraga × urbium* 'Colvillei', a charming white-flowered form of London pride. The overall effect is of quantities of white and pale flowers etched against a continuous backbone of

dark foliage. Even within the general harmony of the picture, though, Miss Jekyll manages to create a subtle transition from the darker end of the border, shaded by the pergola, to the sunnier end below the house. At the one end *Rosa virginiana*, pernettya and the edging of bergenia provide a continuous thread of dark, glossy foliage, whereas at the other the fine, grey-green foliage of white Scotch briars, pale pink damask roses and the neat rosettes of London pride make an appropriate introduction for the softly tinted grey borders just around the corner.

In the wall itself the colouring becomes distinctly softer: long groups of blue and white *Campanula carpatica*, the larger nodding bells of symphyandra, white foxgloves and white columbines furnish much of the wall, with a long drift of *Campanula pyramidalis* (chimney bellflower) near the base, and answering spikes of yellow verbascum near the middle of the wall. A broad drift of fern-leaved *Corydalis lutea* provides a second point of yellow near the sunnier steps. Just beyond the

steps (off the plan), the yellow is repeated by the flat grey cushions of *Achillea compacta* and spires of verbascum in the south-facing wall.

The planting in the shady border at the foot of the east-facing wall is generally low and relies heavily on diversity of form. Hardy ferns spring from the base of the wall (hart's tongues specifically by the steps) and long groups of *Iris foetidissima* add stronger and darker vertical brushstrokes to the picture. Verbascums, foxgloves and, at a lower level, white columbines add their own vertical emphasis over the rounded shapes of skimmia and *Rhododendron ferrugineum* (alpenrose). Much of the border, though, is filled with generous swathes of *Helleborus niger* (Christmas rose) within a low edging of asarum and London pride in its pink and white forms.

This free use of the Christmas rose at Hestercombe, rather than the Lenten rose so often used by Miss Jekyll, is interesting. The foliage of the former, more rounded, smoother and of a softer glaucous green, is less reliably handsome and less

Left Oriental poppies and spikes of kniphofia provide early hints of rich colour in the west-facing border above the Great Plat, while lavender, santolina and other grey plants engender an atmosphere of Mediterranean warmth.

Right The double borders above the east and west walls of the Great Plat are arranged on either side of a grass panel with a central water channel. Lutyens's treatment of the rill on the west-facing side, with its stone edges looping at regular intervals to form small circular tanks, is typical of his lively geometry – well matched by the exuberance of Miss Jekyll's red, orange and yellow borders.

The east-facing wall of the Great Plat

In the beds in the Great Plat, delphiniums, peonies and lilies, within broad bands of bergenias, form a regular but not an obvious pattern. Large arching clumps of perennial miscanthus – Miss Jekyll's favourite grass – have now replaced the more labour-intensive striped maize and cannas of the original plan.

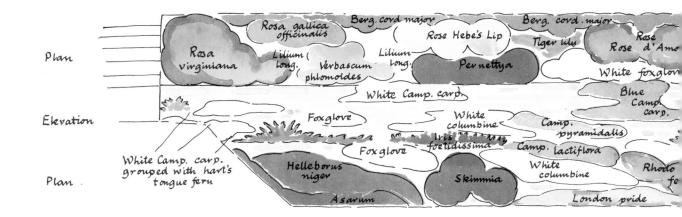

Plan

Elevation

Plan

162

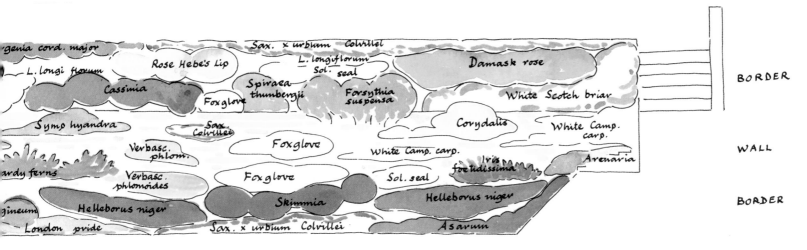

persistent than that of the Lenten rose, which starts as upright fingers of serrated pale green and opens to flat, palmate umbrellas of dark, almost black glossy green. One can only surmise that Miss Jekyll wanted to avoid an over-abundance of the darker foliage (already represented by skimmia, London pride and asarum) and to reflect the much softer hues in the nearby grey border. In this context it is significant that, while three of the four large drifts in the east-facing border are of Christmas rose, the fourth is of white columbine, a plant with elegantly lobed foliage of a green even more glaucous than that of the hellebore. What is beyond surmise, however, is the success of this planting: with generous cultivation, quantities of mortar rubble and the moist but open conditions prevailing at the base of the retaining wall – ideal conditions for Christmas roses – the picture of their snowy white flowers among red-berried skimmias, grey-green mounds of alpenrose and the handsome greenery of London pride would provide delight throughout the dreary winter months.

The south-facing plan shows a symphony of grey, white and blue. Central to the outer border (not shown on the plan) are long groups of *Echinops ritro* (globe thistle), tall and handsome in leaf, with silver-blue spherical spiky flower heads, but soon becoming bedraggled after flowering. To overcome this short-coming each group is accompanied by white everlasting pea and *Clematis × jackmanii*, to be trained in turn over the dying remains of the thistle, garlanding it in milk-white then in deep purple flowers. Between the two groups of echinops is a large

clump of the surprisingly uncommon but undemanding *Clematis heracleifolia* var. *davidiana*, with its bold, deeply toothed and dark green leaves topped in autumn by branching inflorescences of scattered, sweetly scented and pale blue, almost grey, flowers. Unlike the echinops, this herbaceous clematis becomes more and more handsome as the season progresses, until the top growth is finally destroyed by frost. In front of the echinops and flanking the clematis are long drifts of *Eryngium giganteum*, a distinguished sea-holly with the deep blue of its long-lasting flowers diffusing into stem and leaf. This trio of dark-leaved, blue thistle-flowered plants, occupying between them more than half the length of the border, is set in a sea of lavender, santolina, nepeta and gypsophila edged with white pinks, stachys, fleshy *Sedum spectabile* and the sparkling white-felted foliage of *Senecio bicolor* ssp. *cineraria*. A thin group of *Achillea* 'Boule de Neige' is introduced behind the gypsophila, adding a second season of small chalk-white flowers long after the gypsophila itself has faded; and a patch of pale pink godetia is sown at the opposite end of the border – a warming swathe of long-lasting soft colouring to be repeated later in the flat autumn heads of the sedum.

Similar but larger plants fill the border that is immediately above the wall of the Plat. Pinks, nepeta, *Senecio bicolor* ssp. *cineraria* and stachys edge the border; repeated snatches of lavender and santolina are supplemented by darker olearia and rosemary; groups of echinops and *Clematis heracleifolia* var. *davidiana* play a relatively less important role in this larger

The south-facing wall of the
Great Plat

The giant grey thistle
Onopordum acanthium
harmonizes with the grey walls
at Hestercombe. The sword-
like fans of iris leaves below
and branches of rosemary
emerging through the
balustrade above continue the
theme with grey foliage of a
rather darker tone.

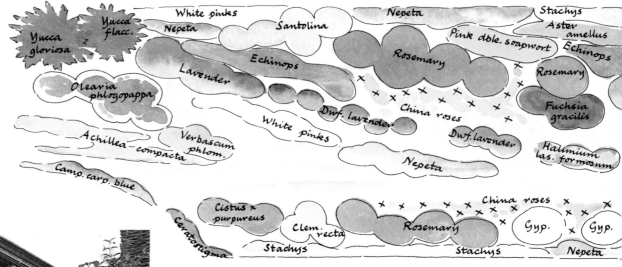

border, their place being taken by spiky colonies of *Yucca recurvifolia* and the smaller *Y. flaccida*, silhouettes repeated in a somewhat gentler way by the repeated spires of white tree lupins at the end of the border. Although the flower interest of these primarily foliage plants is not inconsiderable in itself, the quantity of flower is increased in this larger border by the inclusion of more specifically flowering plants, the tree lupins, pale blue asters (Michaelmas daisies), pale pink double soap-wort (with the steel-grey swords of *Elymus arenarius* in close attendance), thistle-flowered *Berkheya purpurea* and fuchsias, and quantities of China roses.

Planting on the south-facing wall is kept very simple. Lavender, santolina, olearia and berkheya flow over the top of the wall from the border above. Long drifts of nepeta and pinks repeat elements of the pastel planting in the top border, while small groups of upright *Verbascum phlomoides* and wide-spreading *Halimium lasianthum formosum* create brighter points of yellow in their very different ways among equally grey foliage. Thin drifts of blue and white *Campanula carpatica*, of *Achillea compacta* (again with yellow flowers) and of the sparkling blue *Ceratostigma plumbaginoides* are con-centrated near the steps, where the details of leaf and flower can be appreciated at close range.

In contrast to the treatment of the east-facing wall, much of the lower part of the sunny, south-facing wall is left unplanted,

164

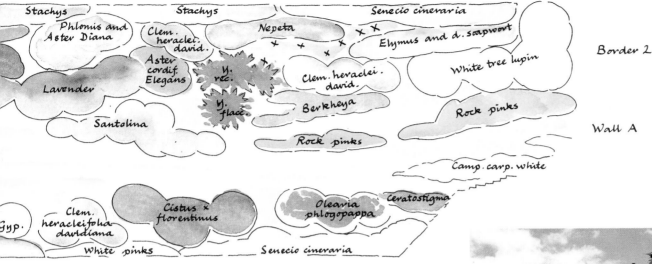

Stachys
Phlomis and
Aster Diana
Lavender
Santolina
Stachys
Clem.
heraclei.
david.
Aster
cordif.
Elegans
H.
rec.
H.
flacc.
Senecio cineraria
Nepeta
Elymus and d. soapwort
Clem. heraclei.
david.
Berkheya
Rock pinks
White tree lupin
Rock pinks
Camp. carp. white
Gyp.
Clem.
heracleifolia
davidiana
White pinks
Cistus ×
florentinus
Olearia
phlogopappa
Ceratostigma
Senecio cineraria

Border 2

Wall A

Broad strokes of globe thistles
and cushions of lavender at the
top of a south-facing wall at
Hestercombe combine with the
grey foliage of eryngium,
santolina and stachys below, to
create an effect of harmony
within diversity. The harmony
is enhanced as blue and pink
flowers emerge, adding to the
delicate froth of the daisy
Erigeron karvinskianus.

because the border at the base, firmly edged with stachys,
pinks, nepeta and senecio again, is filled to overflowing with
the voluminous mounds of gypsophila and *Clematis recta*, and
the rounded bushes of olearia, rosemary, *Cistus × florentinus*
and *C. × purpureus*, with a contrasting statuesque group of
Clematis heracleifolia var. *davidiana* just off centre. These
taller plants would obscure any planting in the wall itself. As in
the border above, these rounded plants are freely interspersed
with pale China roses.

When one remembers that these two schemes form only half
the picture frame of the Great Plat, which has its own
spectacular display of cannas, dahlias, striped maize and scarlet
gladioli, and that equally careful planting continues along the
pergola, in the narrow rill-garden and beyond Lutyens's
'Wrennaissance' orangery in the intricate East Garden described on pages 90–93, Miss Jekyll's achievement as an artistic
gardener is quite breathtaking. Each beautiful garden picture is
carefully composed of a myriad charming details; each detail is
the result of patient experimentation and careful observation.
Miss Jekyll's keen powers of observing, apparent in her
recollections of her London childhood and continuing
unabated until her death at the age of eighty-nine, provided a
firm foundation for her garden designs. We are fortunate that
the benefit of that eighty-five years is still available to us today,
in her books and now in her inspired and inspiring plans.

JEKYLL PLANTS

The plant names that would have been familiar to Miss Jekyll are given (in brackets) after the currently accepted botanical name.

The most valuable of all the lessons to be learned from Miss Jekyll's planting schemes is the benefit that derives from a disciplined and positive use of a few good plants at a time. Her planting was atmospheric, impressionistic: she used harmonious plant associations to convey a strong sense of character in each part of the garden, and in the garden as a whole. Nowhere is this more evident than in her use of plants with grey or silver foliage.

Pages 166–7 Gertrude Jekyll was unequalled in the art of combining plants to form a garden picture. In a modern planting in the Jekyll tradition, at La Malbaie in Quebec, an atmosphere of cool refinement is created by the repeated verticals of blue delphinium spires and yellow ligularias with an occasional foxglove, in a sea of ivory-white flowers. The rhythmic brushstrokes of the plant drifts add to the prevailing sense of harmony, while white birch trunks enhance the perspective and accentuate the impression of a woodland clearing.

GREY AND SILVER FOLIAGE

Mediterranean warmth

Greyness of leaf in plants is usually caused either by a layer of furry white hairs on the surface, or a glaucous waxy coating. In either case, it is an adaptation allowing the plant to survive in hot, dry situations. The outer coat reflects much of the fierce sunlight, keeping the leaf cool and reducing water loss. In the less stressful climate of a cool temperate garden, grey-leaved plants are often short-lived, succumbing to wet or cold winters or simply to too soft a life. However, most are easily propagated and grow quickly to create that impression of sun-baked aridity which is so welcome in a cool, damp climate.

Miss Jekyll used grey foliage freely in narrow borders and terraces near the house, in dry walls and on the sunnier aspects of long flights of steps. In wider borders grey foliage was associated with flowers of pale pink, mauve and purple to paint a picture of warmth and create an ethereal haze.

Carpets of grey and silver

Arabis caucasica (*A. albida*) is one of the lowest of Miss Jekyll's grey plants: its tight, wide-spreading mats of grey-green seldom exceed 15cm/6in high. They bear numerous short spikes of soft white flowers, especially attractive in the double form. This arabis makes an excellent edging in the spring garden, carpeting the ground beneath pale tulips, but it is even more attractive when draped over the edge of a raised border or cascading from the crevices in the face of a drystone wall. On well-drained, alkaline soil in a dry, sunny situation it will remain compact for many years. In richer soil the mats soon become bedraggled, but this can be prevented by shearing the plants almost to the ground after flowering.

Cerastium tomentosum is rather taller (though seldom over 20cm/8in) and distinctly whiter, well deserving its common name of snow in summer. As an edging its rapid lateral growth can soon become a nuisance, unless its spread is restricted by vigorous, clump-forming plants. It is, however, one of the best plants for furnishing drystone walls, rapidly colonizing joints in the stonework with its fine-textured foliage. The spartan conditions of a dry wall help to curb its thuggish growth and the raised situation provides a vantage point for admiring the details of its translucent white flowers, borne in great profusion in early summer.

Stachys byzantina (*S. olympica* and *S. lanata*) is an altogether more controllable plant. Indeed, unless given ideal conditions of reasonably fertile but very well-drained soil in full sun, the spreading mats of foliage soon become patchy and uneven. Lifting and replanting every year or two using young rosettes from the edges of the clumps easily overcomes the problem. Aptly named lamb's ears, the thick, densely furry leaves of stachys, 15cm/6in high, are topped in summer by even woollier 40cm/15in spikes from which peep dull pink flowers, perfect companions for old roses and for the indeterminate blue-grey flowers of such plants as rosemary or eryngium, which also find a home in dry, sunny gardens. When stachys rosettes have flowered they die, accentuating the tendency to patchiness, and for this reason, people often now plant non-flowering forms such as 'Silver Carpet'. However, the repeated vertical lines of a colony of stachys in flower make an attractive feature, worth the effort of removing fading spikes.

Taller plants

Senecio bicolor ssp. *cineraria* (*Cineraria maritima*) is a taller and bolder plant, growing 45cm/18in high and across in its first year, with thick, white-felted leaves deeply toothed along the margins. It is not especially hardy and will soon become woody and untidy even if it does survive the winter, but it is easily raised from seed. Indeed, it is readily available as a half-hardy annual bedding plant. Like many grey-leaved plants, this senecio has daisy-like flowers of a raw yellow, usually best removed before the buds open.

Of similar height to *Senecio bicolor*, but of quite different character, is the cotton lavender, *Santolina chamaecyparissus*. Its minuscule leaves are crowded into dense rounded masses of snowy white. Tiny flowers form brassy yellow spheres on stiff, straight stems, quite decorative where the colour is appropriate, but Miss Jekyll usually recommended removing them. Shearing the plants hard in early spring will prevent them from running to flower, and encourage the dense, compact growth which is such a feature of santolina. Because it responds so well to shearing, cotton lavender can be used to form intricately patterned knots, and it was much used for that purpose in seventeenth-century gardens. A mature effect is quickly achieved but almost as quickly lost, because the plants are not long-lived.

Unlike all the preceding plants, *Othonna cheirifolia* owes its grey-green colouring to a thick, waxy cuticle rather than to a dense covering of hairs. Its fleshy, spoon-shaped leaves, clasping woody stems up to 45cm/18in tall, create a bold, exotic appearance to relieve the woolly effect of most grey plants. Cascading over a wall, spilling from a rock cleft or flowing beneath statuesque clumps of yucca or euphorbia, othonna can be very striking. It is not hard to see why Miss Jekyll admired its bold lines and used it so frequently in rockwork.

Elymus arenarius might best be described as a vigorous, silver-plated couch grass. While it is a potential menace in the border, its stiff 60cm/24in sprays of tapering, metallic foliage spearing though more rounded plants create a marvellous effect. Miss Jekyll usually paired it with double soapwort, *Saponaria officinalis* 'Rosea Plena', a plant of equally vigorous tendencies producing rounded heads of soft pink flowers above glaucous, grey-green foliage – the ideal and irrepressible partnership for a dry bank.

Stachys, santolina and China roses, against a background of lavender punctuated by yuccas, at Hestercombe

Dual-purpose plants

Catmint, lavender and *Iris pallida* ssp. *pallida* might equally be listed among plants with softly coloured flowers, but they are included here because of the particular and lasting value of their grey foliage. Of medium height, but nevertheless suited to the front of the border, catmint, *Nepeta* × *faassenii*, is herbaceous, growing rapidly from ground level each spring to form neatly rounded mounds of pungent, grey-green foliage 30cm/12in high, and topped in early summer by loose spikes of pale lavender flowers. The whole effect is hazy, delightful and very long-lasting, and deadheading (by shearing the whole plant) results in a second crop of fresh young foliage and flowers in late summer or autumn. Miss Jekyll used catmint freely in her own garden. In the grey border it was sheared as soon as the first flowers started to fade, ensuring a second crop in August when the border was at its best. In the aster borders, where its early flowers were particularly welcome in the otherwise leafy garden, shearing was delayed so that the second peak coincided with the similarly soft-coloured flowers of the asters.

The slow-growing bushes of lavender gradually expand into undulating picturesque mounds of grey, aromatic foliage, 45cm/18in high and 1m/3ft or more across, topped in summer by spikes of deep or pale lavender flowers. Old lavender plants respond well to hard pruning, but if this is delayed until spring the plant is more certain to break forth into new growth – and the garden will often be brightened in the winter by goldfinches feeding on the tawny seedheads.

Iris pallida ssp. *pallida* (*I.p. dalmatica*) has more fleeting flowers of palest lavender. Borne on sturdy stems 75cm/30in tall, they have a sparkling, crystalline texture and the most deliciously sweet scent. After flowering, in early summer, the stiff fans of broad, glaucous, sword-like leaves, more durable than the foliage of modern bearded iris, provide the perfect foil for the rounded hummocks of other grey-leaved plants.

DARK FOLIAGE

a handsome framework

Dark masses of glossy green foliage such as those borne by fine-textured yew, Portugal laurel or prickly holly form an ideal backbone for the garden, dividing one compartment from another, providing a foil for colourful flowers and a support for trailing roses, clematis and other climbing plants. In addition, many of the dark-leaved trees and shrubs favoured by Miss Jekyll are tolerant of both shade and a wide range of soils. And while they may be expensive to buy and slow to establish, they lend an indefinable air of dignity and maturity to the garden.

An evergreen background

The hardy hybrid rhododendrons are often considered to be rather dull plants, but this is because they are so frequently seen as dingy, unrelieved masses of coarse foliage. They will eventually grow 2–3m/7–10ft tall, with an equally wide spread. Used as recommended by Miss Jekyll, spaced at least 2.5m/8ft apart in irregular groups and interplanted with graceful ferns, stately foxgloves and shining white lilies, the rhododendrons are handsome and, in their flowering season, spectacularly colourful. Most are also very hardy. Of the many cultivars used by Gertrude Jekyll, the crimson-scarlet 'Doncaster', rose-pink 'Lady Eleanor Cathcart', 'Sappho' with its distinctive white funnels blotched with purple-black, and the purer white, exceptionally tough 'Cunningham's White' occur repeatedly in her plans. Although supplanted in the garden centres by lower and more brightly coloured cultivars, the old hybrids still hold their own in boldness of leaf and elegance of flower. Rhododendrons are more demanding than many evergreens, requiring light but moist acid soil, but they are tolerant of transplanting as mature specimens and respond well to careful pruning to restrict their growth.

At a slightly lower level, growing slowly

Mahonia aquifolium

to 2m/7ft high and wide, laurustinus, *Viburnum tinus*, was one of the shrubs most frequently used by Miss Jekyll, whether in its usual dull green and slightly bristly form or as the glossy, larger-leaved *V. t.* 'Lucidum'. Laurustinus is especially useful because it flowers in the winter. Flat heads of pinkish white flowers open over a period of three months or so while most of the garden is lifeless, before the shrub reverts to its rounded masses of deep green foliage as a foil to summer flowers.

The middle ground

Not all evergreens are large shrubs. *Hebe brachysiphon, Mahonia aquifolium, Daphne pontica* and *Pernettya mucronata* are characteristic of many shrubs of intermediate height used by Miss Jekyll to provide substance in the flower garden.

Hebe brachysiphon (*Veronica traversii*) grows with some rapidity, by evergreen standards, to 1.5m/5ft or more in height, with stiffly upright branches clad in glossy narrow leaves eventually building up to a

dense, rounded dome. In early summer each shoot tip bears several short spikes of white flowers, so the whole effect of the plant becomes light and frothy, but as the flowers fade, the hebe resumes its distinguished glossiness. It is among the hardiest of its genus and grows well in shade.

Mahonia aquifolium (*Berberis aquifolium*) is one of the most adaptable of all plants, growing well in acid soils or on pure chalk, in sun or shade, and spreading slowly into wide colonies of pewter-grey foliage. Miss Jekyll wrote glowing descriptions of the plant, considering its fragrant yellow flowers borne freely in early spring to be 'fuller of bee-music than any other flower'. Left to itself, *M. aquifolium* will readily shoot up to 1.8m/6ft or more, but with stems that are increasingly gaunt and upright. However, given an occasional hard pruning and generous feeding, it will respond with lower, more bushy growth and fresh rosettes of handsome, glossy new foliage.

Daphne pontica is more subtle in its appeal. A low, rounded dome of polished mid-green, it eventually reaches 1m/3ft high and twice that across. Once the plant is established, each extending new shoot produces a whorl of sweetly fragrant yellow-green flowers with thread-like petals. Although never spectacular, this evergreen daphne always has a quiet charm and appears almost to flourish even in the dry, rooty shade beneath trees.

Pernettya mucronata, a relative of the heathers and rhododendrons, is a plant for acid soils only, but when this condition is met it grows steadily into wide colonies of fine-textured and glossy dark green foliage, 1m/3ft or so in height. In early summer this foliage is almost hidden beneath clouds of small, bell-like flowers, followed in autumn and winter (if there are several plants to ensure cross pollination) by berries ranging in colour in its many cultivars from white through pink and pale lavender to deep maroon-purple. The berries are so huge, bright and waxy that a heavily fruiting colony has an almost artificial appearance, but the dense, dark foliage is invaluable for adding weight to fine-textured heathers and for lightening the effect of the coarser rhododendrons.

A firm edging

While dark foliage is mainly thought of as a foil or background, its function as a firm edging to the border is equally necessary in the garden. Miss Jekyll's planting schemes are notable for their use of carefully chosen drifts of glossy green foliage to divide long borders into smaller phrases and to support – both visually and physically – the more slender flowering plants. Bergenias, especially, were enormously important for this purpose but, because of their exceptionally striking foliage, they are described in the section on bold plants. However, wild ginger, London pride and candytuft often achieved the same effect on a more modest scale.

Wild ginger, *Asarum europaeum*, is a cheerful plant, with its low spreading colonies of kidney-shaped leaves overlapping to

form a continuous carpet of glossy green about 10cm/4in high. The foliage is light in colour but handsome and substantial in effect. The maroon flowers, borne at ground level, are visible only to the determined searcher but asarum more than deserves its place in the garden for its foliage alone.

London pride, *Saxifraga × urbium*, is lighter, with leaves toothed to create an elegant scalloped rim to each rosette and slender, upright flower stems branching into light sprays of palest pink flowers with darker veining. As with many Jekyll favourites, London pride is charming *en masse*, its flowers forming a 25cm/10in cloud of pale pink over brightly glossy foliage some 8cm/3in tall, but it is even more delightful when inspected closely. It is more truly evergreen than is asarum, and makes a wonderful picture in winter when each rosette is rimmed with frost.

Perennial candytuft, *Iberis sempervirens*, is a taller and somewhat looser plant, about 20cm/8in high. Its dark green, rather yew-like foliage is borne on upright stems topped in spring with dense round heads of cold white flowers. Although low, it spreads laterally and, especially when hanging over a ledge or flowing between the stones of a rock garden, will soon reach 1m/3ft or more across. On well-drained soil it will live for many years, but where necessary it can rapidly be rejuvenated by shearing to the ground. It is also easily propagated by cuttings taken after flowering.

Roses and peonies

Not all dark green plants are evergreen. Miss Jekyll frequently used *Rosa virginiana* and China roses in her planting schemes, as much for their dark, glossy foliage as for their fragrant flowers. Peonies were also enjoyed for their rich bronze-tinted foliage long after their brief but glorious flowers had shed their heavy petals.

Rosa virginiana (*R. lucida*) is a robust, suckering shrub, 1.8m/6ft tall, especially suited to sandy soils and to the wilder parts of the garden. In midsummer it produces

Viburnum tinus

numerous small, single pink roses with a powerful old rose fragrance. These are followed by dark purple-crimson hips, and in autumn the foliage turns crimson with yellow highlights, before falling to reveal the forest of dark prickly stems.

The China rose, *Rosa × odorata* 'Pallida', is a much more slender plant, bearing a continuous succession of sweetly fragrant pale pink or white flowers from midsummer until autumn. Although it is easily kept to 1m/3ft or so by pruning, it will eventually exceed 3m/10ft against a warm wall. Miss Jekyll usually scattered her China roses in warm borders among rosemary, lavender and other plants of soft colouring, enriching the scheme with the dark coppery rose leaves and adding to it with the frail, blush-pink flowers. Jasmine – the summer-flowering *Jasminum officinale* – frequently accompanied China roses in such situations, benefiting from the warmth of sunny walls and adorning the garden with its abundant dark green foliage spangled with intensely fragrant white flowers.

PALE GREEN FOLIAGE

woodland grace

While grey-leaved plants combined to create a haze of Mediterranean warmth and dark evergreens provided a more solidly handsome effect, Miss Jekyll used pale, fresh green foliage to paint a refreshing illusion of woodland in spring.

Ferns

Ferns are the epitome of this woodland grace, and Miss Jekyll used a range of ferns for the sake of their pale elegance. Male fern, *Dryopteris filix-mas*, with its rusty-backed croziers unfurling into deeply dissected fronds that form handsome cones 1m/3ft high and wide, was the one she used most often. It has the ability to remain remarkably fresh even on dry soils and the old fronds remain well into the winter, only withering when the new cycle of growth begins. Hart's tongue fern, *Asplenium scolopendrium* (*Phyllitis scolopendrium*) has lower but bolder glossy strap-like fronds of delicate pale glossy green. It, too, tolerates a wide range of soils and situations but is especially fine in damp, partially shaded sites where it will produce fronds 60cm/24in or more in length. The common polypody, *Polypodium vulgare*, has a more spreading habit. Its furry brown rhizomes will creep along on the soil surface, on tops of walls or over the rugged bark of old oaks, to produce an ever-widening colony of deeply toothed fronds 25–30cm/10–12in high, dark green above and paler beneath. Like the hart's tongue, polypody is truly evergreen, and the modest scale of both is exploited in many Jekyll plans to soften the lines of walls, steps and paving and to emphasize the contrast between shady and sunny aspects.

The shuttlecock fern, *Matteuccia struthiopteris*, has a lighter grace – 1m/3ft tall, it arranges itself into irregular colonies of narrow, fine-textured cones as skilfully as Miss Jekyll herself might have done! It is, however, quite a demanding plant, requiring a permanently moist, preferably organic and slightly acid soil in light shade.

Fern-like flowering plants

Among the flowering plants, sweet cicely, *Myrrhis odorata*, most closely resembles the ferns, but its pale green, doubly dissected leaves – as aromatic as they are graceful – are topped by flat, lacy heads of creamy white flowers on 45cm/18in stems. Its refreshing delicacy is especially welcome in hot, dry situations, where most ferns would grow reluctantly if at all. Miss Jekyll advised cutting myrrhis to the ground as soon as the flowers start to fade, to prevent seeding and encourage a fresh crop of pale green leafage. She also took care, in her own garden, to maintain a supply of young plants to replace old, congested clumps.

Most of the various plants that Miss Jekyll knew as 'spiraea' are now scattered into other genera by the botanists. Despite differences in name, though, plants such as *Filipendula ulmaria* (*Spiraea ulmaria*), *Aruncus dioicus* (*Spiraea aruncus*) and *Sorbaria tomentosa* (*Spiraea lindleyi*) have in common handsome, dissected foliage of pale green topped by plumes of tiny, ivory-white flowers. *Filipendula ulmaria* is the smallest of the trio, growing perhaps to 1m/3ft high. Its fragrant flowers over boldly ribbed pinnate leaves amply justify its common name of meadowsweet, but the meadows in which it grows naturally are lush and by the waterside; it is not tolerant of dry soils. *Aruncus dioicus*, like meadowsweet a herbaceous perennial, is taller – 1.5m/5ft or more – and more graceful, with tall plumes of greenish white flowers gradually fading to pale straw-

Matteuccia struthiopteris in a woodland setting

brown. Despite its airy grace it is surprisingly tolerant of dry conditions, and is ideally suited to creating the illusion of cool woodland luxuriance where the natural conditions for such luxuriance do not exist – in a shady but dry town garden, for example, or at the edge of a concrete (or, in our modern era, plastic) pool. *Sorbaria tomentosa* is a suckering shrub sparsely clad with deeply veined, pinnate leaves and topped by huge feathery plumes of white flowers, often arching almost to the ground when wet with rain. If neglected it will soon grown into a thicket of gaunt stems 2.5–3m/8–10ft high, but if it is carefully thinned and pruned each year it will retain its exuberant freshness indefinitely.

Smaller plants
Of the lower herbaceous plants, Miss Jekyll often used Solomon's seal, *Uvularia grandiflora* and epimediums. Solomon's seal – either *Polygonatum multiflorum* or *P. × hybridum* – with glaucous, pale green leaves on 75cm/30in arching stems nodding beneath the weight of cool, greenish white flowers, is a picture of woodland grace. Yet this is another plant that will grow in dry, rooty shade, dying away by midsummer when competition from the trees overhead would be at its most formidable. *Uvularia grandiflora* is very similar in stance to Solomon's seal, but it usually carries a solitary pale yellow flower at the end of each arching shoot. It requires more moisture and a lighter, preferably acid soil to give of its best, but that best is very good indeed.

Epimedium is a remarkable plant in many ways. Its flowers range in colour from white and cream through darker yellow to orange and bright red, and are borne with exquisite grace on long wiry stems in early spring. As the flowers expand, more slender stalks bear aloft three-lobed leaves of the palest, translucent green, often flushed with bronze. And as the flowers fade, the thin but now leathery leaves expand into a carpet of pale green 25cm/10in tall, bronzing again as winter approaches but remaining impeccably

Clematis montana

elegant until the new flowers appear. Quite as noteworthy as their colour range and elegant poise is the fact that most epimediums will grow, almost flourish, in dry, shady situations. They are capable of creating a woodland glade in the dingiest of back yards. Indeed, the main difficulty in growing epimediums lies in making the decision as to when the tawny winter foliage should finally be sacrificed to reveal the unfurling spring flowers.

Variegated applemint, *Mentha suaveolens* 'Variegata', is altogether more sturdy than the epimediums, with thick leaves, toothed in outline and soft to the touch. The pale green, white-edged foliage with its refreshing mint aroma adds a sparkle to many Jekyll borders, especially in association with sharp yellow flowers (such as calceolaria or French marigold) and clear blue delphiniums. It is an adaptable plant but grows most vigorously in an open situation and a reasonably moist, fertile soil, where it may exceed 45cm/18in tall. To retain its freshness of colouring throughout the summer months, Miss Jekyll advised shearing the plants as necessary to prevent flowering and encourage a new crop

of young leaves. It is also worth dividing the mint at least biennially (by which time it will usually have strayed far from its appointed place in the border), discarding the dense mat of old rhizomes and replanting only the most brightly variegated young shoots.

The larger scale
On a larger scale, many shrubs and small trees were used by Miss Jekyll for their pale green foliage, usually associated with cool, white flowers. *Magnolia stellata* and the taller *M. denudata* flower on bare branches in spring; the common hawthorn or whitethorn, *Crataegus laevigata* (*C. oxyacantha*) has wreaths of white blossom topping its fresh new foliage and weighing down its stiff, black branches into graceful curves. The Rugosa rose 'Blanc Double de Coubert' forms a large rounded shrub, 1.5m/5ft or more tall, with deeply wrinkled foliage, covered for much of the summer with translucent white flowers – unfortunately turning to an unpleasant brown while still firmly attached to the plant. Pride of place among the pale green, white-flowered shrubs,

though, must go to *Viburnum opulus*. In the wild form, which Miss Jekyll knew as water elder, white lace-cap flowers hover, in late spring, over shoots clad with the freshest pale green grape-like foliage. The flowers are followed by translucent orange berries as the leaves turn from their midsummer green to rich crimson-purple. Equally often, though, Miss Jekyll used *Viburnum opulus* 'Roseum' (still more widely known as *V. o.* 'Sterile'), the guelder rose or snowball tree, a vigorous and more upright shrub often exceeding 3m/10ft tall, with sterile florets clustered into greenish white spheres. Where a nearby wall offered support, the guelder rose would almost invariably be accompanied by swags of *Clematis montana*, not one of the dull pink cultivars so often seen clashing with red brick walls today but the natural – and sweetly scented – translucent white form. The effect of the two plants, so similar in their colouring yet so totally different in growth, mingling together on the shaded side of a wall, captures the whole essence of Miss Jekyll's planting for lightness of effect.

BOLD ACCENTS
focal points in planting

It is surprising that people tend to associate Gertrude Jekyll with the planning of pale, almost insipid, colour schemes, for Miss Jekyll herself recognized that unrelieved fine textures and pale colours would quickly become tedious without the counterpoint of brighter colours and bolder forms. While she arranged her finer-textured plants in long thin drifts, the bolder accent plants were grouped with carefully studied asymmetry, each plant as carefully placed as the stones of the most refined Japanese garden. The positioning of these plants on her plans warrants careful study.

Dramatic distinction
Yucca is the archetype of Miss Jekyll's bold plants. Spiky clumps of *Yucca filamentosa*, *Y. flaccida*, the taller *Y. recurvifolia* and tree-like *Y. gloriosa* spring from Jekyll

borders, make bold and permanent centre-pieces in her rose gardens or punctuate the wilder stretches of rocky hillsides. Although differing somewhat in stature, between 75cm/30in and 1.5m/5ft, all have tough, narrow leaves of dark yet glaucous green, topped, in good summers, by tall branching spires of globular, creamy white flowers – and all have a commanding presence.

Euphorbia characias ssp. *wulfenii* is paler in its colouring and more rounded in outline, but the decisive curve of its thick stems and the size of its pale, lime-green flower heads expanding from spring into midsummer give it an unmistakable air of distinction. This handsome euphorbia, with its glaucous foliage topped by sharp yellow-green inflorescences fading gradually to a softer hue, is equally well suited to either warm grey or cool yellow-green associations, and Miss Jekyll made good use of it in both these situations. It has a further attribute that is especially valuable in our hurried modern age, for it grows rapidly to handsome proportions (1m/3ft high and wide), while seldom becoming too large for even the smallest garden.

Bergenia is another plant that is characteristic of Miss Jekyll's plantings. *B. cordifolia*, with its huge 'elephant's ear' foliage of dark, glossy green, in rosettes reaching 60cm/24in or more across, occurs most frequently on Miss Jekyll's plans, but *B. ciliata* is used too, in those situations where its equally large but softly hairy foliage is more appropriate. *B. ciliata* is a striking plant in summer, but it dies back completely to its thick rootstock in winter, and is suited only to warm, well-drained situations. However, *B. cordifolia* and the many other evergreen species and cultivars of bergenia now available will grow in sun or shade and in a wide range of soils. In *B. cordifolia* itself, the stubby flower spikes that appear in early spring are an unpleasant dingy pale pink; Miss Jekyll advised removing them, so that the plant could throw its whole energy into its magnificent foliage. Many of the newer bergenias have more attractive flowers –

Verbascum, in a border of hot colours

wider-branching heads of rich magenta, clear pink or white, but the foliage is seldom as glossy or densely evergreen. None equal the surprising charm of the flowers of *B. ciliata*, which are pale pink with deeper pink spots. Gertrude Jekyll used bergenias in long, flowing masses, often repeating them several times along a border to form a frame, but they were also used in small groups of three or sometimes five plants where a particular point of emphasis was required.

Especially for summer

Two other spectacular favourites are temporary inhabitants of the garden. Canna, with its banana-like paddle leaves of pale green or deep bronzy crimson, is hardy only in the most sheltered gardens, and even then is slow to recover from the ravages of a typical winter, but if it is lifted in the autumn, stored in frost-free conditions over winter and planted out in rich, well-cultivated soil in early summer, when all danger of frost is passed, it grows rapidly to 1m/3ft or more high, usually producing spikes of red or yellow flowers up to twice that height by the end of summer, creating a tropical lushness among dahlias, begonias and other bright flowers.

Ricinus communis, the true castor oil, and its bronze-leaved form 'Gibsonii', are distinctly tender but they, too grow with astonishing rapidity from large, speckled seeds. If sown in heat in late winter and planted out after frost, the wide-branching plants with their huge, palmately lobed leaves of pale green or bronze will commonly reach 1.8m/6ft high and wide before collapsing in the first autumnal frosts.

Among the herbaceous plants, two were grown especially for their bold leaves. *Trachystemon orientale* (*Nordmannia cordifolia*) has broad, bristly leaves that spread, sometimes a little too readily, into impressive colonies 60cm/24in high and eventually several metres across. It is a plant for shade, and preferably for moist shade, although it does survive in dry conditions, spreading less vigorously. The early blue or pink flowers

are borne in short spikes near ground level and have their own quiet charm, but they are soon overtopped by handsome leafage.

Hostas (known to Miss Jekyll as funkias) are now available in a bewildering number of large and small, plain and variegated forms, but the two most frequently used by Miss Jekyll a hundred years ago are still without peer. *Hosta sieboldiana* has glaucous, blue-grey foliage with spikes of pale lilac flowers. On a good, moist soil the bold crowns of wide leaves will reach 1m/3ft or more across, with flower spikes of much the same height. *Hosta plantaginea*, with similar dimensions, has pale, glossy green leaves, perfectly suited to accompanying ferns in a cool woodland garden. However, this hosta is unlikely to flower well in shade – it is unusual among hostas in preferring sun. In a sunny position its tall spikes of flower are white and delightfully fragrant in late summer or autumn, though sometimes too late to emerge fully before autumn frosts. Both of these large-leaved hostas are quite resilient plants, but they reach their finest stature in rich, well-cultivated soils, benefiting from the painstaking border preparation common in Miss Jekyll's era.

The giant yellow verbascum or mullein, *Verbascum phlomoides*, produces a rosette some 75cm/30in across, wider but flatter than most hostas, with rounded leaves of a soft, downy grey-green. In the second year, each rosette produces a statuesque, branching spire clothed with densely packed yellow flowers set in woolly padding. The plant is biennial and dies after flowering but it is easily raised from seed. Miss Jekyll liked to select self-sown seedlings in the border, observing that plants spared the shock of transplanting would produce the tallest and finest flower spikes – 1.8m/6ft or more tall. The bold rosettes of verbascum flourish on light, dry and preferably alkaline soils.

Many other distinguished plants were used for emphasis in particular circumstances: *Ligularia dentata* (*Senecio clivorum*), for example, for moist conditions, where its large, purple-backed leaves and loose heads

Canna indica 'Purpurea'

of shaggy orange-yellow daisy flowers were needed to provide a high point among other brightly coloured flowers or an accent among green ferns; figs (against a suitable sheltered wall), to provide succulent fruits as well as to conjure an atmosphere of Mediterranean warmth with its bold, lobed leaves; and *Aristolochia durior* to clothe the occasional pergola pillar with huge heart-shaped leaves and intriguing green and purple 'Dutchman's pipe' flowers as a relief from finer-textured roses.

Always, though, Miss Jekyll's plans reveal the careful thought given to the balance and grouping of these spectacular plants among their more demure neighbours.

SOFT FLOWER AND FOLIAGE COLOUR
misty themes

Once the broad outlines of a planting picture had been sketched out with well-chosen foliage, work could proceed on the finer details of the scheme, weaving in plants to be used primarily, but seldom solely, for the beauty of their flowers.

Soft-coloured evergreens

Plants such as rosemary, cistus and the low rhododendrons rank equally as foliage and as flowering plants. Rosemary is the first to flower, with crowds of small, tubular flowers in late spring changing the aspect of the plant from handsome leaden green to hazy grey-blue. Growing quickly to 1m/3ft high and wide, it will eventually reach at least twice these dimensions. The flowering season of the rhododendrons overlaps with that of rosemary, but their flowers are more conspicuously colourful. *Rhododendron ferrugineum* and *R. × myrtifolium*, the two low rhododendrons most frequently used by Miss Jekyll, have funnel-shaped flowers of rose-pink over spreading mounds of rather dark but grey-green foliage. *Rhododendron ferrugineum*, the alpenrose, grows naturally on limestone soils, but both are most at home on moist, sandy and acid soils. Both grow steadily to about 1m/3ft high, spreading rather wider.

Cistus laurifolius and *C. × cyprius* are among the hardiest of their genus. Both grow quite quickly (very quickly by evergreen standards) to 1.8m/6ft high and wide, producing dense mounds of dark, gummy, aromatic foliage and abundant quantities of silky-petalled white flowers. *C. × cyprius* has a dark purple spot at the base of each crumpled petal to create a slightly warmer tone. *C. purpureus* is much lower in growth, more open in habit and has flowers of a light, dusky pink. It is plants like *C. purpureus* and

Wisteria sinensis and *Abutilon vitifolium*

the paler, frailer *C.* 'Silver Pink' that nudge the cistus into the category of flowering, rather than foliage, plants.

Plants for a sunny wall

In contrast to the rounded mounds of all these evergreens, *Abutilon vitifolium* is a distinctly upright shrub. Its appearance in winter is rather nondescript, as it never quite loses all its foliage from the previous year. However, when the new foliage emerges, the plant is transformed into a wide pillar of softest grey-green and among the new foliage appear numerous deeply veined pale lilac flowers. These open to wide circles with a prominent boss of stamens in the centre of each. As might be expected from such a grey apparition, abutilon benefits from a warm, sheltered situation and well-drained soil. Miss Jekyll generally usually used it as a wall plant, training the branches back to clothe the wall in a wide fan 2.5–3m/8–10ft high and thus encouraging the plant to produce even more copious quantities of its pale flowers.

Wisteria sinensis repeats something of the soft colouring of abutilon, but with a very different habit. Trained at a higher level on a sunny wall the twining silver-grey stems will quickly encircle their supports, swelling and merging with each other into statuesque, muscular trunks. In late spring the bare, sinuous trunks contrast dramatically with gracefully pendant racemes of pale lilac and sweetly scented pea-flowers. As the flowers fade and drop, the leaves emerge, translucent silver-green in the first few weeks but soon expanding to a more substantial soft grey-green. Although easily controlled by careful pruning, wisteria is very vigorous and will eventually scramble to the top of tall trees.

Flowering grace

Roses are more easily categorized as flowering plants, although the foliage of many of those used by Miss Jekyll (bright green *R. rugosa*, rich bronze China roses and grey-green Albas, for example) further justifies their place in the garden. The colour range available to Miss Jekyll, as exemplified in the plans of rose gardens shown on pages 98–9 and 100–101, lent itself to soft effects – soft both in colour and in form, with the more vigorous roses trained over pergolas or encouraged to scramble into dark hollies, thorns or old apple trees.

Among herbaceous plants, two very different clematis deserve special mention for their soft colouring. *Clematis recta* produces numerous upright stems bearing elegant, compound leaves of subtle grey-green (deepening to bronzy purple in the best forms of *C.r.* 'Purpurea'). The stems are incapable of supporting themselves but, given the support of twiggy branches or allowed to lean forward over the dying remains of delphiniums, the clematis scrambles to a height of 1.5m/5ft and is crowned in mid-summer by myriads of small, creamy white and fragrant flowers. The greyish foliage and creamy flowers are in perfect accord.

Clematis heracleifolia var. *davidiana* is bolder in form, with sheaves of pale green leaves like those of an exceptionally handsome grape vine. From amid the foliage, tall, straight stems rise to a height of 1m/3ft, branching into open heads of pale, grey-blue (and again sweetly scented) flowers. Both clematis grow best on alkaline soils and the latter, in particular, is tolerant of quite dry situations.

More colourful flowers

The flowers of geraniums are more colourful. *G. himalayense* (*G. grandiflorum*) and the woolly-leaved *G. × magnificum* (*G. ibericum platypetalum*) both produce, in mid- to late summer, masses of delicately veined lilac-purple flowers over 60cm/24in mounds of attractively rounded and scalloped foliage. Nowadays the geraniums are thought of almost automatically as ground-cover plants, and they do indeed make quick-growing and weed-smothering carpets of grey-green foliage, but their practical value should not obscure their attraction as flowering plants, a value apparent in many Jekyll plans.

Aster divaricatus (*A. corymbosus*) is much later in flowering – early autumn rather than late summer, with small, pale mauve daisy flowers individually insignificant in their effect. However, the quantity of flowers in wide, branching sprays, and the dark red-purple colouring of the flower stems give the 45cm/18in inflorescence a delicacy and a distinction that Miss Jekyll much enjoyed. The one great fault of *A. divaricatus* is its tendency to collapse outwards, producing a cartwheel of foliage and flowers around a bare central circle of flattened stems. This can be overcome by staking with branching twigs, but Miss Jekyll preferred to capitalize on the weakness, encouraging the plants to fall forward on to a firm edging of bold, glossy bergenias, highlighting that delicacy which is the aster's greatest charm.

Eryngium × oliverianum is a bolder plant in form, especially suited to warm and well-drained situations where it is a natural partner to softer mounds of grey foliage. Rosettes of dark, glossy leaves veined in lighter green produce stiff 60cm/24in flower spikes which gradually expand into wide heads of deep purple-blue flowers surrounded by holly-like bracts in which dark green, blue-purple and streaks of silver-grey are subtly blended. The purple colouring extends for some distance down the stems, giving the whole plant a distinctive appearance persisting late into autumn.

For the edges of borders of soft purples, pinks and mauves, no plant is better suited than *Campanula carpatica*. Although now known mainly as a pot plant, this low campanula is surprisingly hardy and Miss Jekyll used it freely, in both its blue and its white forms, for the 10–15cm/4–6in mounds of rather grey-green foliage and quantities of charming saucer-like flowers. *C. carpatica* requires well-drained soil and will tolerate dry conditions, but it grows and flowers more freely with an adequate water supply. It was sometimes used as a border edging but it is seen most often in Miss Jekyll's plans near the base of drystone walls where free drainage around the soft stems and a cool moist root-run combine to ensure abundant growth.

Winter colour

All these softly coloured flowers, though charming in their own right, served as components of a general colour scheme whether in borders, rockwork, or walls and steps. Flowering in the depths of winter, *Iris unguicularis* (*I. stylosa*) was unable to associate in the same way, but it played an equally valuable role in continuing the theme of soft colouring into the winter months. In warm spells during the winter its pencil-thin buds, on stems some 40cm/15in tall, open to fragrant, crystalline flowers of pale lavender, a source of great delight at a time when there is little else in flower. Miss Jekyll, who had seen the iris in its native home while exploring the rocky hills of Algeria, took care to place it in her gardens in narrow borders or chinks at the foot of sunny walls or steps in order to bake the plant and thus ensure maximum freedom of flowering. In such situations the iris's fans of narrow grey-green leaves added a gentle vertical emphasis at strategic points, earning their place in the scheme in summer as well as winter.

Geranium × magnificum

177

WHITE FLOWERS AND FOLIAGE

sparkling effects

Miss Jekyll used white in two particular ways. As the predominant colour in a setting of pale green foliage, white flowers and sometimes white-variegated foliage were used to create the spring-like effects discussed on pages 172–4. As a relatively minor element in more varied colour schemes, white provided points of emphasis where lightness or brightness was required.

Fresh elegance

Some examples of plants for the first role – meadowsweet, aruncus and sorbaria, magnolias and water elder – have already been discussed in relation to their pale green foliage. To this short list must be added white foxglove, making soft green rosettes in its first year of growth then expanding in the second year into elegant 1.5–1.8m/5–6ft spires of pure white. Both the colour and the stately form of foxglove made a telling contribution in Miss Jekyll's gardening, in the merging of garden into woodland.

It is significant, also, that two of the plants which she used most frequently as temporary fillers among slower-growing evergreens also have white flowers. White tree lupin bears numerous spikes of soft, milky whiteness, less solidly impressive than the herbaceous lupins but more elegant, because the smaller spikes are borne with greater freedom at a variety of heights on a plant that is much taller (some 1.2m/4ft tall). White broom, *Cytisus albus*, another leguminous plant, has its white pea-flowers ranged in airy sprays on slender, dark green, upright branches. With both the lupin and the broom, young plants flower prolifically but soon become very tall and leggy, often exceeding 2m/7ft. Miss Jekyll recommended hard pruning for rejuvenating the lupin, but her technique with broom was different: the

Gypsophila paniculata and *Achillea* 'Boule de Neige', with *Osteospermum* 'Glistening White'

whole plant was to be pulled forward and down, causing all the branches to break into a cascade of fresh growth and flowers. In both cases, the columns and sprays of white found an ideal backcloth in the dark greens of Portugal laurel, holly or rhododendron, and in return prevented the handsome foliage from becoming sombre.

A lighter note
Foxglove, lupin and broom were also used to fulfil a second role, introducing a lighter note into other colour schemes, but the leading characters in this second situation were white lily and gypsophila. Although Miss Jekyll found it difficult to grow the Madonna lily, *Lilium candidum*, on her dry, acid soil, she never gave up the attempt, planting the bulbs into vertical drain tiles filled with heavy loam then plunging the drainage tiles in the border or at the edge of the wood. There may have been some religious or symbolic significance in her determination to grow this contrary bulb, but the lily's stately 1m/3ft spire of pure white, sweetly scented funnels, warmed by the reflected glow of yellow stamens, provided added incentive. Other lilies were easier and she used *L. longiflorum* and especially *L. regale*, with its glistening white funnels backed with a rich purple flush, freely in many plans. Lily bulbs could be planted in spring among the young growth of peonies and other herbaceous perennials, benefiting from the shade to their bases and support for their graceful stems, and adding a lively sparkle among darker colours.

Miss Jekyll exploited to the full the intriguing versatility of gypsophila (the perennial *G. paniculata*). In her flower borders the first frail grey-green shoots usually emerged among the dying remains of scarlet and orange Oriental poppies, expanding steadily into myriads of chalk-white flowers on thread-like stems. The effect was so light that she described the gypsophila as 'cloud like masses . . . settling down on the border'. As the plant came into full flower, reaching 1.2m/4ft when well established, seeds of nas-turtiums were sown around the base and, as the diaphanous mounds changed slowly from white to pale straw-brown, the nasturtiums threaded their way up to drape the gypsophila in strands of scarlet, repeating the earlier effect of the poppies.

While gypsophila faded from white to brown and eventually supported trails of scarlet, Miss Jekyll frequently used white everlasting pea, *Lathyrus grandiflorus*, in other parts of the same border to conceal and adorn the dying remains of delphiniums or anchusa, thus maintaining sufficient presence of white to balance the colour scheme.

Leucanthemum maximum (*Chrysanthemum maximum*) found a place in many schemes, too. Many people dismiss the trouble-free Shasta daisy as common, but Miss Jekyll did not consider its easy disposition to be a fault. In high summer, when there tends to be something of a gap in the floral calendar, rosettes of dark foliage sport liberal quantities of large, snow-white daisies on 75cm/30in stems, and if the plants are dead-headed after flowering the polished foliage continues to make a significant contribution to the border until the end of the year.

Achillea ptarmica is rather more of a problem, not because it is difficult to grow but because it grows too freely: its wandering habit can become a nuisance. However, with regular division and replanting its spread will be checked and it will produce taller and finer heads of flowers. The 75cm/30in stems are clad with whorls of narrow dark green leaves topped by loose, rounded heads of small chalk-white flowers. The most widely grown cultivar is 'Boule de Neige' (still more generally known as 'The Pearl', the name under which it appears on Miss Jekyll's plans). This has its white florets closely packed into tight hemispherical buttons. The sight of these dense but delicate white heads, carried uniformly above the ground on a forest of stiff, straight stems some 60cm/24in tall, insinuating themselves among clumps of brighter flowers illustrates beautifully the benefits to be derived from the careful use of white flowers.

BRILLIANT COLOURS IN THE GARDEN
light and bright

In the opening paragraphs of *Colour Schemes* Miss Jekyll described the wonderful effect of yellow forsythia and white magnolia against the clear blue sky of a sunny spring day in her garden. That same balance of blue, yellow and white provides a recurrent theme in her planning of flower borders. Although blue is usually thought of as a soft, recessive colour, the effect of clear, deep blue flowers blended with sharp yellow and the occasional highlight of white flowers or white-variegated foliage provides one of the most sparkling and delightfully refreshing of all colour schemes.

The blues
Good blue flowers are relatively few in number, but the immense, towering spires of stately pale and deep blue delphiniums 1.8–2.5m/6–8ft tall, the more slender 1–1.2m/3–4ft spikes of Belladonna delphiniums and the frail butterfly flowers of *D. grandiflorum* (*D. chinense*) on branching 45cm/18in stems provide a good start. Miss Jekyll grew her own delphiniums from seed to escape the vagaries of the nurseryman's colour descriptions, but, for gardeners with less patience, good clear blues of varying intensity are available from specialist growers. The fact that plants can now be bought in flower offers added reassurance.

Delphinium is in many ways the archetypal herbaceous perennial. It demands a moist, well-drained and fertile soil, and it revels in the painstaking cultivation that was commonplace in Miss Jekyll's era. If the plant is to produce high-quality spikes, the young shoots must be carefully thinned and the shoots remaining after thinning must be carefully and regularly tied in to sturdy stakes. After a relatively brief flowering season the old stems and foliage quickly

Delphiniums against *Acer shirasawanum* 'Aureum'

anchored, the rest of the stem will support itself in most weather conditions, dividing again and again to form a wide dome, 1.2m/4ft high, of bristly foliage topped with a succession of brilliant blue flowers in early summer. 'Opal' is a paler form.

Of more graceful habit are the irises, and especially the slender, rich blue *Iris sibirica* with its fountains of pale grey-green foliage. *Iris sibirica* is reputedly a plant for the waterside, but it grows well even on dry soils over chalk or limestone. It quickly forms large, impressive clumps 1m/3ft high and wide, but the effect is more elegant if the clumps are divided regularly, and the divisions scattered irregularly as bright accents through drifts of more rounded plants.

Later in the year come the blue salvias: the low (45cm/18in) and leafy *Salvia patens* with individually large, brilliant deep blue flowers, and the taller (1.2m/4ft) *S. guaranitica* 'Blue Enigma' (*S. ambigens*), with slender spikes of pale blue flowers. Both are best propagated afresh each year (from cuttings, or, in the case of *S. patens*, from seed) to ensure vigorous, free-flowering plants, although they will survive several winters in sheltered gardens. The willow gentian, *Gentiana asclepiadea*, flowers in early autumn, producing 45–60cm/18–24in spires of vivid blue gentian flowers over mounds of bright, yellow-green foliage when most other flowers in the garden are beginning to look distinctly jaded. Lastly, the season closes with ceratostigma. The wide-spreading, herbaceous *Ceratostigma plumbaginoides* (*Plumbago larpentae*) seems each year to have forgotten how to flower, until, as the autumn evenings close in and the leaves of the ceratostigma begin to turn from pleasant leaden green to rich plum-purple, the mats of 20cm/8in trailing stems suddenly become spangled with small, brilliant blue flowers. This was a favourite plant for narrow, sunny borders at the base of walls: the hot, dry conditions encouraged the most prolific and earliest flowering, while the ceratostigma softened the angularity of the stonework.

become mildewed and dishevelled, presenting a sorry sight in the border. However, for the month or so that it takes for the solidly filled but elegantly tapering flower spikes to open their long succession of charming long-spurred blue flowers, the effect of its massed spires is quite breathtaking – well worth the effort and the occasional agony of seeing promising young spikes dashed by a heavy summer storm. It was around the delphinium and its weaker points that Miss Jekyll developed her ideas of clothing the remains of early perennials in fresh, flowering trails of white pea, purple *Clematis × jackmanii* and ivory-white *C. flammula*.

Anchusa azurea, though less demanding than delphinium, is still challenging to grow well. It requires a well-drained soil and even then is not very long-lived. Its main weakness, though, lies in the instability of the wide-branching flower stems, so easily flattened by wind or rain. The only safe solution is to stake each stem firmly just above its weak point at ground level. If the base is

Clear yellows

For the yellow accompaniment to blue, Miss Jekyll resorted to both flowers and foliage. Forsythia has already been mentioned, for its clear yellow flowers in spring. *Kerria japonica* follows closely on the heels of forsythia. It is remarkable in having two quite distinct forms: the better known is the stiffly upright double form, with pompom flowers of egg-yolk yellow on a vigorous suckering plant 2.5–3m/8–10ft tall. The single form has paler flowers, like small single roses on slender bright green stems, and is a charming – and very hardy – plant for the shrub border or wild garden. It grows to 1.5m/5ft tall and 2–2.5m/7–8ft across.

Foremost among the summer flowers are the many daisy relatives, *Anthemis tinctoria* in its pale and deep yellow forms, and fine-leaved *Coreopsis verticillata* for the front of the border, each growing 45–60cm/18–24in tall, with the coarser rudbeckias and helianthus, growing to 1.5m/5ft or more, at the back. Helianthus, in particular, was often pulled forward over the dying remains of earlier flowers, encouraging the normally gaunt stems to produce numerous side-shoots and thus transforming the plant into a sheet of glorious colour.

Achillea filipendulina is also a member of the daisy family, but its tiny flower heads are compressed into broad, flat plates of bright, hard yellow on stiff 1.2m/4ft vertical stems clad in finely dissected bright green foliage. The flower heads are exceptionally long-lasting, remaining attractive even in winter when the sharp yellow flowers have turned to a warm brown. Like the other yellow daisies it is easy to grow in a wide range of soils, but benefits from frequent division and replanting in fresh soil to maintain its youthful vigour.

Golden foliage

In Miss Jekyll's original scheme for the gold garden, described in *Colour Schemes*, she used golden holly, golden privet, and other yellow-leaved or yellow-variegated plants to create the background and structure for yellow flowers. In her flower borders, golden privet, *Ligustrum ovalifolium* 'Aureum', in particular, played an important role in providing bright, greenish yellow foliage for much of the year. Although much less vigorous than green privet, it will eventually reach sufficient height (2–2.5m/7–8ft) to set off the blue spires of delphiniums; at the same time it is amenable to hard pruning so can be kept low enough for the middle or foreground of the border.

Golden elder, *Sambucus racemosa* 'Plumosa Aurea', was used less frequently but was not uncommon in her schemes. It is particularly welcome in the garden for the delicacy of its deeply divided foliage as well as for its clear fresh colour. From a distance it could be mistaken for golden Japanese maple but it survives in cold, exposed situations which would instantly disfigure the maple. For the brightest foliage golden elder is usually pruned hard each year, growing up again to 1.5–2m/5–7ft, but if some plants in a group are pruned in alternate years the older branches will produce creamy white elder flowers followed by large clusters of decorative red fruits. The older leaves also develop a reddish tinge, creating a generally warmer effect.

At a much lower level, frequent use was made of the 25cm/10in golden feverfew, *Tanacetum parthenium* 'Aureum' (*Parthenium tanacetifolium* 'Aureum'), as an edging plant, together with French marigolds or sometimes blue lobelia. The white flowers of feverfew are an attractive bonus, but their appearance seriously shortens the life of the plant. Cutting it back to about 5cm/2in from the ground when the first buds appear will result in a new crop of fresh feathery foliage, prolonging the useful life of the plant. This cutting down can be done several times during the course of a year if necessary. If the occasional plant in each group is left unshorn it will soon run into flower and seed, on 45cm/18in stems, providing an abundance of seedlings that can be thinned *in situ* or transplanted elsewhere for the following year.

RICH COLOUR SCHEMES
fiery splendour

It is difficult to understand how the inevitable link between the name of Gertrude Jekyll and borders of pastel colours ever came about. In practice and on plan, she showed great enthusiasm for bold, rich colour schemes, and used a wide variety of plants, from annuals to shrubs, to achieve a fiery splendour.

Glowing colours

In many a Jekyll scheme the season starts with Oriental poppies, *Papaver orientalis*, of orange and scarlet, verging on crimson, with their crumpled silk petals and immense bosses of sooty black stamens on bristly 75cm/30in stems. These poppies collapse as soon as the flowers are finished, but in the Jekyll border they would be quickly concealed beneath emerging shoots of gypsophila and later nasturtiums, or interplanted with dahlias to provide a continuous succession of red and orange flowers. The old double crimson peony, *Paeonia officinalis* 'Rubra Plena' (*P.o.* 'Flore Plena'), with its dark foliage mounding 75cm/30in high and wide, also appears on Miss Jekyll's plans, offering an opulent start to the year.

There is a plethora of glowing flowers that might follow. Double orange daylily, *Hemerocallis* 'Flore Pleno', produces its fat buds from early sheaves of lime-green foliage. *Monarda* 'Cambridge Scarlet' has its vivid colouring diffused into the bracts and upper stem for long-lasting ornament, although the colour is soon lost beneath mildew on dry soils. Both grow up to 1m/3ft tall. Evening primroses – oenotheras – of several kinds were used in warm colour schemes. Although the flowers are often rather pale yellow (especially in the delightful trailing *O. missouriensis*) the stems and buds are usually spotted or flushed with red. *Helenium autumnale* in its various cultivars extends the raw yellow of helianthus and the stronger colouring of rudbeckia to deep gold, copper and mahogany-red, on plants up to 1m/3ft tall.

Dusky tones

This rich blend of deep yellow, orange and red might be intensified with a 30cm/12in edging of red-flowering heuchera, or with Miss Jekyll's favourite 'satin leaf', the bronzy *Heuchera americana*, interplanted with spikes of red penstemons or dark antirrhinums. Among these bright and mainly strong colours, though, Miss Jekyll was careful to add the duskier tones of pink: valerian, *Centranthus ruber*, making large mounds of pale or deep rose-pink on 75cm/30in stems over glaucous foliage; *Polygonum affine* with trailing 10cm/4in mats of dark green foliage covered in autumn by slender spikes of pink deepening to subdued crimson; *Sedum telephium* with bold, flat heads of pink fading to warm

brown, and remaining as statuesque dead heads for much of the winter, long after the pale, fleshy leaves have withered.

Dark foliage

Lastly, the effect might be deepened still further by dark foliage, ranging from *Heuchera americana*, already mentioned above, to the purple-leaved plum, *Prunus cerasifera* 'Pissardii', usually seen as a medium-sized tree but hard-pruned in Miss Jekyll's schemes to keep it as a large shrub with long wands of rich-hued foliage. *Clerodendrum bungei*, now rarely seen in gardens, has a particular value in the border of strong colouring. In sheltered gardens, against a sunny wall, this rather tender clerodendrum will sometimes grow into a shrub 2–3m/7–10ft tall. More normally it is cut back to the ground by frost each winter, to emerge in spring as a wide-suckering 1m/3ft colony of handsome, heart-shaped reddish purple

foliage. The foliage alone would earn it a place in the border, but in late summer or autumn each sturdy stem is terminated by a flat head of bright, lilac-pink flowers set in a dusky rosette of young leaves. Studied at close range the foliage and flowers clash quite badly – the more so when clouds of orange butterflies settle on the flat heads on a still autumn day – but the overall effect of the plant in full flower is both rich and subdued.

This richness of colouring would be supplemented further by bold clumps of yucca, or dark canna, castor oil, or the darker-leaved dahlias, and interplanted with numerous orange, scarlet and crimson annuals – marigolds, antirrhinums, nasturtiums. With such a broad palette of gorgeous colours and striking forms so evident in Miss Jekyll's planting schemes, the origin of her reputation as a designer only of pastel effects becomes increasingly mystifying.

Monarda 'Cambridge Scarlet'

Paeonia officinalis 'Rubra Plena' and *Heuchera sanguinea*

A WIDE COLOUR RANGE

a rainbow of flowers

The prevailing character of Gertrude Jekyll's planting was a sense of harmony, and harmony requires an element of repetition in the planting. In the colour-graded border, though, repetition of form can only be achieved by the use of those plants that are available in a range of colours.

A spring rainbow

Wallflowers and tulips fulfilled this requirement admirably in the spring. Miss Jekyll never resorted to serried ranks of bedding plants, but thin trails of white, yellow, pink or red tulips and long drifts of fragrant wallflowers in primrose, deeper yellow, red, purple and brown played an important part in her enchanting spring gardens, among the paler foliage and pale flowers of arabis or aubrieta, and the dark foliage of sage and bronzy heuchera. For gentle variations on a theme, she used columbine, *Aquilegia vulgaris*, in purple, lilac and pink, as well as clear ivory-white. The colour range of the long-spurred hybrid aquilegias is very wide, so it is not difficult to raise one's own rainbow of these charming flowers. The plants may be moved to appropriate places in a colour scheme even when in flower, if a little care is taken to water them in. Alternatively, they can be labelled in the nursery during their first flowering season, then lifted and divided after flowering to provide a larger stock of plants for setting out in the following autumn or spring. The clouds of long-spurred flowers, like a host of butterflies on 75cm/30in straight stems over 30cm/12in mounds of grey-green foliage, capture the essence of late spring, and the foliage remains attractive until well into summer.

Pride of place for its extensive colour range must go to the iris – appropriately for a flower named after the Greek goddess of the rainbow. Specific lessons from Miss Jekyll's use of bearded iris are difficult to draw, for two reasons. First, the plant itself has changed dramatically in the course of the twentieth century, with breeders producing an enormous number of new cultivars ranging in colour from white through various tones and combinations of yellow, blue, pink, orange, brown and purple to nearly black. Only a few of the types used by Miss Jekyll still linger on in specialist collections. Secondly, she supplied many or most of the plants used in her commissions from her own garden and, either for convenience or because names had been lost over the years, she referred to many of the iris on her plans by number. If stock was taken from her summer garden near the Hut at Munstead Wood, they were labelled 'Hut 1', 'Hut 2', and so forth, and one can only guess at the colours by relating the plans thus labelled with other plans on which named iris were used in particular contexts of colour. Such problems are largely academic, however. Although the original Jekyll irises may not be available, and might not bear comparison with their modern counterparts if they were, the example of Miss Jekyll's repeated use of iris in her planting schemes, changing in colour to harmonize with its neighbours in the various parts of the border but retaining the rhythm of its pale 45cm/18in fans of sword-like leaves, is still highly relevant.

The summer spectrum

In summer, the tuberous begonia provides large, round flowers of white, yellow, orange and red on fleshy-stemmed plants 40–45cm/15–18in tall. Today these large-flowered begonias are too often restricted to patio pots. Planted in quantity within a setting of glossy bergenia leaves, they make a splendid rather than a garish display, and are capable of switching the mood of a planting scheme instantly from fiery red and orange to sherbet-cool yellow and white.

Hollyhocks in white, pale and deep yellow, pink, red and blackish crimson were important constituents of Miss Jekyll's longer borders. Sadly, with the outbreak of hollyhock rust at the beginning of the

Wallflowers at Great Dixter

Hollyhocks at Lindisfarne

century, it became difficult to grow the hollyhock as a reliable perennial with lofty 2.5m/8ft spires of flowers exuding their cottage-garden charm, but good strains of hollyhocks suitable for growing as annuals or biennials and growing nearly as tall have become available.

Most dahlias, including those seized upon by exhibitors of show flowers, have, when grown *en masse*, a depressing uniformity in their rounded habit and coarse, potato-like foliage. When distributed along a border, though, among more varied foliage and occasional spikier flowers, they are invaluable for their freedom of flower, their immense colour range and the considerable size to which plants will grow, given good cultivation, between planting out in early summer and the lifting of the blackened remains after the first autumn frosts. As with iris, it is difficult and rarely necessary to discover the specific cultivars used by Miss Jekyll. Her example can be interpreted with the modern cultivars ranging in height from 3m/10ft giants to 45cm/18in or less.

Antirrhinum, more frequently referred to as 'snapdragon' in Jekyll plans, was the other plant used most frequently for its colour range. The upright but elegant spikes of white, yellow, pink, rose or red, were particularly useful because the plants ranged in height from 40cm/15in dwarf forms through intermediates to 1.2m/4ft tall cultivars. It was therefore possible to weave antirrhinums of appropriate colouring through the front, middle and occasionally to the back of the border in order to exploit their distinct, emphatic rhythm. At one time plant breeders appeared to be infatuated by aberrant snaps, dwarf plants forming smug puddings instead of sturdy spikes, and penstemon-flowered types in which the essence of the snapdragon – the way it will 'snap' on to a child's finger – was lost. Fortunately, though, antirrhinum-flowered antirrhinums have remained available in seed catalogues, and trays of self-coloured plants are beginning to appear once more among the trays of mixed colours in garden centres.

EPHEMERAL PLANTS

flowers for a season

Ephemeral plants – annuals, biennials and tender perennials – played a special part in extending both the range and the exuberance of Miss Jekyll's more elaborate planting schemes. Some ephemerals have been mentioned already for their particular qualities – the bold foliage of canna, for example, or the rainbow hues of dahlias and antirrhinums. Most others would fit equally logically into the various colour themes discussed in the previous pages, but it seems fitting to group certain of these short-lived but versatile plants together, as a reminder of their particular role. Although they involve much effort in sowing, thinning and transplanting, or in overwintering of rooted cuttings, they pay a handsome return in both the freedom and the duration of their flowering.

The dividing line between ephemeral and permanent is not a hard and fast one. Antirrhinum and hollyhock were grown for centuries as perennials, but now they soon deteriorate because of the ravages of rust and so are better raised annually from seed. Dahlia and canna can be grown as herbaceous perennials in the mildest gardens, but they are more reliable and more vigorous in growth if overwintered under cover and planted out as divisions or rooted cuttings early in the following summer.

Soft harmonies

To fill gaps in borders of soft colouring Miss Jekyll used especially the fluffy lavender heads of ageratum, pink godetia and heliotrope ranging in colour from pale lilac, almost white, to deep purple. Ageratum is a half-hardy annual, to be sown under glass and planted out in the garden after frost. Most modern ageratums are compact, sometimes excessively so (15–20cm/6–8in), but the taller strains (the old-fashioned and cheaper cultivars considered 'inferior' for bedding) will produce more graceful plants

with an informal undulation of flowers more appropriate to the gentle colouring.

Godetia is a hardy annual, one of the easiest to grow from seed sown where the plants are to flower. Dense domes of flowers reach 30–60cm/12–24in, depending on the strain. Most modern strains are of mixed colours, but the range of pink, rose and red flowers is harmonious within itself. Where a particular colour is required, good results can usually be had by sowing a mixture, thinning the young plants to 10cm/4in apart then thinning a second time when the plants start to flower, leaving only those of the desired colour or colour range.

Heliotrope was grown at the beginning of the century as a tender perennial, propagated by cuttings overwintered in heated glasshouses and sometimes trained into pyramids or standards 1m/3ft or more tall. Many hundreds of cultivars provided loose,

Heliotrope 'Princess Marina'

Godetia

Felicia amelloides

rounded heads of sweetly fragrant 'cherry pie' flowers over handsome rich green foliage. A few of the old cultivars survive in specialist nurseries but heliotrope is one of the more difficult tender perennials to over-winter and is now usually raised from seed. The readily available cultivars are deep purple with dark, rich, purple-tinged foliage in dense 35–45cm/15–18in mounds. Fortunately, they retain the rich scent of older cultivars.

Colourful schemes

For brighter colour schemes Miss Jekyll used low, trailing carpets of lobelia, or the rich blue kingfisher daisy, *Felicia amelloides*, pale lemon French marigolds and vivid yellow calceolaria, to supplement *Delphinium grandiflorum* (a short-lived perennial but better grown as a half-hardy annual), *Salvia patens*, anchusa and the yellow daisies. The contrast between the way Miss Jekyll used lobelia, calceolaria, marigold and other 'bedding' plants and the standard Victorian pattern of concentric rings of contrasting colours could hardly be greater.

In her borders of richer colouring, the ephemerals really showed their merits. Orange African marigolds, red antirrhinums, scarlet salvias and the varied reds and salmon-pinks of penstemons and pelargoniums (zonal geraniums) were woven among dahlias, cannas and perennial kniphofias. Yellow, orange and scarlet nasturtiums did their own weaving into the fading mounds of gypsophila, or scrambled up into curtains of Virginia creeper.

One of Miss Jekyll's favourite annuals, though, was mignonette, *Reseda odorata*. The quiet charm of its pale green foliage and solid 40cm/15in green spikes of honey-scented flowers was used as an edging to many brighter schemes, a timely reminder of the need for measured contrast to maintain the vitality of the boldest planting.

A finishing touch

Sometimes whole garden compartments were dedicated to ephemerals, as at Munstead Wood itself, of course, and at Little Cumbrae. More often, though, the brightly coloured ephemeral plants provided the finishing touches to permanent herbaceous perennials and shrubs. Their long season, their freedom of growth, and the sense of joy they bring, enriched many memorable garden pictures. Miss Jekyll's consummate skill in raising and in placing ephemeral plants, the skill of a gardener and a painter in one, is an appropriate note on which to end this account of her contribution to garden making, and of the inspiration she is still able to evoke in the present day.

ZONE RATINGS

The usefulness zones quoted in the list below suggest the range of zones in which a plant may be successfully grown. The lower figure represents the coldest zone in which the plant will be hardy without winter protection; the higher figure, which is relevant in the United States and Australia, but not in the cool temperate climates of the United Kingdom or New Zealand, indicates the limit of its tolerance of hot summer weather. It is important to remember that any zone list can give only approximate guidance. Microclimates within any particular zone can vary widely, and the survival of a plant also depends on a great many other factors, including the depth of its roots, its water content at any given time, the force of the wind and the duration of cold or hot weather.

Approximate range of average annual minimum temperatures
  1 below −45°C/−50°F
  2 −45°C/−50°F to −40°C/−40°F
  3 −40°C/−40°F to −34°C/−30°F
  4 −34°C/−30°F to −29°C/−20°F
  5 −29°C/−20°F to −23°C/−10°F
  6 −23°C/−10°F to −18°C/0°F
  7 −18°C/0°F to −12°C/10°F
  8 −12°C/10°F to −7°C/20°F
  9 −7°C/20°F to −1°C/30°F
10 −1°C/30°F to 4°C/40°F
11 above 4°C/40°F

Abutilon vitifolium Zones 8–9
Achillea filipendulina Zones 4–8
Achillea ptarmica Zones 4–8
Anchusa azurea Zones 4–8
Anthemis tinctoria Zones 4–8
Aquilegia vulgaris Zones 5–8
Arabis caucasica Zones 4–7
Aristolochia durior Zones 5–8
Aruncus dioicus Zones 3–8
Asarum europaeum Zones 4–7
Asplenium scolopendrium Zones 4–8
Aster divaricatus Zones 4–8
Bergenia ciliata Zones 6–8
Bergenia cordifolia Zones 3–8
Campanula carpatica Zones 4–7
Centranthus ruber Zones 4–8
Cerastium tomentosum Zones 2–7
Ceratostigma plumbaginoides Zones 5–8
Cistus 'Silver Pink' Zones 8–10
Cistus laurifolius Zones 8–10
Cistus purpureus Zones 9–10
Cistus × *cyprius* Zones 8–10
Clematis flammula Zones 7–9
Clematis heracleifolia var. *davidiana* Zones 4–9
Clematis montana Zones 6–8
Clematis recta Zones 3–9
Clematis recta 'Purpurea' Zones 3–9
Clematis × *jackmanii* Zones 4–9
Clerodendrum bungei Zones 7–10
Coreopsis verticillata Zones 4–9
Crataegus laevigata Zones 5–7
Cytisus albus Zones 6–8
Daphne pontica Zones 7–8
Delphinium grandiflorum Zones 4–9
Dryopteris filix-mas Zones 4–8
Elymus arenarius Zones 4–9
Epimedium pinnatum Zones 5–9
Eryngium × *oliverianum* Zones 5–8
Euphorbia characias ssp. *wulfenii* Zones 7–10
Felicia amelloides Zones 8–9
Filipendula ulmaria Zones 3–9
Gentiana asclepiadea Zones 6–9
Geranium himalayense Zones 4–8
Geranium × *magnificum* Zones 4–8
Gypsophila paniculata Zones 4–9
Hebe brachysiphon Zones 8–10
Helenium autumnale Zones 4–8

Hemerocallis 'Flore Pleno' Zones 3–9
Heuchera americana Zones 4–8
Heuchera sanguinea Zones 3–8
Hosta plantaginea Zones 3–9
Hosta sieboldiana Zones 3–9
Iberis sempervirens Zones 5–9
Iris pallida ssp. *pallida* Zones 4–8
Iris sibirica Zones 4–9
Iris unguicularis Zones 7–9
Jasminum officinale Zones 8–10
Kerria japonica Zones 5–9
Lathyrus grandiflorus Zones 6–9
Leucanthemum maximum Zones 4–8
Ligularia dentata Zones 4–9
Ligustrum ovalifolium 'Aureum' Zones 6–8
Lilium candidum Zones 4–9
Lilium longiflorum Zones 7–8
Lilium regale Zones 3–8
Magnolia denudata Zones 6–8
Magnolia stellata Zones 5–9
Mahonia aquifolium Zones 5–8
Matteuccia struthiopteris Zones 2–8
Mentha suaveolens 'Variegata' Zones 6–9
Monarda 'Cambridge Scarlet' Zones 4–8
Myrrhis odorata Zones 4–8
Nepeta × *faassenii* Zones 4–8
Oenothera missouriensis Zones 5–8
Othonna cheirifolia Zones 8–9
Papaver orientalis Zones 4–9
Paeonia officinalis 'Rubra Plena' Zones 3–9
Pernettya mucronata Zones 7–9
Polygonatum multiflorum Zones 3–9
Polygonatum × *hybridum* Zones 4–9
Polygonum affine Zones 3–9
Polypodium vulgare Zones 5–8
Prunus cerasifera 'Pissardii' Zones 5–8
Reseda odorata Zones 8–9
Rhododendron ferrugineum Zones 4–7
Rhododendron × *myrtifolium* Zones 5–7
Ricinus communis Zones 9–10 (an annual elsewhere)
Rosa rugosa Zones 2–8
Rugosa rose 'Blanc Double de Coubert' Zones 2–8
Rosa virginiana Zones 3–7
Rosa × *odorata* 'Pallida' Zones 8–10
Salvia guarantica 'Blue Enigma' Zones 9–10
Salvia patens Zones 8–9

Sambucus racemosa 'Plumosa Aurea'
 Zones 4–7
Santolina chamaecyparissus Zones 7–9
Saxifraga × urbium Zones 6–7
Sedum telephium Zones 4–9
Senecio bicolor ssp. *cineraria* Zones 8–10
Sorbaria tomentosa Zones 7–8
Stachys byzantina Zones 4–9
Tanacetum parthenium 'Aureum'
 Zones 6–8
Trachystemon orientale Zones 5–9
Uvularia grandiflora Zones 5–9
Verbascum phlomoides Zones 5–9
Viburnum opulus Zones 4–8
Viburnum opulus 'Roseum' Zones 4–8
Viburnum tinus Zones 7–10
Wisteria sinensis Zones 5–8
Yucca filamentosa Zones 4–9
Yucca flaccida Zones 5–9
Yucca gloriosa Zones 7–9
Yucca recurvifolia Zones 7–9

LIST OF PLANS

Barton St Mary, Sussex, East Grinstead, 1906
Edwin Lutyens for Munro Miller

Bowerbank, Wimbledon, London, 1914
Walter Hewitt for Arthur Carr

Brackenbrough, Calthwaite, Cumbria, 1904
Robert Lorimer for Mrs Harris

Brambletye, East Grinstead, Sussex, 1919
Forbes & Tate for Mrs Guy Nevill

Busbridge Park, Godalming, Surrey, 1904
Ernest George for P.N. Graham

The Deanery, Sonning, Berkshire, 1901
Edwin Lutyens for Edward Hudson

Drayton Wood, Drayton, Norfolk, 1921
W. & J. Dunham for Lt. Col. O'Meara

Durmast, Burley, Hampshire, 1907
For Miss Baring

Elmhurst, Cincinnati, Ohio, 1914
For Glendinning B. Groesbeck

Field House, Clent, Clwyd, 1914
Forbes & Tate for A. Colin Kenrick

Fox Hill, Elstead, Surrey, 1923
For Mrs Hamilton

Frant Court, Tunbridge Wells, Kent, 1914
Arthur Charlton & Sons for Miss Thornton

Grayswood Hill, Haslemere, Surrey, 1922
J.W. Howard for S.J.H. Whittall

Greenwich, Connecticut (Cotswold Cottage), 1925
For Mrs Stanley Resor

Hascombe Court, Godalming, Surrey, 1922
C. Clare Nauheim for Sir John Jarvis

Hawkley Hurst, Petersfield, Hampshire, 1914
Granville Streatfield for Mrs Clive Davies

Hestercombe, Kingston, Somerset, 1904–1908
Edwin Lutyens for Hon. E.W.P. Portman

Highcroft, Burley, Hampshire, 1906
For Miss Sarrin

Highmount, Guildford, Surrey, 1909–11
For Walter Neall

Hydon Ridge, Hambledon, Surrey, 1912
Stanley Towse for C.E. Denny

Little Aston, near Birmingham, 1914
Bateman & Bateman for J.J. Birch

Little Cumbrae, Bute, Strathclyde, 1916
C.E. Bateman for Evelyn S. Parker

Marshes, Willowbrook, Eton, Berkshire, 1927
Edwin Lutyens for E.L. Vaughan

Monkswood, Godalming, Surrey, 1912
Forsyth & Maule for J.A. Moir

Munstead Wood, Godalming, Surrey, 1883–1896
Edwin Lutyens for Miss Jekyll

Newchapel House, Lingfield, Surrey, 1916
For H. Rudd

The Old Glebe House, Woodbury, Connecticut, 1926
For Miss A.B. Jennings

The Old Parsonage, Gresford, Clwyd, 1919
Forbes & Tate for G.C. Bushby

Pednor House, Chesham, Buckinghamshire, 1919
Forbes & Tate for H.S. Harrington

Pollards Park, Chalfont St Giles, Buckinghamshire, 1905
For A. Grove

Presaddfed, Holyhead, Gwynedd, 1909
For Mrs W. Fox–Pitt

Rignalls Wood, Great Missenden, Buckinghamshire, 1909
Adams & Holden for Sir Felix Simon

Sandbourne, Bewdley, Worcestershire, 1912
For Mrs Wakeman–Newport

Upton Grey, Hampshire (The Manor House), 1908
Wallis & Smith for Mr Best

Walsham House, Elstead, Surrey, 1920–1929
For A.C. Kenrick

Warren Hurst, Ashtead, Surrey, 1913
Percy Leeds for Henry Sams

The White House, Wrotham, Kent, 1919
For Miss M. Rowe and Miss Edith Taylor

INDEX

ACKNOWLEDGMENTS

Author's Acknowledgments

Although technical credits to staff at Frances Lincoln Limited are given elsewhere, I should like to express my personal thanks to Jo Christian and Louise Tucker for help well beyond the call of duty in producing *The Gardens of Gertrude Jekyll*. Tony Lord also rendered valuable assistance in dealing with the ever-changing world of plant names. Andrew Lawson was responsible for the specially commissioned photography.

Most of the gardens described in these pages are no more, so the world owes a debt of gratitude to Ros Wallinger for restoring and maintaining the garden at Upton Grey with such energy and diligence. I am especially grateful to her for sharing her garden so willingly.

Behind every frantic author is a neglected family. My most sincere thanks and apologies go to my wife, for holding the fort so magnificently, and to my long-suffering children, for managing without the cycle rides, football games and outings which they richly deserve.

Photographic Acknowledgments

All photographs by Andrew Lawson, except for the following:
Country Life Library: 8–9, 11, 12, 13, 21
Geoff Dann © FLL: 126
Mick Hales: 166–7
Georges Lévêque: 116, 128
Tony Lord: jacket flap (UK edition only), 28, 43, 45, 50, 77, 86, 98, 99, 101 *left*, 101 *right*
Clive Nichols: 62, 63, 78 *left*
By kind permission of Penelope Hobhouse: 66
Reproduced from *Some English Gardens* by Gertrude Jekyll and G.S. Elgood: 67
Reproduced from *Wood and Garden* by Gertrude Jekyll: 20
Harry Smith Horticultural Photographic Collection: 88

Publishers' Acknowledgments

The publishers would like to thank John Elsley, Sue Gladstone, John Laing, Katherine Lambert and Caroline Taylor for their help in the production of this book.

Watercolour illustrations by Liz Pepperell
Calligraphy by Mary Dachowski
Horticultural Consultant Tony Lord
Editor Jo Christian
Art Editor Louise Tucker
Picture Editor Anne Fraser
Production Adela Cory

Editorial Director Erica Hunningher
Art Director Caroline Hillier
Production Director Nicky Bowden